BATTLEFIELDS
OF THE FIRST WORLD WAR

A TRAVELLER'S GUIDE

TONIE AND VALMAI HOLT

PARKGATE
BOOKS

...ACKNOWLEDGEMENTS

There are scores of friends that we would like to acknowledge whose help over many years has contributed to this book. Sadly we cannot mention them all here. There are some, however, that we *must* name: Steve Bench, Philip Guest, Derek Hayles, Alf Jenkins, Rosalie McFerran, Tom Miles, Mike Scott and Charlotte Zeepvat.

The staff of the Commonwealth War Graves Commission have always been extremely helpful. So too has Serge Barcellini of the Secretariat d'Etat Chargé des Anciens Combattants et des victimes des Guerre, and Lt. Col. Santa Clara Gomes, Military Attaché at the Portugese Embassy in Paris.

Finally our thanks to Jean Pierre Thierry and other staff at the Historial at Peronne.

First published by Pavilion Books Ltd, 1995
This edition published in 1998 by

Parkgate Books Ltd
London House, Great Eastern Wharf
Parkgate Road
London SW11 4NQ
Great Britain

3 5 7 9 8 6 4 2

British Library Cataloguing in Publication Data:
A catalogue record for this book is available from the British Library.

ISBN 1 902616 29 4

Designed by Clare Clements
Maps drawn by Wendy Hough

Printed and bound in China by Sun Fung Offset Binding Company Limited.
Produced in association with the Hanway Press, London.

Reprinted 1999

CONTENTS

LIST OF MAPS

HOW TO USE
THE GUIDE

This book may be read at home as a continuous account, used en-route as a guide to specific battles and battlefields, dipped into at any time via the index as a source of fascinating detail about the First World War or kept as a reminder of past visits to the sites described.

Fifteen of the most significant battlefields are included and the continuity of the story is maintained through sections named, 'Opening Moves' which precede the battlefield tours.

Each battle is separately described under the heading 'What Happened' and can be read alone. To remind readers of the salient features of every battle so that the details may be more readily understood, each is prefaced by a 'Summary' which provides a framework upon which the accounts that follow may be hung.

At the front of each chapter are one or more quotations from people who were involved in the war and these have been chosen to give a relevant personal flavour to the detailed accounts. Those already familiar with the First World War will find the chapter quotations apposite before reading further, while those less familiar will find it worth while to read the quotations again at a later stage.

The battlefield tours cover features that in almost two decades of guiding parties across them have been the most requested. None is exhaustive, but in combination with the 20 specially drawn maps, they provide a compact and illuminating commentary upon the events of the time, from glimpses of the Grand Designs, through individual acts of heroism to the memorials that now mark the pride and grief of a past generation. The time given for the tours excludes stops for meals but covers all suggested visits and all travelling over the route.

There are recommended commercial maps for each tour and it is vital that the traveller buys them, or their nearest updated equivalent, before setting out. These maps, used in conjunction with the sketches in this book, make it possible not only to navigate efficiently but also to understand what happened where – and sometimes 'why'. It is a good idea to mark the tour route and stops on the map before setting out.

At the end of the book the 'Tourist Information' section gives tips on how to prepare for your journey, where to eat or stay, and where you will find information and help. The 'War Graves Organizations' section describes the dedicated associations which tend and administer the war cemeteries and memorials that you will visit following the tours.

This book does not seek to glorify war. No one who has visited the war cemeteries could ever do that. It is right, though, to remember with gratitude the sacrifice made by those who have gone before in the hope that the price that they paid might make us pause and rethink before each potential conflict. The world today gives little sign of that. If you go out along the Western Front then as your journey ends recall the words on the memorial to the Second Division that fought at Imphal and Kohima.

When you go home, tell them of us and say
For your tomorrow we gave our today.

COUNTDOWN
TO WAR

'The lights are going out all over Europe,
we shall not see them lit again in our lifetime'
Edward, Viscount Grey of Fallodon

On 28 June 1914 Archduke Franz Ferdinand and his wife were assassinated at Sarajevo in Bosnia. The Archduke was the heir apparent to the throne of the Austro-Hungarian Empire, then ruled by the Emperor Franz Josef. He had gone to Austrian-occupied Bosnia on a tour designed to bolster up the Empire which was cracking under a rising tide of ethnic nationalism. The assassins were Serbs and the Austrians immediately accused the Kingdom of Serbia of harbouring the killers and others like them, and determined upon revenge. It also seemed an opportunity to crush the growing strength of the Serbs.

On 23 July the Austrians sent an ultimatum to Serbia demanding that anti-Austrian propaganda should be banned in Serbia and that the man behind the assassination be found and arrested. To these points the Serbs agreed, but they did not agree to having Austrian officials in their country to supervise the proceedings. On 28 July the Austrians, considering the response to be unsatisfactory, declared war on Serbia.

Now the dominoes began to fall as old loyalties, tribal relationships and treaties toppled country after country into one armed camp or the other. Germany sided with Austria, Russia with Serbia. The French, still hurting from their defeat by Prussia in 1870 and determined to regain from Germany their lost provinces of Alsace-Lorraine, saw a victorious war as a method of achieving that objective.

On 31 July Russia ordered general mobilization followed that same day by Austria. The British Foreign Secretary, Sir Edward Grey, asked both France and Germany if they would observe Belgian neutrality. France replied 'Yes'. The Germans remained silent and the Belgians ordered that mobilization should begin the following day.

On 1 August the French ordered mobilization, Belgium announced her intention of remaining neutral and Germany declared war on Russia. On 2 August German troops invaded Luxembourg and made small sorties into France. Belgium refused to allow German forces to cross her soil with the object

1

of 'anticipating' (as the Germans put it) a French attack and the King of the Belgians appealed to King George of Britain for help.

On 3 August, Bank Holiday Monday, Germany declared war on France, while in Britain bright sunshine warmed the holiday crowds and Sir Edward Grey told Parliament, that 'we cannot issue a declaration of unconditional neutrality'.

On 4 August, just after 0800 hours, German forces crossed into Belgium. The British issued mobilization orders and the British Ambassador in Berlin told the Chancellor that unless Germany withdrew her troops by midnight their countries would be at war with one another.

The Germans did not withdraw. It was war.

THE SCHLIEFFEN PLAN

The German plan for the conquest of France began to evolve in the early 1890s under the direction of the chief of Staff, Field Marshal Count von Schlieffen. France and Russia were allied against possible German aggression under the Dual Alliance of 1892 and so Schlieffen had to devise a plan that avoided fighting both enemies at the same time. According to German military intelligence estimates the Russians would be unable to mobilize fully for six weeks after the beginning of a war. Therefore, reasoned Schlieffen, if France were to be attacked first and defeated within six weeks, Germany could then turn around and take on Russia. That logic, however, only moved the goal posts to uncover another challenge: how to defeat France in six weeks?

Schlieffen had the answer to that too. The key element to a quick victory was surprise and simplistically the plan aimed to convince the French that they should maintain their major forces in the area of Alsace-Lorraine to counter an invasion directly from Germany around Metz, while the actual assault descended on France from the north via neutral Belgium.

Ten German divisions were nominated to keep an eye on the Russians, while 62 were assembled to take on the French. Of these latter, five armies were assembled in a line facing west and stretching northwards from Metz (see Map 1) to form a door hinged upon Switzerland. This door was to swing in a massive anti-clockwise movement through Belgium. At the top of the door was von Kluck's 1st Army and von Schlieffen had enjoined that the very last soldier at the end of the swing should 'brush the Channel with his sleeve'.

Von Schlieffen died in 1912, saying on his deathbed, 'Above all, keep the right wing strong'. His successor was Helmut von Moltke, nephew of the von Moltke of the 1870 War and made of different stuff to his eminent ancestor. A cautious man, lacking the ruthlessness upon which Schlieffen's plan depended and frightened by the possibility of a strong counter-attack by the French in the area of Alsace-Lorraine, he strengthened the hinge end of the door, weakening the force that was planned to sweep through Belgium.

Nevertheless, when the invasion began, von Moltke had almost 1½ million men forming his door and at the far end of his extreme right wing, there was the 1st Army, commanded by General von Kluck, who saw himself as Attila the Hun. On 4 August 1914 the door began to swing and Attila invaded Belgium.

MAP 1

THE ARMIES MOVE TO MONS
AUGUST 1914

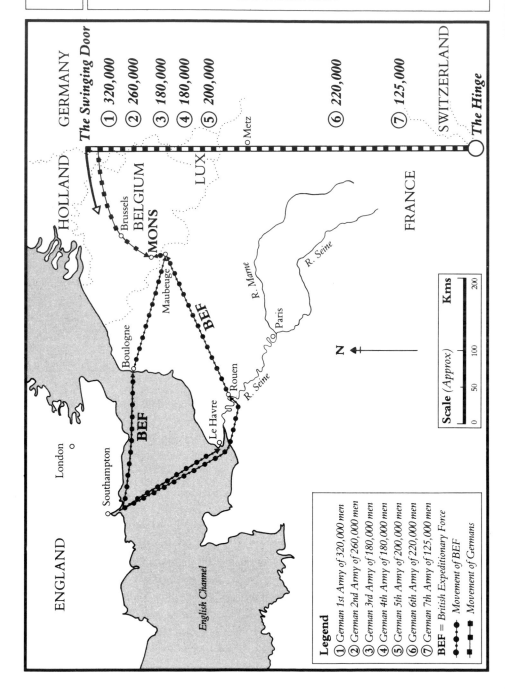

Legend
① German 1st Army of 320,000 men
② German 2nd Army of 260,000 men
③ German 3rd Army of 180,000 men
④ German 4th Army of 180,000 men
⑤ German 5th Army of 200,000 men
⑥ German 6th Army of 220,000 men
⑦ German 7th Army of 125,000 men
BEF = British Expeditionary Force
•—• Movement of BEF
■—■ Movement of Germans

Scale (Approx)   Kms
0   50   100   200

MONS
23 AUGUST 1914

'Our men have come to believe that every one of you
carries a portable Maxim with him'
A German officer to an 'Old Contemptible'

SUMMARY OF THE BATTLE

This was the first battle of the war for the British Expeditionary Force (BEF),
which faced the invading German armies along a defensive line based upon the
Condé Canal running through the northern outskirts of the Belgian town of
Mons. The German attack began at 0830 from the north and by mid-afternoon
the British were forced to withdraw with 1,600 casualties. German casualties are
variously estimated at between 3,000 and 15,000.

OPENING MOVES

On 4 August 1914 the Germans invaded Belgium and headed for Liège,
expecting only a token resistance. They were wrong. The forts around Liège
held out until 7 August, the same day that advance parties of the BEF began to
land in France en route to Belgium.

On 20 August the Germans marched through Brussels and headed onward
towards Mons and the Franco–Belgian border, less than 40 miles away. Early on
the morning of 23 August their artillery came within range of the Mons-Condé
Canal, which lay between them and France, and they began shelling the crossing
points. Along the canal, unknown to the Germans, waited the men of the BEF.

Following the order to mobilize on 4 August, the British knew exactly what
to do, because everything was written down in the 'War Book'. In anticipation
of future conflicts, political and radical thinkers had envisaged as many different
scenarios as they could and recorded in millions of words of instructions just
what was to be done when any particular prediction came to pass. Thus, in
August 1914, the section of the War Book entitled 'In the Event of War with
Germany' was opened and its instructions concerning the BEF were followed.

The Expeditionary Force (EF) was one of the three elements of the Army that
came out of the Haldane Reforms of 1906/7. The other two elements were the
'Forces Overseas' and the 'Territorial Force' designated for Home Defence. The
EF was made up of a core of Regular units stationed at home, but trained and

prepared to move overseas to any trouble spot. Militia battalions of men having six months' training formed a 'Special Reserve' to fill out the EF in the event of general war, 70,000 Special Reservists were recalled in August 1914.

The Allied plan required the British to take up a position at the extreme left of the French line and to assemble in the area of the old fortress of Maubeuge, some 12 miles south of Mons. Following the War Book instructions, training and equipping (only one pair of boots) of militia reinforcements began immediately and in Britain on 9 August the main bodies of the BEF marched to their local train stations early in the morning to catch the evening boat from Southampton to Boulogne, Le Havre or Rouen. The movements of one battalion over this period were:

9 AUG	7 am March to station
	Afternoon. Arrive Southampton
	Evening. Sail from Southampton
10 AUG	Afternoon. Arrive Le Havre
	March to rest camp
11 AUG	Midnight. March to station
	Slow trains north for the next five days
17 AUG	7 mile march to Maubeuge area
20 AUG	15 mile training march
21 AUG	18 mile training march
22 AUG	11 mile training march
23 AUG	0100 hours. 14 mile march to Mons to take up defensive positions

The promised strength of the BEF was six infantry divisions and one large cavalry division, but Lord Kitchener, appointed Secretary of State for War on 5 August, mistrusted the French plan and kept back two divisions so that, when concentration of the BEF was complete at Maubeuge on 20 August, the force under Sir John French's command totalled about 80,000 men divided into two corps of two divisions each, plus an independent brigade and a cavalry division.

Early on the morning of 23 August, the BEF made its final moves into its defensive positions along the Mons-Condé canal. I Corps, under General Douglas Haig moving well to the east of Mons, and II Corps, under General Smith-Dorrien, a survivor of the massacre at Isandlwana in the Zulu War, covered the canal west from Mons to Condé, Mons itself and the canal to Obourg (see Map 2). Thus they waited for von Kluck's legions to arrive. It wasn't a long wait.

WHAT HAPPENED

Von Kluck's troops were moving fast. The II (Ger) Corps at the end of the swinging door had marched 140 miles in 11 days. Just after first light on the morning of 23 August German divisional cavalry were tapping at the British II Corps forward positions. At 1030 hours the IX (Ger) Corps artillery opened up in the area of Obourg and together with the III (Ger) Corps artillery quickly dominated the British line through Nimy along the canal towards Jemappes in the west.

At 1100 hours a massed infantry attack was made towards the canal bridges at Nimy, held by the 4th Royal Fusiliers and at Obourg, held by the 4th Middlesex (the 'Diehards', a name derived from the exhortation of their dying CO at Albuhera in 1811), both of the 3rd Division. This frontal assault by the 18th (Ger) Division, coupled with a flanking movement by the 17th (Ger) Division which had crossed the canal at an undefended spot east of Obourg, forced a British withdrawal to begin at around 1300 hours to intermediate positions in and around the town of Mons.

Along the canal to the west the Germans made multiple small crossings and at mid-afternoon another major attack developed, forcing further withdrawal along the whole British line. It was the beginning of the 'Retreat from Mons'.

The Battlefield Tour

The tour begins in Mons and visits the memorials to the first and last British actions of the war, the sites of the actions of the 4th Royal Fusiliers and the 4th Middlesex, the memorials at the Binche (la Bascule) crossroads and ends at the Saint Symphorien Commonwealth War Graves Commission cemetery.

Total distance   27 miles
Total time   4 hours
Map   IGNB M736 Sheet 45. 1:50,000

Drive to the central square of Mons and park outside the Town Hall. Walk through the archway of the Town Hall. The War Museum is beyond the gardens and to the right.

THE WAR MUSEUM In the archway of the Town Hall are memorial tablets to the 5th Royal Irish Lancers who fought in both battles of Mons and to the Canadians whose 3rd Division liberated Mons on the morning of 11 November 1918.

The War Museum was established by the Mons local authority in 1930 and today occupies the ground floor and third floors of what was, in 1625, the town pawn shop. The eight rooms on the ground floor are given over to the First World War and have sections devoted to the British, the French, Canadian, Belgian and Italian forces, plus exhibits chronicling the life of the people under German occupation. The presentation is a fascinating and slightly damp mixture of hardware and ephemera, designed with the old-style enthusiasm to display everything available.

One day, no doubt, the new professional class of curator will replace most exhibits with coloured lights and panels and Mons will have a museum like all the others. Meanwhile, be prepared to spend at least 45 minutes absorbed in the wealth of memorabilia. Inside, normally over the entrance, is a large oil painting depicting the legend of the 'Angels of Mons'. During the evening of 23 August,

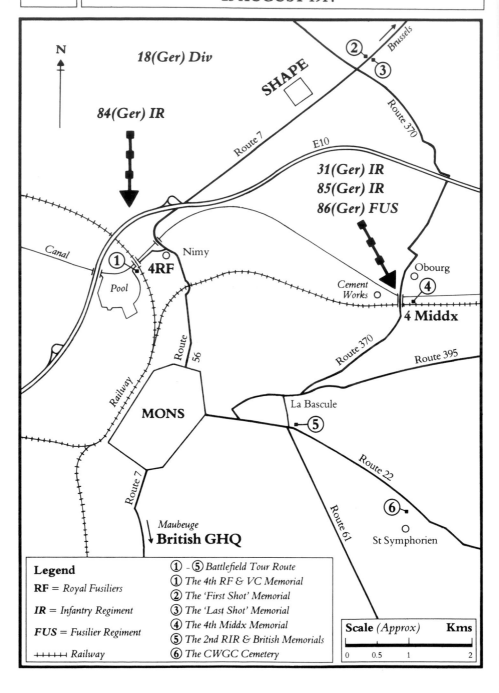

| MAP 2 | **THE ACTION AT MONS**
The First British Shots of the War
23 AUGUST 1914 |

N

18(Ger) Div

SHAPE

② → Brussels

③

84(Ger) IR

Route 7

Route 370

E10

31(Ger) IR
85(Ger) IR
86(Ger) FUS

Canal

Nimy

① 4RF

Pool

Obourg

Cement
Works

④

4 Middx

Route 56

Railway

Route 370

Route 395

MONS

La Bascule

⑤

Route 7

Route 22

Route 61

Maubeuge
↓ **British GHQ**

St Symphorien

⑥

Legend

RF = Royal Fusiliers

IR = Infantry Regiment

FUS = Fusilier Regiment

++++++ Railway

① – ⑤ *Battlefield Tour Route*
① *The 4th RF & VC Memorial*
② *The 'First Shot' Memorial*
③ *The 'Last Shot' Memorial*
④ *The 4th Middx Memorial*
⑤ *The 2nd RIR & British Memorials*
⑥ *The CWGC Cemetery*

Scale *(Approx)* **Kms**

0   0.5   1   2

bowmen 'angels' allegedly appeared in the sky over Mons and prevented the Germans from annihilating the British. Although many sworn affidavits from highly respectable 'witnesses' were produced verifying the heavenly intervention, it was all an invention of Arthur Machen, a journalist with the *Evening News*, which published the story on 29 September 1914. He wrote it to relieve his despair at the retreat of the British Army. Later he admitted that the stories of the angels were 'every one of 'em lies, sir'.

On the third floor is a Second World War section housed in two large rooms containing an excellent collection of German weaponry as well as examples of Allied military equipment, plus details of concentration camps and resistance activities. There is a small entrance charge and opening hours are published as 1000–1230 and 1400–1800, every day except Monday. Check current times with the Tourist Office in the Grand Place (main square).

On leaving the museum, go to the Tourist Office to collect their excellent maps and tourist literature and establish the best walking route (a 5-minute puff up a steep hill) to the area of the Belfry tower, which stands on the Castle Hill behind the Town Hall. In the surrounding gardens is the main British 14–18 War Memorial.

THE BRITISH WAR MEMORIAL   This was inaugurated in 1952 by Field Marshal Lord Alexander of Tunis and commemorates the two battles of Mons – 1914 and 1918. It consists of a memorial panel flanked by two Tuscan pillars. There have been discussions about moving the memorial to the Binche crossroads which are visited later in this tour.

Face north beside the memorial. A good overview of the battlefield may be had depending upon the foliage on the trees and general visibility. On the horizon is the east-west motorway that runs from Liège to Valenciennes. At this point it runs parallel to and just behind (north of) the line of the canal defended by II Corps. Straight ahead, i e at 12 o'clock, a pool beside the canal may be visible. That is the area of Nimy defended by the Fusiliers. To the right, at 2 o'clock, a cement factory on the horizon marks the canal site defended by the Middlesex.

THE BELFRY TOWER   The seventeenth century belfry and area around it have been undergoing renovations and may not be fully accessible until well into the 1990s. At the top of the tower is a panorama describing the battles of 1914, 1918, 1940 and 1944, and in a cavity at the base was buried some soil taken from graves of British and Canadian soldiers killed at Mons in the First World War. During the ceremony, on 3 November 1935, a small silver replica of the tower was given to the British Ambassador as a gift for HM King George V.

Return to your car and take the Rue de Nimy following signs to Bruxelles/Ath/SHAPE and head for Nimy. Just before the road crosses the canal there is an open space on the left – the Place de Nimy. Either park there or, if strong-hearted, ignore the 'No Entry' signs and drive down the small road beyond the Place (Square) and past the Mairie (Town Hall) towards the canal. In either case make your way left along the canal to the railway bridge over it. Stop.

THE NIMY CANAL BRIDGES   *Stand on the bank to the west of the bridge with your back to the canal. In the distance the belfry tower at Mons can be seen and to your immediate right is the water pool that you may have been able to pick out earlier. You are facing away from the enemy who approached from the other side of the river.*

The railway bridge and the road bridge up the canal in the direction from which you came were the responsibility of the 4th Royal Fusiliers to defend and were given to C Company commanded by Captain Ashburner. Following some casualties from the Germans' early shelling, the Company had a brief encounter with a German cavalry (Uhlan) patrol and took prisoner Lieutenant von Arnim, son of the general commanding IV (Ger) Corps.

Shortly after the skirmish with the patrol the German infantry attack began. A solid mass of soldiers in columns of fours came on towards the canal from the north. The Tommies were astounded. Their opponents moved as if on parade, as if taking part in some Napoleonic war game. They were ducks in a shooting gallery to the riflemen of the BEF who were trained to fire fifteen aimed rounds a minute and capable of almost double that with such a target. Although their first attacks failed, the Germans came on, pausing to direct machine gun fire on to the Fusiliers' positions and to co-ordinate their attack with artillery fire. The two machine guns commanded by Lieutenant Dease, sited on the top of the embankment where you are standing at the southern end of the bridge, wreaked terrible havoc among the grey horde, but the Fusiliers were suffering too.

Captain Ashburner was wounded in the head and, despite reinforcements brought up from the battalion reserve in the Place, by midday the situation was becoming serious. Only one machine gun was now operating and that was being fired single-handed by Lieutenant Dease, despite his having been hit three times. Inevitably Dease died (he is buried in St Symphorien cemetery, which is visited at the end of this tour) and Fusilier Private Frank Godley volunteered to take over the weapon. For a whole hour he held off the German attack as the Fusiliers began a withdrawal down the road to Mons (the road along which you drove to Nimy).

He too was wounded and just before being overwhelmed by the Germans he dismantled the gun and threw it into the canal. Three months later, while in POW camp, Frank Godley learned that he and Lt Dease had each been awarded the Victoria Cross (VC), the first ones of the Great War. After the war Godley, who had a large 'walrus' moustache, dressed as Bairnsfather's 'Old Bill' and raised funds for the Royal British Legion. At the end of the day the Fusiliers counted some 250 casualties, about half the number of Germans they had killed.

Below the bridge on the southern side is a bronze plaque commemorating the action and the awards. The French blew up the bridge in 1940 damaging the plaque which was recovered by a villager from Nimy who looked after it until the end of the war. The bridge was blown up again in September 1944 and the plaque was placed on the present bridge on 12 November 1961.

Return to your car and continue your journey along the Rue Grande following signs to SHAPE *(which you will pass on your left) or to Brussels. After* SHAPE*, and immediately following a crossroads controlled by traffic lights, is a rise with a stone memorial beside the road on the left and an isolated building on the right. Stop on the left hand side of the road.*

THE FIRST AND LAST SHOTS MEMORIALS It was near this spot that Corporal E. Thomas of C Squadron 4th Royal Irish Dragoon Guards (4th RIDG) fired the first British shot of the war, an event commemorated by the cairn which was unveiled on 20 August 1939. Not since Waterloo had the British fired a shot on the Continent of Europe. The memorial stands where the 4th RIDG began their charge upon the enemy.

General Allenby's cavalry had crossed into Belgium on 21 August and at about 0700 hours on 22 August, while riding out from Mons the RIDG, part of the division, made contact with the enemy along this road. Two troops of the Dragoons were involved – 1st Troop who engaged with sabres and 4th Troop who used their rifles. Corporal Thomas, who was in 4th Troop, described what happened:

'I saw a troop of Uhlans [German cavalry] coming leisurely down the road, the officer in front smoking a cigar. We were anxiously watching their movements when, quicker than I can write here, they halted, as if they had smelt a rat. They had seen us! They turned quickly back. Captain Hornby got permission to follow on with the sabre troop and down the road they galloped.'

Hornby's 1st Troop charged into the middle of the Germans, who included three cyclists, Hornby himself running a German lieutenant through with his sabre. Meanwhile, as the enemy dismounted and scattered, 4th Troop came up and dismounted too. Corporal Thomas's account continued:

'Bullets were flying past us, and possibly because I was rather noted for my quick movements and athletic ability in those days, I was first in action. I could see a German cavalry officer some four hundred yards away standing mounted in full view of me, gesticulating to the left and to the right as he disposed of his dismounted men and ordered them to take up their firing positions to engage us. Immediately I saw him I took aim, pulled the trigger and automatically, almost as it seemed instantaneously, he fell to the ground, obviously wounded, but whether he was killed or not is a matter that I do not think was ever cleared up.'

In all eight Germans were killed. There were no British casualties and Captain Hornby was awarded the DSO.

Cross the road to the plaque on the building opposite.

The plaque commemorates the place where, at 1100 hours on 11 November 1918, an advanced post of the 116th Canadian Infantry Battalion welcomed the cease-fire. The Canadian Corps had liberated Mons earlier that day and had continued their advance to this spot where Corporal Thomas had fired the first shot four years before.

Return to your car. Drive back to the first traffic light junction and turn left onto the

Voie d'Hayons following the road under the motorway to Obourg. Drive over the canal and the railway and take the first left sharply backward to the railway station. Stop. The cement works which you may have been able to make out from the Belfry viewpoint is on the canal to the west of you. Walk over the footbridge to the centre platform and what seems to be an isolated square wall. There is a plaque on the northern face.

THE ACTION AT OBOURG RAILWAY STATION The plaque, unveiled on 9 September 1951, commemorates the stand of the 4th Middlesex here and the bravery of a lone British soldier who held the Germans at bay from the roof of a building which once stood on this spot. The area has changed since 1914 but the line of the old houses on the northern bank and the line of the road on which you have parked give a clear indication of the position of the original bridge.

The Middlesex had taken up fire positions all around the village on 23 August. D Company commanded by Captain Glass covered the bridge and B Company in the station was commanded by Lt Wilmot-Aliston following the death of the company commander and his 2IC in the storm of German artillery fire that began around 0800 hours. It was probably in this area that Private J. Parr, the first British soldier to be killed, met his fate. He is buried in St Symphorien cemetery. Lt Wilmot-Aliston became the first British soldier to be taken prisoner by the Germans.

The Middlesex machine guns and rapid fire caused appalling casualties in the thickly packed grey ranks of the six assaulting battalions. As at Nimy, the Germans paused and regrouped, adopting tactical movements co-ordinated with machine gun and artillery fire. Despite support from two companies of the 2nd Battalion RIR at around midday, the Middlesex were forced to withdraw shortly afterwards. Latest reports of Captain Henry Glass were that, despite two legs shattered by machine gun bullets, he remained propped up against a wall of the railway station overseeing the withdrawal of his men. The unknown soldier on the roof covered his comrades as they moved out until he was killed by the advancing Germans. The Middlesex had suffered badly. At the beginning of the day they had been almost one thousand strong. At evening roll call under three hundred answered their names.

Return to your car and continue along the Rue d'Obourg some 2km to traffic lights. Turn left along the Avénue Reine Astrid. About 1km later as the road rises you reach a crossroads. There are two memorials on the left. This is la Bascule.

THE LA BASCULE MEMORIALS As the BEF fought their way back from the canal line they made a stand here around the crossroads. The keystone of the defence was a small group of some 40 men gathered together by RQMS Fitzpatrick of the 2nd Battalion Royal Irish Regiment (2nd RIR) and this key crossroads position, so important to the safe withdrawal of the BEF was held until nightfall. At midnight RQMS Fitzpatrick and 18 survivors continued the withdrawal, thus completing an action for which Fitzpatrick was later awarded the DCM.

The first memorial, a Celtic cross, was unveiled by Sir John French on 11 November 1923. It commemorates the actions of the 2nd RIR.

The second memorial claims that 'here' the forces of the British Empire fought the first and last battles of Mons. The memorial was originally in the Belfry garden and was moved here in August 1986. There are rumours that the 'Lord Alexander of Tunis' memorial may be moved here too. The junction is sometimes referred to as the 'Binche crossroads'.

On the corner diagonally opposite are the grounds of Gendebien Château, now the residence of the C–in–C at SHAPE. At the time of the battle the building was used as a British medical station and was set alight by German shelling..

Return to your car and continue along Reine Astrid, taking the left fork, Route de Binche, signed St Symphorien. After some 2km you will see signs to the British cemetery. Follow them.

SAINT SYMPHORIEN CWGC CEMETERY This is one of the, if not *the*, most unusual cemeteries on the Western Front. It was begun by the Germans immediately after the battle in the remains of an old potash mine and the layout of the cemetery follows the contours of the spoil heaps, with trees and bushes forming leafy glades connected by small paths.

At one side of the entrance is the bronze box which contains the visitors' book and the cemetery register (in alphabetical order) of all the British soldiers buried here and on the other side is a box containing German information, for men of both sides lie in this cemetery – true 'comradeship in death'.

The German graves have grey granite markers grouped regimentally, often with different headstones for officers and men, while the British have the standard white Portland stone headstone. (Harder Italian Carrera-style stone is now used when headstones are replaced.) Among the almost 400 British are some graves of particular note:

LIEUTENANT MAURICE DEASE VC, generally accepted as having won the first VC of the war, though four VCs were won on the first day of the battle.

PRIVATE J. PARR, said to be the first British soldier killed in the war. There is considerable argument about the date of his death: whether it was 22 or 23 August, the date on the headstone having been altered. Two RFC men buried in Tournai Commonwealth War Graves Commission cemetery, 2nd Lieutenants Waterfall and Bayley, were killed on 22 August 1914. Bayley was a distant relative of Gordon of Khartoum and a friend of Lanoe Hawker.

PRIVATE J. L. PRICE, the last soldier to be killed in the Great War. He was shot by a German sniper at 1058 hours on 11 November 1918 while holding flowers given to him by Belgian civilians grateful for their liberation. He was Canadian.

PRIVATE G. E. ELLISON, of the 5th Royal Irish Lancers, who was the last British soldier to be killed in the War, also on 11 November 1918.

The Germans erected a number of memorials in the cemetery – to the 'Royal' Middlesex Regiment (a column surmounted by a sphere), to the Royal Fusiliers (a curved stone seat), to the Royal Irish Regiment, and an obelisk to the dead of both armies. Details and locations of all of these are given in the cemetery register.

Please sign the cemetery visitors' book. The work – and hence the funding – of the Commonwealth War Graves Commission is partly judged by the number of visitors to its cemeteries.

LE CATEAU

26 AUGUST 1914

'Early on that memorable day the Cornwalls, after a
wretched night, stood to arms. It was still dark
and their clothes were sodden with rain: many had
not slept at all . . .. Stand To was the worst hour
of the day: chilled through and drowsy . . ..'
DCLI Regimental History

SUMMARY OF THE BATTLE

Following its defeat at Mons on 23 August 1914 the BEF fell back to the south,
pursued by the Germans. Just after dawn three confused days later, on the
anniversary of the Battle of Crécy, von Kluck's army caught Smith-Dorrien's
tired II Corps at le Cateau from where, after a morning's battle, the retreat
continued. British casualties were about 8,000 men and 38 guns. German
casualties are estimated at 9,000.

OPENING MOVES

The plan of the French Commander in Chief, General Joffre, to counter the
German invasion was known as 'Plan 17'. Its essential idea was that of a massive
counter-attack through the German centre to the south-east of Belgium. What
came out of Plan 17 was a series of four major engagements known as 'The
Battle of the Frontiers'.

In three of the battles in Lorraine, the Ardennes and on the Sambre, the
French, following their tactical doctrine of *l'attaque à l'outrance* (attack to the
extreme), threw themselves forward into the maelstrom of German machine-
gun and artillery fire without apparent regard to tactical caution.

The French offensive stopped in bloody confusion with over 300,000
casualties and the armies began to withdraw.

The fourth 'Battle of the Frontiers' was the stand of the BEF at Mons on 23
August and as night fell Sir John French, the British Commander-in-Chief, had
in mind to continue the defence the following day.

The French 5th Army to the immediate right of the BEF was under the
command of the 62-year-old General Lanrézac who, believing that the security
of his whole army was threatened, that same night of 23 August gave the order

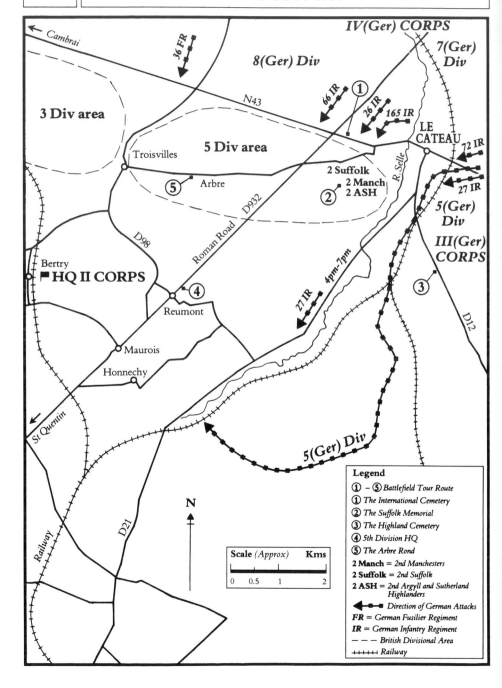

MAP 3

II CORPS STAND AT LE CATEAU
Showing the German Attacks
26 AUGUST 1914

IV(Ger) CORPS

Cambrai

36 FR

8(Ger) Div

7(Ger) Div

N43

66 IR

①

26 IR

165 IR

3 Div area

5 Div area

LE CATEAU

72 IR

Troisvilles

2 Suffolk

R. Selle

⑤

Arbre

2 Manch
2 ASH

27 IR

②

5(Ger) Div

Roman Road

D932

III(Ger) CORPS

D98

Bertry

HQ II CORPS

27 IR

4pm-7pm

③

D12

④

Reumont

Maurois

Honnechy

St Quentin

5(Ger) Div

N

Railway

D21

Scale *(Approx)* **Kms**

0   0.5   1   2

Legend

① – ⑤ *Battlefield Tour Route*
① *The International Cemetery*
② *The Suffolk Memorial*
③ *The Highland Cemetery*
④ *5th Division HQ*
⑤ *The Arbre Rond*
2 Manch = *2nd Manchesters*
2 Suffolk = *2nd Suffolk*
2 ASH = *2nd Argyll and Sutherland Highlanders*
◀■■ *Direction of German Attacks*
FR = *German Fusilier Regiment*
IR = *German Infantry Regiment*
– – – *British Divisional Area*
++++ *Railway*

for a general retreat without telling Joffre – or the BEF. Fortunately there was a British liaison officer with the 5th Army who brought the news of the with-drawal to Sir John in his HQ at le Cateau just before midnight. Orders were sent immediately for the BEF to retire.

General Haig's I Corps, which had not been in action, received its orders by wire at 0200 hours on 24 August and was underway before dawn. General Smith-Dorrien's II Corps HQ was not in telegraphic contact, having been in battle all day, and its orders did not arrive until 0300 hours. As II Corps began to move it was once more under fire.

Sir John French oscillated between innocent optimism and extreme pessimism about the military situation. The British high command did not trust the French and Lanrézac's retreat reinforced that attitude. When Lord Kitchener had briefed the British C-in-C on the responsibilities of the BEF he had said that it was 'to support and co-operate with the French Army' but had added 'you will in no case come in any sense under the orders of any allied general'. Sir John had met Lanrézac on 17 August, a week before Mons. Neither spoke the other's language and the meeting ended uncomfortably. Thus nation to nation there was hardly accord in the adjoining allied forces.

Yet things were just as bad within the BEF. Douglas Haig, commanding I Corps under Sir John, wrote in his diary, 'I know that (Sir John) French is quite unfit for this great command', while Sir John was not at all pleased at the appointment of Horace Smith-Dorrien to command II Corps. He had named General Plumer to take over after the original Corps commander died, but Kitchener chose Smith-Dorrien, who himself wasn't the greatest fan of the C-in-C. These antipathies laid reins over the course of the coming battle and led to unpleasant post-war altercations as to whether the battle of le Cateau need ever have been fought.

At 2025 hours on 24 August Sir John French issued 'Operation Order No. 7'. It said in part:

'The army will move tomorrow, 25th inst, to a position in the neighbourhood of le Cateau, exact positions will be pointed out on the ground tomorrow . . ..'

It was a long march. I Corps were to take the eastern half of the position and II Corps the western. On average the troops had to march between 20 and 25 miles. I Corps routes were very complex, crossing and recrossing the River Sambre, and they were also occupied here and there by the retreating French. Thus I Corps fell behind II Corps and communication between the corps was lost.

At 2100 hours on 25 August Smith-Dorrien received orders from GHQ to continue the withdrawal on the following day and not to make a stand. Yet II Corps actually stood and fought. The reader is invited to consider the circumstances in which the decision to fight was made and for that purpose should now assume the identity of General Smith-Dorrien. Imagine that it is

0200 hours on the morning of 26 August. Your corps has been on the move for 24 hours, marching along roads thick with refugees. It is dark. It is raining. You have no communications with I Corps but you have heard rumours that they are behind (to the north) of you and that they are under pressure from the Germans.

Your troops are tired and are now approaching the town of le Cateau, which offers a certain solidity for defence and some comfort from the elements. You may get an idea of the conditions from this account by Frank Richards, a soldier in the Royal Welch Fusiliers, who described how he got to the town from Mons: 'We marched all night and the greatest part of the next day and dug trenches . . .. We were only in those trenches a few hours before we were on the march again . . .. We marched all night again and all next day . . .. We arrived in le Cateau about midnight, dead-beat to the world. I don't believe any one of us at this time realised that we were retiring, though it was clear that we were not going in the direction of Germany. Of course the officers knew, but they were telling us that we were drawing the enemy into a trap. Le Cateau that night presented a strange sight. Everyone was in a panic, packing up their stuff on carts and barrows to get away south in time. The Royal Welch camped on the square in the centre of the town. We were told to get as much rest as we could. The majority sank down where they were and fell straight asleep.'

General Allenby suddenly arrives at your HQ and says, in effect, 'The high ground before le Cateau that I planned to hold to cover your retreat tomorrow has been taken by the enemy. I cannot contact General French and in my opinion the Germans will attack you at first light unless you can get away now and in the dark.' You are also out of contact with GHQ which has moved back to St Quentin. It is up to you alone to decide what to do. You call in your divisional commanders to report to you. They virtually say, 'Many men are separated from their units' or 'The men are too weary to move before the morning', or 'The roads are jammed with refugees', or 'Some roads have been washed out by the storm.'

What would you decide to do? Would you obey your order to continue to retreat? Smith-Dorrien decided to disobey his orders and to stay and fight on the ridge which runs behind the town and roughly parallel to the le Cateau-Cambrai road.

WHAT HAPPENED

Shortly after dawn on 26 August, German troops of the left hand column of III (Ger) Corps entered le Cateau and came up against elements of 5th Division – the Duke of Cornwall's Light Infantry (DCLI) and East Surreys – near the railway bridge, when after a short fire fight conducted from the windows of the houses the British withdrew to the high ground behind the town.

Realizing that the British meant to stand and fight, von Kluck decided to mount a frontal attack with IV (Ger) Corps behind an artillery barrage on the main British line behind the Cambrai–le Cateau road, and to send III (Ger) Corps to the east to outflank the BEF (see Map 3). The British line consisted of 5th Division on the high ground astride the Roman road covering from le Cateau to Troisvilles, 3rd Division to the west up to Caudry and the newly arrived 4th Division beyond that.

An early German cavalry attack on the extreme left of the BEF was checked and German small arms activity then focused upon the 5th Division area through the morning, with infantry pressing forward tactically across the broken ground with machine guns, and using the spire of le Cateau church as an Observation Point (OP). By mid-morning the Germans controlled the high ground to the east of the River Selle and had uncovered the end of the British position.

The morning had been an artillery battle above all else, with some 230 Royal Artillery pieces ranged against about 550 of the enemy along the total frontage of about 13 miles. The 5th Division area from the le Cateau spur to Troisvilles was about 4½ miles and consisted mostly of cut cornfields with patches of beet and clover, dramatically different to the houses and slag heaps of Mons. With the exception of the broken ground behind the railway station the general aspect was one of gently rolling Atlantic waves of open fields. There was little opportunity to find cover for guns or for men.

The Germans continued to concentrate their efforts upon the le Cateau spur across which the Roman road struck straight through to St Quentin. A break-through at le Cateau could divide and perhaps destroy Smith-Dorrien's Corps. The main strain of the attack fell upon the King's Own Yorkshire Light Infantry (KOYLI) and the Suffolks and an attempt to reinforce them by the Manchesters and two companies of the Argylls failed. Nevertheless, at midday the British line still held.

Inexorably von Kluck's forces built up against the open right flank and by 1300 hours the British on the exposed spur were under artillery fire from three German divisions and under frontal and flank attacks by a dozen infantry battalions. It was time to get out.

Smith-Dorrien decided to withdraw by divisions from right to left, i.e. 5th Division would be the first to move. His order was issued at 1340 hours but much of the line communication had been destroyed by the artillery bombard-ments and the message had to be delivered by runner. 5th Division HQ received the order at 1400 hours, forward units got it at 1500 hours. 2nd KOYLI and 2nd Suffolk never got it at all and by 1600 hours they were surrounded and wiped out.

The Royal Artillery had suffered badly. Not a single battery left on the ridge was capable of sustained action, being damaged or without horses or ammunition. But some guns could be saved – had to be saved – and, in volunteering to return to the ridge and recover the remaining two guns of 37

(Howitzer) battery, drivers Fred Luke and Job Drain, as well as their officer, Captain Douglas Reynolds, won the vc.

Thus II Corps withdrew from le Cateau, having stopped the German advance for half a day in a battle that many, including Sir John French, said should never have been fought. Others believed that the fight had saved the BEF and even the C-in-C in his Despatch dated 7 September 1914 wrote, 'I cannot close the brief account of this glorious stand of the British troops without putting on record my deep appreciation of the valuable services rendered by General Sir Horace Smith-Dorrien. I say without hesitation, that the saving of the left wing of the Army under my command on the morning of August 26 could never have been accomplished unless a commander of rare and unusual coolness, intrepidity and determination had been present to conduct the operation personally.'

Later French was to vilify the II Corps Commander (who was extremely popular with his men and whose cheery smile was recorded as being a great morale-raising factor during the Retreat) and accuse him of disobeying orders at le Cateau. In 1915 he had Smith-Dorrien recalled to England.

However, contact with the Germans had been broken. They did not immediately pursue and the BEF was able to breathe a little more easily as it fell back towards Paris and the Marne. Le Cateau cost over 8,000 casualties and 38 guns.

THE BATTLEFIELD TOUR

The tour begins at the International Cemetery immediately to the north of le Cateau and visits the Suffolk memorial on the le Cateau ridge, the Highland Cemetery, 5th Division HQ building at Reumont and the site of the *arbre rond*. If the weather is wet, wellingtons would be advisable.

Total distance   15 miles

Total time   2 hours 30 minutes

Map   IGN 2607 1:25,000 or 1:50,000 le Cateau est

Drive to the main crossroads, immediately to the west of le Cateau, of the D932 and N43 and continue north on the D932 for 500 yards following the green CWGC signs to the 'le Cateau Military Cemetery.' Stop.

LE CATEAU MILITARY CEMETERY   This is also known as the International Cemetery because of the considerable number of British, German and Russian burials. The ground was laid out by the Germans in February 1916 with separate plots for their own and for the British dead. There are over 5,000 Germans buried here (most are buried in a mass grave) including some females. There are a number of large German memorials including a pyramid structure on which is embossed SEI GETREU BIS DEN TOD (Faithful unto Death). Curiously a very similar pyramid is to be found on the 1942 battlefield of El Alamein to commemorate German fighter pilot Captain H. J. Marseille. Also in this cemetery is a memorial column erected by the Leibkurassier Regiment which names its casualties on the day of the battle. Thirty-four Russian prisoners lie together in a separate plot. The British burials number some 640 buried in sections representative of 1914 and 1918, including the grave of Lance Corporal John William Sayer, VC who won his award for an action on 21 March 1918. This general area formed a focus for the attacks of the 7th (Ger) Division and from here the German artillery had clear views over the British positions.

Walk to the southern border of the cemetery.

The view to the south is directly towards the high ground of the le Cateau ridge beyond the town and over which runs the Roman road (a southern extension of the road you have just used) and on which 5th Division made its stand. Note the white water tower on your left. It is a useful reference point.

Return to your car, drive to the crossroads and turn left towards le Cateau. Using the recommended IGN map fork right before the town as the road goes downhill and make your way to the College buildings at les Essarts (point 109). Drive up the track to the right of the perimeter fence as far as mud will allow. Park. Continue to walk past houses on the left following the sunken lane and keep right at the next track junction. The track that you are following is shown on the map. When you reach a memorial among a group of trees, stop. You are on high ground of point 139.

THE SUFFOLK MEMORIAL (see Map 3)   This marks the centre of the Suffolk's position, one of the four infantry regiments that made up 14th Brigade, part of 5th Division. The other regiments were the 1st East Surreys, the 1st Duke of Cornwall's Light Infantry and the 2nd Manchester Regiment.

The original II Corps order issued from Corps HQ at 2215 hours on 25 August, just over an hour after Sir John French's withdrawal order arrived, envisaged the retreat continuing on 26 August and early that morning the Suffolks had already started to withdraw when, at 0600 hours in thick morning mist, they were stopped and told to hold the spur. Half of the Brigade did not receive that order and were in the skirmish action near the railway station. The Suffolks therefore had no choice of position and had to scratch shallow trenches where they stood, taking up thin firing lines on the forward slope of the feature you have just climbed and facing in an arc generally to the north and north-east.

The supporting artillery, 11th, 52nd and 37th (Heavy) batteries of 15th Brigade Royal Field Artillery (RFA), was lined up some 200 yards behind the Suffolk's trenches but in front of reserve troops so that the guns were actually sited among the infantry. As you can see the position is totally exposed. The only camouflage available to the gunners were stooks of corn which they lashed to the gun wheels. By facing north you can see the white water tower referred to at the International Cemetery, and to the east the skyline marks the high ground beyond the valley of the River Selle, ground that the Germans occupied very early in the morning and thus opened II Corps' right flank. The initial forward movement of von Kluck's forces was towards you from the right of the tower as you look at it and German forces worked their way south along the valley of the River Selle. German machine guns were sited in the area of the tower.

Lt–Col Stevens commanding 15th Brigade RFA told 52nd Battery, 'We will fight it out here and there will be no retirement', and before the guns could be properly dug in they came under rifle fire. Soon after 0600 hours German artillery opened up causing considerable casualties among the gunners and the drop–shorts fell on the Suffolks in their shallow trenches.

At about 1000 hours a German infantry attack began to develop from the area of the River Selle (see Map 3 for orientation) just south of le Cateau and 52nd Battery inflicted considerable damage on the enemy despite having several limbers set on fire by a German HE shell. Another infantry attack began at noon from the ground left and inclusive of the white water tower. Once again it was discouraged by the artillery. The gunners' fire controller had his OP well forward in the front line of the Suffolk trenches and his instructions to the guns were relayed back by a chain of orderlies lying out in the open because all telephone wires had been destroyed.

The volume of noise beating down on the trenches was horrendous. German HE shells from some one hundred guns were bursting overhead and our own guns, between 100 and 200 yards away, added their own cacophony as they returned fire.

Despite attempts at reinforcement by the Manchesters and Argyll and Sutherland Highlanders, the courageous tenacity of the gunners and the steady markmanship of the Suffolks, the German effort built up steadily against this flank, moving ever closer and at mid–morning an aerial observer reported that a 6–mile long column of German infantry was moving down the Roman road towards the crossroads (near the International Cemetery which you visited earlier).

As targets appeared the artillery engaged them but, of the four British batteries supporting the positions on the ridge, only one remained intact at the end of the morning and most of the ammunition in the lines had been used. 52nd Battery fired over 1,100 rounds in the action. At 1330 hours a message was received ordering the guns to withdraw, but heavy casualties among the horses, let alone both men and guns, made this no easy task.

'One of the saddest things I have seen was the wounded horses trying to keep themselves on their legs by leaning against the stooks of corn', said one Sapper officer.

Lt Col. Stevens who had earlier told 52nd Battery that there would be 'no retirement' (the word 'retreat' had not yet come into use in the BEF) decided that he needed confirmation of the order to withdraw before acting upon it and it was not until 1400 hours that the guns of the Brigade were told to move. There was no escape for the 52nd, however, because their CO, Major A. C. R. Nutt, did not receive any order at all.

German infantry were attacking to the right of the Suffolks and working clear round them. A hail of machine gun fire poured down from the guns near the water tower. The British field guns fired singly as best as they could, most of the men being dead or wounded, and the last minutes were described by Lt Col Stevens as follows:

'About 2.40 pm some cheering was heard on our right about 300 yards away and over the crest. About five minutes afterwards we heard 'Stand Fast' and 'Cease Fire' sounded and whistles blown. Then it was shouted down the line from the right, 'You are firing on friends'. All firing stopped at once. On standing upright and looking just over the crest we found everyone standing up and the firing line being rounded up by Germans. The position was lost, considerable numbers of the enemy being round our right and right rear.

The fight had lasted eight hours. The memorial, a cenotaph, commemorates the actions of the Suffolks, the Manchesters, the Argylls and the supporting batteries of the Royal Artillery.

Return to your car and drive into the centre of le Cateau Park.

LE CATEAU   In the Town Hall may be found one of the British field guns that took part in the 1914 action – though if it is not there it may be found in the entrance to the school buildings that lie just to the right of the last crossroads in the town on the Landrécies road. On the opposite corner, at that crossroads, in the Rue de la Fontaine a Gros Bouillons is a stone horse trough used as a flower bed which is the memorial to the British 66th Division which liberated the town in 1918. (It's a long walk from the town centre.) Incorporated into the town cemetery is the British le Cateau Communal Cemetery which was used in August and September 1914 and the last three months of 1918. There are some 150 burials including thirteen Australians.

(9km out of town along the Landrécies road, 2km north of the bridge over the Sambre Canal, is the Commonwealth War Graves Communal Cemetery at Ors. Two VCs, 2 Lt James Kirk and Lt-Col James Neville, are buried here, as well as the war poet Wilfred Owen. All three were killed in the opposed canal crossing on 4 November 1918, the news of Owen's death reaching his parents on 11 November 1918 as the Armistice bells were pealing. On the bridge over the canal in the centre of the village is a memorial to Owen placed by the Wilfred Owen Society and the Western Front Association.)

Leave the town on the D12 road to Wassigny. After going under the railway bridge look out for signs to the Highland Cemetery. Stop and walk to the back wall of the cemetery.

HIGHLAND CEMETERY   At the back wall look right along the wall of the cemetery and just to the left on the skyline are two distinct poplar trees. This is the area of le Cateau Station where the first German attacks began. Left of the poplars is a line of trees and just on their left, as they end, the Suffolk memorial may be visible on the skyline.

Further left is a factory complex which indicates, to a first approximation, the route of the valley of the Selle and left again a large single bushy-top tree on the skyline indicates the village of Reumont where 5th Division had its HQ. It is readily seen from here how the German 5th Division's advance from the railway station area up the Selle River Valley outflanked the Suffolk's position. The skyline running right to left is the route of the Roman road and indicates the line taken by the British 5th Division as it retired on the afternoon of 26 August.

Rudyard Kipling called these military cemeteries 'Silent Cities' and a look at a number of graves here shows the diverse nature of some of them:

PRIVATE OSBORNE, an Australian, he was wounded, commissioned, invalided out, rejoined and then killed;

RIFLEMAN KING, a deacon, the son of a priest, who had to obtain his Bishop's permission to enlist;

LIEUTENANT SKEMP, Professor of English at Bristol University;

PRIVATE SUPPLE, a 19-year-old boy;

PRIVATE TORGERSON, an American from Minnesota.

The cemetery was begun by the 50th (Northumbrian) Division in October 1918 and the name comes either from the high ground on which the cemetery stands or the 32 graves of the Black Watch that are contained within it. Altogether there are some 620 burials.

Return towards le Cateau and at the crossroads beyond the railway bridge turn left on to the D21 towards Busigny. Follow signs to Honnechy on the D115 and thence to Maurois on the D932 Roman road. Drive into and through Reumont and stop at the last building on the right – a pair of semi-detached cottages.

5TH DIVISION BATTLE HQ   The right-hand house of the pair was used by the divisional commander, General Sir Charles Fergusson, as an HQ. Until a few years ago the building was marked with a plaque which has since been stolen. General Fergusson watched most of the battle from the roof of this house, from where he could clearly see the parlous state of our right flank as the Germans worked forward along the Selle Valley.

At noon Smith-Dorrien arrived here and the commanders discussed the possibility of retirement. One hour later Genearl Fergusson sent a message to II Corps HQ at Bertry saying that 5th Division could not hold out much longer and at 1320 hours added that he ought to begin to move unless reinforced.

General Smith-Dorrien ordered the move of two reserve battalions to Bertry to come under Fergusson's command and told the divisional commander to withdraw when he thought fit, after which 3rd and 4th Divisions would follow. Fergusson issued his orders around 1400 hours. Forward battalions did not get them until 1500 hours. Some never got them at all, in particular the KOYLI of 13th Brigade who, despite an heroic stand by Major Yate for which he was awarded the VC, were overwhelmed, only eight officers and 320 men answering the roll that evening.

By 1700 hours the whole of II Corps was in retreat – but in good order with flank guards established. At 1800 hours darkness and rain settled over the long moving column and the German pursuit lost contact.

Continue north along the Roman road to the crossroads below the International Cemetery and turn left on the N43 towards Cambrai. As you drive you are effectively in No Man's Land with the German assaults coming from your right towards 5th Division positions on your left. Also on your left in the middle distance a solitary bushy-top tree should become apparent. Immediately after the auberge on your right take the D98 to Troisvilles keeping left of the calvary in la Sotière. At the crossroads below the cemetery turn left and follow the track to the bushy top tree. Stop. This is point 138, l'Arbre Rond, on the IGN map.

THE 'ARBRE ROND' At the time of the battle trees were few and far between in the area and the tree that stood here was about 40 ft high. It was marked on the maps that the Germans had and they used the tree as a marker on which to range their artillery.

15th Brigade of 5th Division held this area with Brigade HQ nearby in the cutting. 1st Norfolk were tasked to prepare the defences – and they wanted the tree down so that the German guns could not range upon it. They set about sawing it through but never quite finished the job.

There are various accounts about the fate of the tree and the reported planting of a sapling in the late 1950s, but the romantic can scrutinize the gnarled trunk and be convinced that healed saw cuts can be found.

| MAP 4 | **FIRST YPRES** *18 October – 11 November 1914* |

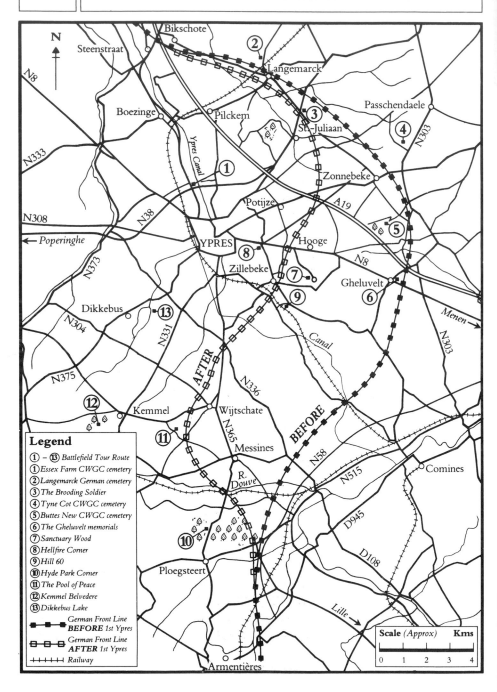

Legend

① – ⑬ *Battlefield Tour Route*
① *Essex Farm CWGC cemetery*
② *Langemarck German cemetery*
③ *The Brooding Soldier*
④ *Tyne Cot CWGC cemetery*
⑤ *Buttes New CWGC cemetery*
⑥ *The Gheluvelt memorials*
⑦ *Sanctuary Wood*
⑧ *Hellfire Corner*
⑨ *Hill 60*
⑩ *Hyde Park Corner*
⑪ *The Pool of Peace*
⑫ *Kemmel Belvedere*
⑬ *Dikkebus Lake*

German Front Line **BEFORE** 1st Ypres
German Front Line **AFTER** 1st Ypres
＋＋＋＋＋ *Railway*

Scale *(Approx)*   **Kms**
0   1   2   3   4

THE FIRST BATTLE
OF YPRES
18 OCTOBER 1914–11 NOVEMBER 1914

*'Shall I ever forget this day? It will be indelibly
stamped on my memory. How anyone
survived to tell the story is a mystery to me.'*
An infantry Captain at Gheluvelt.

SUMMARY OF THE BATTLE

In an attempt to break through the rapidly stabilizing allied line and to reach
Calais, von Falkenhayn launched the 4th and 6th (Ger) Armies against the BEF at
Ypres on 18 October 1914. The fighting, toe to toe, staggered on with no real
advantage gained by either side until heavy rains brought the contest to an end
on 11 November. The British lost 2,350 officers and 55,800 soldiers. German
losses were more than 130,000.

OPENING MOVES

Following II Corps' brief encounter at le Cateau the BEF continued its retreat
from Mons and crossed the River Marne on 3 September. Von Kluck, believing
that the allies were beaten, altered the main thrust of his attack to come east of
Paris and crossed the river only a day after the BEF. This change of direction
exposed his right flank (doubtless von Schlieffen turned in his grave) and on 6
September the French 6th Army struck at it with 150,000 men, while the
remainder of the Allies, including the BEF, about faced and drove the Germans
40 miles back to the Aisne River. The Schlieffen Plan was finished. Its failure
was probably due to Molke's steady weakening of the German right wing,
contrary to Schlieffen's death-bed plea to 'keep it strong'. On 14 September he
was replaced by General Eric Von Falkenhayn.

That same day, 14 September, General Joffre began an attack on the German
positions beyond the Aisne with the BEF and the French 5th and 6th Armies. The
gains against the well-entrenched Germans were small and after two days Joffre
began moving forces to the north-west in an attempt to get around the end of
the German line. Von Falkenhayn responded by moving reserves to outflank the
outflankers who responded in similar measure. The line grew and grew in a 'race
to the sea' which ended when the Allies reached the coast at Niewpoort in
Belgium in the first week of October 1914.

The BEF moved north in the 'race' in two parts. II Corps went directly to la Bassée and immediately came into action on 11 October in the 25-mile gap south of Ypres and I Corps went first to St Omer where the C-in-C, Sir John French, had to make a choice. Either I Corps should go further to the north where thinly stretched French forces together with the recently arrived British 7th Division were maintaining their hold on Ypres and their contact with the Belgians on the coast, or he should reinforce II Corps at la Bassée. He sent I Corps to Ypres and the First Battle began.

WHAT HAPPENED

Le Cateau was the last of the old-style one-day battles. The fighting at Ypres was never so simple. The title 'First Ypres' seems to describe a clear-cut contest, over a set period, with an agreed victor, yet by the end of 1914 the measure of victory was changing. It was no longer 'he who held the ground' but 'he who had the will to fight' who prevailed, and the will depended upon many things, including national reserves of manpower. 'Kill the enemy' became not just a tactical requirement but a strategic necessity. Everywhere, all the time, each side was intent upon killing the other. 'All Quiet Along the Potomac Tonight', goes the haunting song from the American Civil War, which goes on to intone that the loss of 'a private or two now and again will not count in the news of the battle'. That daily loss, even when there was no official 'battle' in progress, became significant during the First World War.

It was never 'All Quiet on the Western Front'. The BEF would lose hundreds of men by 'natural wastage' every day from 1915 onwards, yet every so often the enemies lumbered dinosaur-like into battle against each other and engaged in periods of ferocious killing that were graced with distinctive names. So it was with 'First Ypres', where the blood of a quarter of a million soldiers began etching a line of trenches that would stretch from the North Sea to Switzerland. Yet when the battle began (and historians cannot agree on the exact date) the leaders were still hoping for a great victory, a decisive battle. It was not to be.

The armchair analyst can divide First Ypres into neat and separate parts:–

Battle of Armentières	13 Oct.–2 Nov.
Battle of Messines	12 Oct.–2 Nov.
Battle of Langemarck	21 Oct.–24 Oct.
Battle of Gheluvelt	29 Oct.–31 Oct.
Battle of Nonne Boschen	11 Nov

These classifications are geographical and the actions associated with them are best described during the battlefield tour (p.97) which for simplicity covers First, Second and Third Ypres simultaneously. Lumping together the October and November actions, the 'First' Battle of Ypres is generally accepted to have opened on 18 October 1914 when the Germans began a three-week period of repeated mass attacks against the British positions. The British occupied a salient which bulged forward with a 16 mile-long perimeter into the German line (see Map 4). The heart of the Salient was Ypres, its defence now the responsibility of I Corps, and German attacks were concentrated along the axis of the Menen Road which enters Ypres from the east, passing as it does so the hamlet of Gheluvelt, barely 8 miles from Ypres Cathedral.

On 31 October Gheluvelt was lost and the Germans were on the brink of breaking through the line, outflanking the BEF and making a run for the Channel ports. In one of the most remarkable actions of the War, the 2nd Worcesters charged the enemy at Gheluvelt and saved the day. The Germans made one more major effort along the same axis when on 11 November 12½ divisions attacked across a 9-mile front with almost 18,000 men against 8,000. It wasn't enough. On that day, weighted down with mud and casualties, the First Battle of Ypres ended. The Salient perimeter had shrunk to 11 miles; but Ypres had not fallen. It never would.

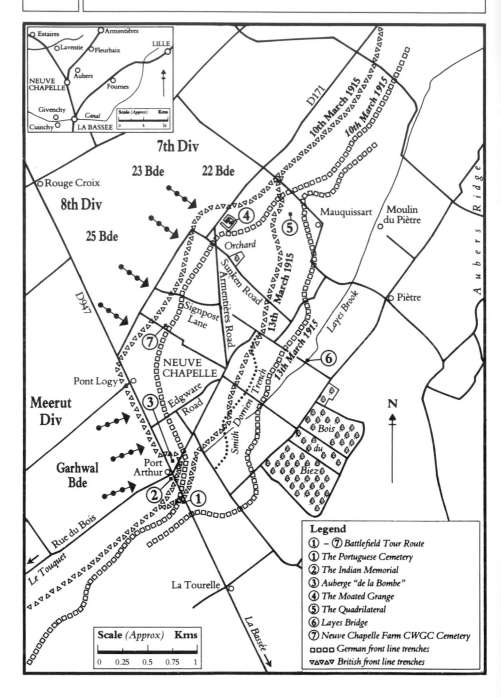

| MAP 5 | NEUVE CHAPELLE 10 – 13 MARCH 1915 |

Estaires
Armentières
Laventie
Fleurbaix
LILLE
NEUVE CHAPELLE
Aubers
Fournes
Givenchy
Canal
Scale (Approx) Kms
Cuinchy
LA BASSEE

7th Div

23 Bde
22 Bde

Rouge Croix

8th Div

25 Bde

Mauquissart
Moulin du Piètre

Orchard

Piètre

Aubers Ridge

D947

Sunken Road
Armentières Road

Signpost Lane

NEUVE CHAPELLE

Pont Logy

Meerut Div

Edgware Road

Smith Dorrien Trench

Layes Brook

Bois du Biez

N

Garhwal Bde

Port Arthur

Rue du Bois

Le Touquet

La Tourelle

La Bassée

Legend
① – ⑦ Battlefield Tour Route
① The Portuguese Cemetery
② The Indian Memorial
③ Auberge "de la Bombe"
④ The Moated Grange
⑤ The Quadrilateral
⑥ Layes Bridge
⑦ Neuve Chapelle Farm CWGC Cemetery
▯▯▯▯ German front line trenches
▽△▽△▽ British front line trenches

Scale (Approx) Kms
0 0.25 0.5 0.75 1

NEUVE CHAPELLE

10–13 MARCH 1915

'The attack which we are about to undertake is of the first importance to the Allied Cause. The Army and the Nation are watching the results, and Sir John French is confident that every individual in the IVth Corps will do his duty and inflict a crushing defeat on the German VIIth Corps which is opposed to us'.
Written note from General Rawlinson commanding IV Corps given to every soldier before Neuve Chapelle.

'The G.O.C. the Division desires me to convey to you and all ranks under your command his deep appreciation of the splendid work performed by your battalion during the last few days' hard fighting. For my own part I find it difficult to express adequately my admiration for the way in which you have fought. I mourn with you for our gallant comrades who have fallen, but the splendid cause for which they have fought, and the brave way in which they have died, must always be the greatest comfort to those whom they have left behind, and stimulate them to fresh efforts'.
Message passed after Neuve Chapelle to the 13th Bn London Regiment ('The Kensingtons') by Brigadier Lowry-Cole commanding 25 Brigade.

A Summary of the Battle

This was the first British-initiated offensive of the war and was prompted by French doubts about British commitment to the conflict. Following a massive but short bombardment, General Haig's 1st Army attacked the village of Neuve Chapelle which was taken on the first day. However, von Falkenhayn's rapid movement of reserves and a British shortage of ammunition prevented a breakthrough. British casualties were about 13,000, the German 14,000.

OPENING MOVES

On 15 February 1900 General French led a dashing cavalry charge to complete the relief of Kimberley after a 5-month siege by the Boers. Fifteen years later, now commanding the British Expeditionary Force on the continent of Europe, he once again seemed to have in mind a cavalry charge through enemy lines, something which, like the Kimberley affair, he hoped would have great publicity and morale benefits.

By the end of 1914 the trench system behind which each opposing army sheltered was well defined along the Western Front and the prospect of huge casualties from frontal attacks had been signalled by First Ypres. Fertile minds like Winston Churchill were seeking alternatives to mutual mass bludgeoning in Europe as a way of settling the war and by 1915 the Gallipoli alternative was taking shape. The French, however, unlike the British, had the enemy on their soil which concentrated their minds to a much shorter focal length and in January and February they engaged in aggressive and successful operations in Champagne, retaking important ground from the Germans.

The Champagne offensives generated benefits in that large bodies of German troops were diverted from the Eastern Front, but they also had a tactical lesson that was to colour the next four years of warfare. The French had won back territory by a new and sophisticated use of artillery. First they chose a sector to attack where surprise was possible. Then, by massing their artillery, they pounded the enemy front line into oblivion. At a pre-determined hour, the barrage lifted and moved behind the front line to drop between it and the German reserves. Thus reinforcements were prevented, by a curtain of steel, from moving to the front. Meanwhile the French infantry advanced and captured the German front line positions.

At the beginning of March 1915, the Belgians held the line from the North Sea to Dixmuide and the French from Dixmuide to the top of the Ypres Salient. West of Neuve Chapelle were IV Corps under General Rawlinson and the Indian Corps under General Willcocks, both part of the 1st Army. The BEF had expanded to some 18 divisions, three times its original strength of August 1914 and was now divided into two armies. Sensitive to French innuendo that the British were not pulling their weight, the C-in-C decided to mount the first British offensive of the war, an attack with General Haig's 1st Army. He gave as his reasons for offering 'a vigorous offensive movement', 'the apparent weakness of the enemy in my front . . . holding as many hostile troops as possible in the western theatre (and) . . . the need of fostering the offensive spirit in the troops under my command'.

It was decided to attack the German salient at Neuve Chapelle with a view to taking the high ground around Aubers Ridge to the east of the village and to effecting a breakthrough. There were to be two phases: (1) take the village and the line known as 'Smith-Dorrien trench' to the east of the village (see Map 5);

and (2) enlarge the gap in the enemy line and make towards the Aubers Ridge. On 9 March General Haig finished his Special Order for the Day with these words, 'To ensure success each one of us must play his part and fight like men for the honour of old England.' At least half of the fighting, however, was to fall to the Indian Division and not the men of old England.

What Happened

At 0730 on 10 March almost 500 guns opened fire on the German lines over a length of 2 miles. Thirty-five minutes later the guns lifted and the iron curtain fell across the village of Neuve Chapelle itself. Simultaneously the Garwhal Brigade, the assault formation of the Indian Corps, 'swarmed over the parapet and doubling over the intervening space of from 100 to 200 yards reached (except one battalion) its first objective without a check'.

On the north western flank of the salient the assault by 8th Division met with similar success, only the Middlesex being held up just south of the Moated Grange. Complete surprise had been achieved and the village and Smith-Dorrien trench were taken. Now was the time for urgency, to move on quickly to Phase 2, but communication between the two Corps commanders was confused, each waiting for the other to act, and it was five hours before General Haig ordered the attack to continue. The Germans had reacted quickly, bringing up reinforcements through thin British artillery fire. It was thin because the front had been widened but mainly because the British did not have enough ammunition to continue the bombardment at an effective rate. The shortage developed into a public outcry known as 'The Shell Scandal', which led to the appointment of Lloyd George as Minister of Munitions with the task of sorting things out. One of his actions was to introduce liquor licensing laws in an attempt to reduce absenteeism due to alcohol. Even today, therefore, some effects of the battle of Neuve Chapelle remain.

The results at the end of 10 March were, however, considerable. A front of 4,100 yards from Port Arthur to just beyond the Moated Grange had been taken and to a depth in places of 1,200 yards. The whole of Neuve Chapelle village had been captured. Little more was thereafter gained. The Germans mounted a counter-attack at dawn on 12 March with 16,000 men against the Indian Brigade and the front of 8th Division, but this failed to make any advance. It did however pre-empt any further offensive action of substance by 1st Army so that on 13 March both sides settled down to consolidate the positions that they held.

The battle was over, but now the British felt themselves to be more substantial than just an adjunct to the French forces, the French had proof that the British were willing to fight, the Germans began to strengthen their lines opposite the British and everyone adopted the destructive artillery barrage as being standard practice for the battles to come.

THE BATTLEFIELD TOUR

The battlefield tour begins at the Portuguese memorial immediately south of Port Arthur on the D947. The Indian memorial is next, followed by the Moated Grange, the Quadrilateral, Layes Bridge, Neuve Chapelle Farm CWGC Cemetery, and the tour ends at the le Touret memorial to the Missing.

Total distance   10 miles

Total time   2 hours

Maps   IGN 2404 Est 1:25,000 plus IGN 2405 Est 1:25,000

Drive north from la Bassée on the D947 for 3 miles until you reach the clearly signed Portuguese cemetery on the left. There is a chapel opposite. Stop and beware of the traffic.

THE PORTUGUESE MEMORIAL   This has no connection with the battle of 1915 but relates to the Kaiser's offensive of 1918. Since the memorial is on our route, and the Portuguese did come into action here on 9 April 1918, it has been included.

The two division Portuguese Army was dispirited by 1918. A change of government had meant that they no longer had political support at home and their morale was low. Anticipating a German offensive, the British area commander withdrew one of the Portuguese divisions and before it could be replaced by a British force, the enemy struck directly at the one remaining Portuguese division, now holding a double frontage. Unlike their forbears at Busaco in 1810, they broke, some taking the machines of a British cyclist battalion and pedalling their way to safety, but many others fought well against overwhelming odds. Their losses were heavy – some 7,000 were killed in the action known as the Battle of the Lys during which Neuve Chapelle was lost – and they are commemorated with pride by their countrymen.

The cemetery on the left contains 1,831 burials, of whom 239 are unidentified. The entrance gate, inspired by Léal de Camara, is unfortunately usually locked. Over the road is a small chapel to Notre Dame de Fatima, built in the 1970s by the local Portuguese immigrants' association to honour their compatriots killed during the First World War.

During the Battle of the Lys the Portuguese, for divine protection, carried into their trenches a damaged statue of Christ, with legs broken off at the knees, the right arm broken and the chest wounded. When they were forced to leave the trenches they abandoned the statue and it was later retrieved by the Bocquet family who had originally erected it in 1877. When the village of Neuve Chapelle was rebuilt, the old statue was propped up beside a new calvary, and remained in situ throughout the Second World War. In 1958, on the 40th anniversary of the Lys battle, the French Government awarded Portugal's Unknown Soldier with the Croix de Guerre and the Légion d'Honneur and the Bocquets agreed to allow the statue to travel to the commemorative monastery of Batallha (founded in 1385). Great ceremony and pomp attended the delegation (which included Portuguese veterans who had settled in France) which flew to Lisbon on a military plane bearing a message from President Rêné Coty to President Salazar. On 9 April 1958 the 'Christ of the Trenches' was erected above the tomb of the Portuguese Unknown Soldiers (one from the First World War, one from Africa) where it remains to this day.

Continue north to the next crossroads. The Indian memorial is on the left. Stop

NEUVE CHAPELLE INDIAN MEMORIAL This is Port Arthur crossroads, the southern end of the Indian Corps' front on 10 March 1915. The intended main thrust of the attack here (by the 1/39th Garhwalis) was west to east, enveloping the entire crossroads. The 1/39th was the one Indian battalion which didn't make its objective. Immediately on leaving the trenches the attack veered right towards the Portuguese memorial area and entered part of the German line which had not come under the preparatory bombardment. The 1/39th suffered heavy casualties, all six British officers who were in the assault were killed. The Indian Corps consisted of two divisions, the 3rd (Lahore) and the 7th (Meerut), both of three brigades. Each brigade contained one British and three Indian battalions, a total Corps strength of some 24,000. The Corps had seen action at Neuve Chapelle in October 1914 and by the end of the year had suffered 9,500 casualties, 7,100 from Indian units. In the 1915 battle the Corps lost one-fifth of its strength and this is therefore an appropriate site for their memorial.

Designed by Sir Herbert Baker, it is circular, with a lotus-capped 50ft high column flanked by two tigers, the whole complex acknowledging the connection with India, from the screen wall to the two domed chattris (loggia). The names of over 5,000 dead with no known grave are carved on the wall, arranged in unit order.

Drive north at the crossroads towards Neuve Chapelle, passing the Auberge de la Bombe on the left.

AUBERGE DE LA BOMBE The café's name has nothing to do with the war. Studious research at the bar (and with the local history society) by the authors established only that the name originated in the Middle Ages and has some connection with the smuggling that went on at that time. However, over the door of the café is the name 'Port Arthur' and the date '10 mars 1915', the opening day of the battle.

Continue through the village and just after a sharp bend right at the junction of the D171 with the D170 there is a small courtyard farmhouse on the right with iron gates. On current maps it may be called 'Ferme de Lestre'. Stop.

THE MOATED GRANGE This is not the original building, though it is on the original site and broadly to the same design and of the same size. It is the northern (left hand) end of the attack frontage for 10 March 1915. At the time of the battle it had been a strongpoint in the German line. The trenches in front of the Middlesex, just below the Grange, held by the 11th Jager Battalion were not bombarded effectively, owing to the late arrival of the artillery. The leading waves of the Middlesex were cut down and the battalion had to be reinforced with two companies of the West Yorks for a later attack. The orchard (see Map 5) immediately south of the Moated Grange (the orchard is no longer there) was, however, finally taken by the Middlesex and the West Yorks just after noon on 10 March. During the morning, 24th Brigade Trench Mortar Battery had dropped over 230 mortar bombs on to the Grange and when the West Yorks worked north from the orchard the German survivors surrendered. Two days later the 13th and 15th (Ger) Infantry Regiments counter-attacked the Grange but were held off, in great measure due to the activities of the newly trained 'bombing' (grenade-throwing) detachments. One bomber, Corporal W. Anderson of the 2nd Green Howards, won the vc for his part in the action for leading three men in a bombing raid against a large group of the enemy.

Continue to the next crossroads and turn right towards Mauquissart and Piètre on the D168.

THE QUADRILATERAL One hundred yards to your right, two hundred yards along the road, was the German defensive area known as the Quadrilateral which was taken by the 2nd Scots Guards on 12 March together with 400 prisoners. It was sadly one of the few places where the pressures of war and harsh military discipline led a soldier to desert. Private Isaac Reid left the forward areas the day before the Quadrilateral action, he was caught, court-martialled and executed in front of the Regiment on 9 April 1915.

Continue through Mauquissart, do not turn right in the village. At Piètre crossroads turn right and take the next right just before the Bois du Biez. After 200 yards there is a small bridge over a stream. Stop.

LAYES BRIDGE This is the centre of the battlefield and the line of the stream, Layes Brook, which features strongly in detailed accounts of the fighting, can be seen clearly to north and south. The Germans had turned this area into a redoubt with barbed wire and 15 machine guns. On 12 March, under the impression that the German line had been broken, General Haig brought up cavalry units and ordered that the infantry attack be pressed forward 'regardless of loss'. It was pressed, but the soldiers were tired, ammunition was short and the German defenders were fresh reinforcements. The Layes Bridge redoubt was never taken and the attack petered out overnight and during the following morning.

Continue to the crossroads with the D171. Turn left and just before the church in Neuve Chapelle turn right down the Rue du Moulin to the second British cemetery sign. Stop.

NEUVE CHAPELLE FARM CWGC CEMETERY There are 35 identified British soldiers buried here and 21 of them are from the 13th Battalion the London Regiment, known as 'the Kensingtons'. The Regiment was typical of the proud Territorial forces that came to the Colours, its origins deriving from the Volunteer forces of 1859. Like most, its gestation was complex. However, the Haldane reforms of 1908 created the Battalion via the amalgamation of the Kensington Rifles (4th Middlesex) and the 2nd (South) Middlesex and in 1913 it became 'Princess Louise's Kensington Regiment'. On 2 August 1914 the Kensingtons arrived at Salisbury Plain for their annual training. That night they were woken up and ordered to return to their drill hall immediately. There they were told to be ready for mobilization, which came two days later. Over the next fortnight the battalion was equipped and brought up to strength and on 16 August it left with other Territorial units for war training in Hertfordshire. Early on the morning of 3 November 1914, led by the band, they marched to Watford station and at 1100 entrained for Southampton. After a long wait they sailed on the 'SS Matheran' at 0100 hours on 4 November, reaching le Havre that same afternoon and marching to St Martin's rest camp on the hill. By foot and train they moved to the area of Laventie and spent the winter manning trenches in what was known as a quiet sector, even exchanging souvenirs with the enemy during an unofficial truce on Christmas day. Nevertheless, by the beginning of March the battalion had 96 casualties, 27 of whom were killed. Then came Neuve Chapelle.

The Kensingtons were in reserve with 25th Brigade. Their task was to follow up the assault battalions. They had a hot meal with the rest of the brigade at Rouge Croix, filled their water bottles with tea and with two extra bandoliers of ammunition each and their rations in a sandbag, marched forward in great anticipation 'of making a decisive step towards the winning of the war'. They never came into contact with the enemy because after the first day the attack made no progress, though they began to suffer casualties from enemy artillery fire. On 11 March they were reinforced with a draft of 133 men, including Lt M. A. Prismall, son of Captain A. Prismall commanding B Company. For three more days they suffered under continuous bombardment and then came the order to move out. As the battalion was about to leave Captain Prismall was killed by a shell. He lies in this cemetery with the other volunteers. He was 53.

Another battalion which suffered severely and with bravery in the Battle of Neuve Chapelle was the 2nd Scottish Rifles, who went into the battle on 10 March some 900 strong of whom 700 went 'over the top'. Six days later, only 143 were fit enough to parade for roll-call after the battle. The story is well-documented in John Baynes' book *Morale: A Study of Men and Courage*.

Continue to the T junction. Turn left and return to Port Arthur. There turn right and continue about 3 miles to a major British cemetery on the left.

LE TOURET MEMORIAL AND CWGC CEMETERY   The memorial commemorates those missing with no known grave in this area over the period from the arrival of the BEF to the eve of the Battle of Loos. Their names are inscribed inside the colonnade in Regimental order. The cemetery, begun in November 1914 by the Indian Corps, was used continually until taken by the Germans in April 1918. There are over 900 burials, including that of Lt Cyril Alfred William Crichton who, until 1925, was buried under a special private memorial near where he fell opposite the Auberge de la Bombe. He was a Territorial.

| MAP 6 | **SECOND YPRES** *22 April – 25 May 1915* |

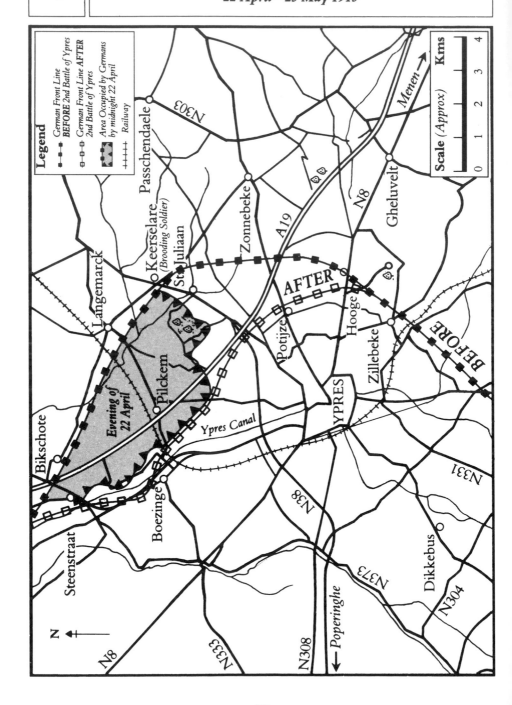

Legend

- German Front Line **BEFORE** 2nd Battle of Ypres
- German Front Line **AFTER** 2nd Battle of Ypres
- Area Occupied by Germans by midnight 22 April
- Railway

Scale (Approx) Kms

Passchendaele

N303

Keerselare
(Brooding Soldier)

St Juliaan

Langemarck

Zonnebeke

A19

N8

Gheluvelt

AFTER

Menen →

Pilckem

Evening of 22 April

Potijze

Hooge

BEFORE

Bikschote

Zillebeke

Ypres Canal

YPRES

N331

Boezinge

Steenstraat

N38

N373

Dikkebus

N304

Poperinghe →

N308

N333

N8

N

SECOND YPRES
22 APRIL 1915–25 MAY 1915

'There was a curious smell, which was quite noticeable
– we all remarked on it – and then after a time the
casualties started coming in. It was most dramatic:
long, long lines of Canadian soldiers, single file, each
man with his hand on the shoulder of the man in front.
There would be a man in front who could see – all these
other chaps couldn't; hundreds and hundreds of these
chaps stumbling along, single file.'
A First World War doctor

SUMMARY OF THE BATTLE

At around 1700 hours on 22 April 1915 the Germans attacked the north-eastern
edge of the Ypres Salient using poison gas in what is generally accepted as the
first major use of gas in warfare. Subsequent defensive fighting against repeated
gas attacks resulted in a shortened Salient, but no breakthrough. Allied casualties
were about 60,000, German 35,000.

OPENING MOVES

At the end of 1914, the German General Staff decided that, having failed to
defeat France quickly and now being faced by enemies in both the east and the
west, they would concentrate upon the Russian front. General Erich von
Falkenhayn considered that Russia, struggling with internal political discontent,
was the weaker of his two immediate protagonists and would succumb to
concentrated German might. As far as the Western Front was concerned he
instructed his commanders only to do enough 'lively activity' to keep the enemy
occupied. One of the things that seemed likely to 'occupy' the French and
British was to try out poison gas on them.

Article 23 of the 1907 Hague Convention, which Germany had signed,
forbade the use of 'poisons or poisonous weapons', but before April 1915 the
Germans had already tried out gas. Shrapnel shells containing a form of chemical
irritant were tried out near Neuve Chapelle in October 1914 and tear gas shells
had been used at Bolimow in Poland in January 1915, but neither trial produced
any significant result. Von Falkenhayn was, however, supportive of the idea of

developing a gas weapon and extensive testing was carried out at the Kummers-dorf artillery ranges near Berlin. In the Second World War another secret weapon was tested there – von Braun's V2 rocket.

Germany possessed the most powerful chemical industry in the world and it was not difficult to consider other ways than shelling in which an enemy might be enveloped in a gas cloud. What was more difficult was to decide where to use the gas and several German commanders considered the use of such a weapon to be unethical. However, Falkenhayn persisted and keeping in mind his need to draw attention away from his intended effort in the east, he looked for a sensitive spot on the Western Front. Ypres was such a place.

The 4th (Ger) Army had been on the edge of breaking through during First Ypres (cf. Gheluvelt p.97) and the Salient was the only significant piece of Belgian soil not yet occupied. Added benefits were that the BEF had been decimated in defending Ypres and any activity there would demand whole-hearted British attention as well as the fact that the French knew full well that holding Ypres was the key to keeping the Germans out of the Pas de Calais. Therefore Duke Albrecht of Wurttemberg and his 4th (Ger) Army facing Ypres were chosen to try out the new weapon. Preparations began in February 1915.

The simplest method of delivery of the gas was by cylinder, since that was the standard commercial container. Train loads of the heavy 3.5-ft long objects were brought into the lines. It is estimated that some 30,000 cylinders were brought up into the forward areas and inevitably some were damaged – by accident or enemy action – so that the presence of the gas weapon was fairly common knowledge among German soldiers as time went on. Now and again German prisoners were taken who spoke about the presence of gas. However neither the French nor the British authorities took the reports seriously enough to take any precautions, though early in April Canadian troops were warned about the possibility of a gas attack following the mention of gas in the 10th (French) Army's 30 March intelligence bulletin.

The cylinders were dug into their firing positions in groups of 20, each group covering 40 yards of front and, 24 hours ahead of the intended assault time, the German soldiers were given their final briefings. At 0500 hours on 22 April 1915 everything was ready – except the wind. It was blowing the wrong way.

WHAT HAPPENED

As the German infantry waited, hoping for the wind to change direction, their field artillery pounded the front line defences and heavy 17-inch guns bom-barded the rear areas. When the day matured it became warm and sunny, perhaps lulling the defenders into a degree of laxity and certainly making the Germans hot and uncomfortable in their heavy equipment. By late afternoon the attack was in the balance. Soon it would be dark. The offensive could not be made at night. Then, soon after 1600 hours a breeze began to develop from the north-east and one hour later the Germans opened the nozzles of thousands of gas cylinders and a fog of death rolled slowly across No Man's Land.

Below the Pilckem Ridge was the Canadian 3rd Brigade and alongside them, north of the ridge, the French Algerian 45th Colonial Division and it was upon these two formations that the fog descended. Sir Arthur Conan Doyle described what happened: 'The French troops, staring over the top of their parapet at this curious screen which ensured them a temporary relief from fire, were observed suddenly to throw up their hands, to clutch at their throats, and to fall to the ground in agonies of asphixiation. Many lay where they had fallen, while their comrades, absolutely helpless against this diabolical agency, rushed madly out of the mephitic mist and made for the rear, over-running the lines of the trenches behind them. Many of them never halted until they had reached Ypres, while others rushed westwards and put the canal between themselves and the enemy.'

By 1900 hours there was no organized body of French troops east of the Yser Canal. Between the Belgians (who held the ground north of the 45th Division's area) and the Canadian 3rd Brigade there was now a gap of 8,000 yards. The way to Ypres was open. The German advance (four reserve divisions – the 45th, 46th, 51st and 52nd) was cautious and limited. Their objective had been to take the Pilckem Ridge and no more and by the time they reached it darkness was falling. Thus it was not until the following morning that they realized how successful their attack had been and just how close they were to Ypres, which they could now see quite clearly ahead of them (see Map 6). The Canadians around St Julien, meanwhile, had reacted to the gas with determination despite the fact that the French panic had left their northern flank unprotected. Brigadier General R. E. W. Turner commanding the Canadian 3rd Brigade ordered his reserve battalion, the 14th, into line beside the already postioned 13th and 15th battalions and held strong German attacks north of Keerselare (cf 'The Brooding Soldier' page 97) until they finally stopped at about 1830 hours. Two platoons of the 13th fought to their last man and L/Cpl Frederick Fisher of the battalion won a posthumous VC for his actions that day. His citation as published in the *London Gazette* gives the date of his action as the 23rd, but Canadian authorities say that this is incorrect. Sir Max Aitken, the Canadian Record Officer, later (as Lord Beaverbrook) wrote *Canada in Flanders*, the story of Canadian actions to 1916, including an entire chapter, with maps, covering the gas attacks.

Curiously, the fact that the Canadians stood and fought through the gas attack meant that they suffered less from it than they might have done had they followed the example of the French colonial troops and streamed back to the rear. *The Official History* explains: 'It early became evident that the men who stayed in their places suffered less than those who ran away, any movement making worse the effects of the gas, and those who stood up on the fire step suffered less – indeed they often escaped any serious effects – than those who lay down or sat at the bottom of a trench. Men who stood on the parapet suffered least, as the gas was denser near the ground. The worst sufferers were the wounded lying on the ground, or on stretchers, and the men who moved back with the cloud.'

General Smith-Dorrien commanding the Second Army first heard news of the attack at about 1845 hours on the 22nd and immediate moves were made to bring up reinforcements to plug the line. General Foch heard at midnight what had happened and reacted typically with three steps that should be taken: (1) hold; (2) organize for a counter-attack; (3) counter-attack. In fact counter-attacks did begin that night and following Foch's proposals it was agreed that 'vigorous action' east of the canal would be the best way to check any German attempts to advance. The enemy, however, struck first and on 24 April following a one-hour heavy bombardment the Germans released a gas cloud at 0400 hours immediately to the north-east of Keerselare and on a front of 1,000 yards against the Canadian Division. Throughout the day pressure on the Canadians forced them to withdraw to second-line positions, Keerselare being captured early in the afternoon. The following day, Sunday, 25 April 1915, the day of the Gallipoli landings, the Germans made a fierce effort to break the British lines. They made gains, but they did not break through.

The struggle continued in a series of engagements classified as the Battle of Gravenstafel, 22–23 April; Battle of St Julien, 24 April–5 May; Battle of Frezenberg, 8–13 May and Battle of Bellewaerde, 24–25 May. The Germans did make net gains overall. On 4 May the British made tactical withdrawals in order to shorten their lines, reducing their frontage from 21,000 yards to 16,000 yards and shortening the greatest depth of the Salient from 9,000 to 5,000 yards. In the World of 'If', the Germans might have taken Ypres and then the Channel Ports. If they had not used the gas just as a tactical distraction, but part of a major attack, if they had had reserves ready to follow up the initial success, if the wind had been in the right direction early on 22 April they would have seen how successful the gas had been and could have called up forces to exploit the break in the French lines. If they had used their secret weapon properly, say many, they could have won the war with it. The 'after-the-event' experts say the same thing about the British use of the tank on the Somme. Perhaps the most relevant 'If' belongs to the Canadians, courtesy of Rudyard Kipling, because they kept their heads when all about were losing theirs.

LOOS

25 SEPTEMBER 1915–8 OCTOBER 1915

'Our new armies entered into action for the first
time and fought with conspicious valour,
and tens of thousands of them fell in the futile
carnage of the Loos offensive.'
Lloyd George, War Memoirs

'I had come to the conclusion that it was not fair
to the Empire to retain French in command.
Moreover, none of my officers commanding corps
had a high opinion of Sir John's military ability. . ..'
General Haig in his diary

'My Darling Darling we've had such terrible losses
which made me very depressed and sad. . ..'
General French in a letter to his mistress during the battle.

' "What's happened?" I asked. "Bloody balls-up," was
the most detailed answer I could get.'
Robert Graves, Goodbye to All That

SUMMARY OF THE BATTLE

On 25 September 1915 as part of the French Artois offensive, Douglas Haig's 1st
Army attacked German positions at Loos. The British used gas for the first time
causing many casualties to their own side. There were no significant positive
results and the affair provoked the forced resignation of Sir John French. British
casualties were 43,000, German 20,000.

OPENING MOVES

Even halfway through 1915 it had not been a good year for the Allies. There had
been the heavy British casualties at Neuve Chapelle, the disaster at Gallipoli and
the steady reverses on the Russian front. General Joffre had prompted his forces
into a number of attacks along the Western Front in what he called the 'war of
stabilization'. This could perhaps be likened to a boxer moving around the ring,
feeling out his opponent's strengths, before attempting a knock-out blow.

| MAP 7 | THE LOOS BATTLEFIELD
25 September 1915 |

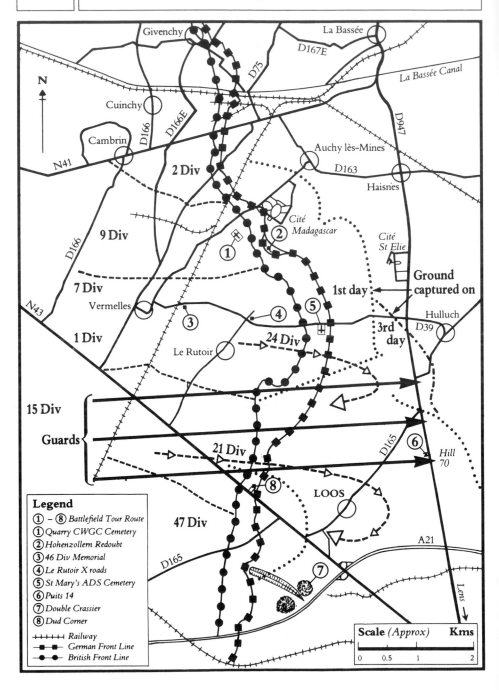

N

Givenchy
D167E
La Bassée
D75
La Bassée Canal

Cuinchy
D166E
Cambrin
D166
N41
2 Div
D947
Auchy lès-Mines
D163
Haisnes

9 Div
Cité Madagascar
②
①
Cité St Elie
Ground captured on

7 Div
Vermelles
③
1st day
Hulluch
D39

1 Div
Le Rutoir
④
⑤
24 Div
3rd day

15 Div

Guards
21 Div
D165
⑥
Hill 70

⑧
LOOS
A21

Legend
① – ⑧ Battlefield Tour Route
① Quarry CWGC Cemetery
② Hohenzollern Redoubt
③ 46 Div Memorial
④ Le Rutoir X roads
⑤ St Mary's ADS Cemetery
⑥ Puits 14
⑦ Double Crassier
⑧ Dud Corner
┼┼┼┼┼ Railway
▪━▪ German Front Line
●━● British Front Line

47 Div
D165
⑦
Lens

Scale *(Approx)*   **Kms**
0   0.5   1   2

In June 1915 Joffre proposed his knock-out blow: a two-pronged offensive. One attack, the main one, was to be in Champagne and entirely French. The other was a joint Franco-British affair in Artois. Each prong was to break through the German lines. A general offensive would follow along the entire Franco-British front that Joffre believed could 'possibly end the war'. The Artois offensive was also to be a two-pronged affair with the British 1st Army attacking just north of Lens at Loos and the French 10th Army just south of Lens.

General Haig toured the area allocated for the 1st Army's attack and declared it to be unfavourable because the flat open ground would be swept by machine gun fire from the enemy's front trenches. Joffre refused to change the plan and Kitchener, visiting Sir John French in August, told him that co-operation was essential and the 'we may suffer heavy losses'. Haig, conscious of what had happened at Neuve Chapelle because of the shortage of artillery, decided that the only way in which he could get enough concentration of fire to neutralize the German machine guns was by adopting a very narrow frontage for the attack.

Accordingly he planned to attack with two divisions only, the 15th and the 9th. While the two division assault was being planned a new weapon became available – British poison gas. Haig immediately saw gas as a means of neutralizing those enemy defences that he did not have enough artillery to take on and extended the attack frontage to six divisions in line, their flanks to be protected by smoke screens. On 16 September he wrote to Sir William Robertson, General French's Chief of Staff, 'in my opinion under no circumstances should our forthcoming attack be launched without the aid of gas.' He was over-ruled and told that because of the need to co-ordinate the offensive with the French 10th Army the attack had to be made and that it would go in on 25 September. Haig therefore produced a plan with two options: one for a wide front, one for a narrow front.

1. Wide Front. If the weather conditions were favourable on 25 September the attack, with gas on the whole front, would take place on that day with 6 divisions.

2. Narrow Front. If the wind did not permit the use of gas . . . a two division assault would be made . . . the wider attack with gas to be postponed until favourable conditions on the 26th or 27th or not at all.

All that remained was for the Allies to agree the time that their infantry would assault. The British wanted to go over the top as early as possible in the morning so that positions gained could be consolidated by nightfall. The French didn't want to leave their trenches before 1000 hours, so that they could visibly control the last phase of their bombardment. In the event the French attack went in 5½ hours after the British. Something similar would happen again on 1 July 1916 on the Somme.

WHAT HAPPENED

The preliminary bombardment which covered the 18-mile frontage of the 1st Army (i.e. covered the main assault and diversionary actions north and south of it) was carried out by 110 heavy guns, and 84 guns and howitzers began at first light on 21 September and continued day and night until the moment of the assault on 25 September. As a precaution against the enemy finding out about the gas it was given a codename – 'the accessory'.

In England and along the front line observers anxiously monitored the wind direction. Four times a day the Met Office in London sent reports and 40 specially trained gas officers stationed along the assault trenches sent in hourly reports during the night of 24 September. The required wind direction for a gas attack was from somewhere between north-west and south-west and at 2145 hours on 24 September, having received a favourable forecast, Haig ordered that the gas attack should take place on the morrow. The exact time would be 'notified later during the night'.

Early on the 25th, although the general forecast remained favourable, things looked changeable and the meteorologist, Captain E. Gold, attached to Haig's staff, advised that the sooner the gas was released the better. At 0500 hours Haig went on to the battlefield rear area and asked his ADC Major Alan Fletcher to light a cigarette. The smoke drifted north-east, a borderline but acceptable direction. Fifteen minutes later the General ordered the attack to go ahead. Robert Graves, who was in the battle (see below) wrote that one front-line report at 0530 said, 'Dead calm. Impossible discharge accessory', to which the reply was, 'Accessory to be discharged at all costs.' At 0550 hours the gas was released, emissions continuing on and off for 40 minutes. As there wasn't enough gas available to allow a continuous gas cloud, the gas cylinders were turned on and off and smoke candles burned in between to fool the enemy.

At 0630 hours the infantry scrambled out of their trenches and headed across No Man's Land in a haze of smoke and gas. There were six divisions in line, the 2nd, 9th (Scottish), 7th, 1st, 15th (Scottish) and 47th (London Territorial). Two separate divisions, the 21st and 24th, were kept back in reserve, but they were not under command of General Haig. General French kept them under his control. On the extreme right 47th Division rapidly reached the area of the double *crassier* (coal tip) while on its left the 15th Division made spectacular progress, advancing completely around Loos to the north of, then later taking, the town after all-night street fighting. The remaining division of Rawlinson's IV Corps, the 1st, had mixed fortunes. Some units reached as far as the village of Hulluch and others retreated under enemy shell fire. South of the corps boundary, the Vermelles to Hulluch road, the gas had proven its worth, but further north in Gough's 1 Corps area alongside the la Bassée Canal the officer in charge of gas on 6th Brigade's front decided not to turn on the gas because the wind wasn't right. General Horne ordered it turned on and many men were poisoned by their own gas. Eventually Horne listened to his brigade commanders and stopped the attack.

Overall, particularly at Loos itself, the first day had gone well. There was a potential break in the German line to be exploited. Now was the time to punch through the weakened enemy defences with our fresh reserves. Where were they? They were too far away, too tired and too new to mount a successful follow-up assault. Why? Whose fault was it? The generals blamed each other.

The broad sweep of the British plan had been agreed at least one month before between Joffre and General French at a conference at Chantilly – including the formation of a two divisional infantry reserve. Yet instead of forming the reserve from seasoned divisions already in France, General French nominated two raw, untried 'K' (Kitchener volunteers) Divisions, the 21st and 24th, which had arrived in France in September. They had never been in the trenches or under fire and they were held many miles to the rear under Sir John's control as part of XI Corps, which also included the newly formed Guards Division. On the night of 24 September, the two K Divisions marched 10 miles through rain to within five miles of the front line. It took over six hours. The previous night they had rested, but on each of the two nights preceding that they had marched more than 20 miles.

Sir Douglas Haig had assumed that the two reserve divisions would move forward at 0630 hours together with the main assault and come under his control ready to follow up a breakthrough. They did not. Sir John French said that he put the divisions under Haig's command at 0930 hours. Haig didn't agree that that had been done. On 29 September he wrote to Lord Kitchener, 'No reserve was placed under me. My attack, as has been reported, was a complete success . . .. The two reserve Divisions (under C-in-C's orders) were directed to join me as soon as the success of the First Army was known at GHQ. They came on as quick as they could, poor fellows, but only crossed our old trenchline with their heads at 1800 hours. We had captured Loos 12 hours previously and reserves should have been at hand THEN'. . ..

At first, despite their tiredness, when they did eventually arrive the reserve divisions had some success but German counter-attacks forced them back, only the arrival of the Guards Division on 27 September preventing what might have been a headlong retreat of the novice soldiers. The battle ventured on without concentrated central effort until the first week in October. Two months later Prime Minister Herbert Asquith wrote a secret letter to Haig saying that Sir John French had resigned and 'I have the pleasure of proposing to you that you should be his successor.'

BATTLEFIELD TOUR

The tour begins at Quarry CWGC cemetery and then follows the centre line of the British attack from Vermelles, the 46th Division memorial, the Rutoir

MAP
8

BATTLE OF LOOS
Attack of the 2nd Worcestershire
26 SEPTEMBER 1915

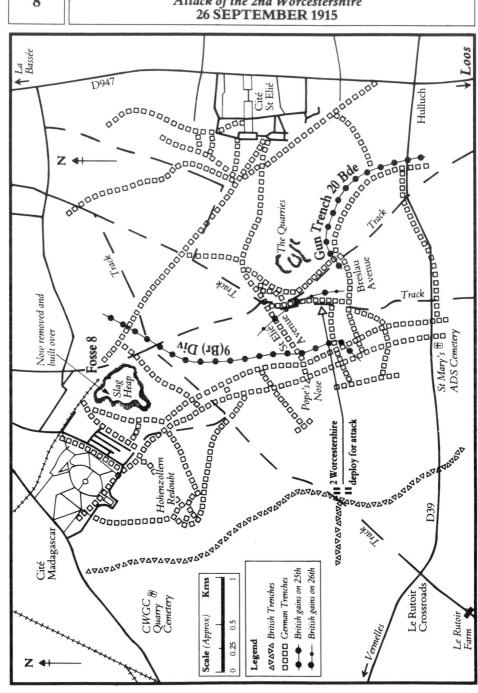

La Bassée

D947

Cité St Elié

Loos

Hulluch

N

The Quarries

Gun Trench 20 Bde

Track

Breslau Avenue

Track

Track

St Elié Avenue

9(Br) Div

Now removed and built over

Fosse 8

Slag Heap

Pope's Nose

St Mary's ADS Cemetery

2 Worcestershire deploy for attack

Hohenzollern Redoubt

Cité Madagascar

CWGC Quarry Cemetery

D39

Le Rutoir Crossroads

Le Rutoir Farm

Vermelles

N

Scale (Approx)   Kms
0   0.25   0.5   1

Legend
△▽△▽ British Trenches
▢▢▢▢ German Trenches
●━━● British gains on 25th
●──● British gains on 26th

crossroads, St Mary's Advanced Dressing Station CWGC cemetery, Hulluch, the area of Hill 70 and the double crassier ending at Dud Corner north-west of Loos. The battlefield has changed very little in the intervening years and particularly rewards the use of a good map.

Total distance   11 miles
Total time   2¼ hours
Maps   IGN 2405 Est. Lens 1:25,000

Take the N41 west from la Bassée and turn left on to the D163 into Auchy les Mines, a built-up area.

It was in this area of 28th Brigade, that the gas blew back over the British lines and caused many casualties. The failure of the brigade to advance negated the success of 26th Brigade to whose area you are travelling. It was also in this area that the poet-author-raconteur Robert Graves, serving with the RWF, observed the muddled and tragically ineffective gas attack. His memories of the loosing of the 'accessory' are graphically and often amusingly described in his gossipy, and sometimes imaginative, autobiography, *Goodbye to All That*. It should be compulsory reading for anyone studying the Loos battle.

Drive slowly seeking signs to Vermelles and/or Cité Madagascar and when found turn right heading south-west. As you are about to leave the built-up area – and may be about to give up – the cemetery is signed. Park and be prepared to walk 200 yards. It can be muddy. You are at Point 29 on the recommended map.

QUARRY CWGC CEMETERY   As you walk down the track you are walking towards the front line of 26th Brigade of 9th Division and are in No Man's Land. On 25 September the Division attacked west to east across the track. To your left you may be able to define a slightly higher feature of ground with some trees and bushes on it. It lies under the power cables. That was the Hohenzollern Redoubt, a major German defensive position. It was taken by 9th Division on 25 September and they pushed on beyond, towards the village of Haisnes. This remarkable achievement was the result of careful planning and the digging forward of Russian saps (tunnels barely below ground that can rapidly be converted into open trenches) so that when these were opened, and their heads joined by a trench, the assault line was only 150 yards from the redoubt. The attack was led by the 7th Seaforths and the 5th Cameron Highlanders, all wearing glengarries. Sadly, at mid-morning, Lt Col Gaisford commanding the Seaforths was killed. The Germans recaptured the Hohenzollern on 3 October.

The cemetery contains burials from the fighting in the area of the Hozenhollern Redoubt and was used mostly between July 1915 and June 1916. It was badly damaged by shell fire and not all of the 140 burials are individually marked because the original graves were lost. Therefore some headstones say, 'Buried near this spot', and the register lists only 129 war graves. Many of the graves are those of cavalrymen who were used in the dismounted role and there is one German soldier. The 'Quarry' referred to is the one in which the burials have been made, which is an old chalk pit about 10 ft deep and reached by steps. It is not connected with the 'Quarries' which featured in the fighting near Hulluch.

Continue south to the village of Vermelles and seek out the D39 to Hulluch. Basically it is the first left on entering Vermelles, but it isn't that simple on the ground.

VERMELLES   The village sits like a lollipop head at the western end of its stick the D39 Hulluch road, the Corps boundary. IV Corps were south, exclusive of the road, I Corps north. It was in areas like Vermelles that final arrangements were made before battalions moved forward through communication trenches to the front line. Tea would be brewed, hot meals served (on rare occasions), orders issued, heavy kit left behind, routes signed and 'farewell' notes written. As you drive now you are following exactly the route taken by 7th Division as it moved into its forward trenches.

Drive out of the village on the D39. As you leave the built-up area there is a memorial on the right. Stop.

46 (NORTH MIDLAND) DIVISION MEMORIAL   This commemorates an action on 13 October 1915, the week following the 'official' end of the Loos offensive. 138th and 139th Brigades of the Division set off to recapture the Hohenzollern Redoubt (to the north-east). Their gas cloud was weak and the artillery bombardment had not destroyed the German wire. The Hohenzollern was not taken, though parts of it were entered by the Midlanders, and the Division lost heavily – 180 officers and 3,500 men.

Continue to the next crossroads at which there is a small calvary. Stop. You are at Point 33 on the D39. The farm to your right down the track is le Rutoir.

LE RUTOIR CROSSROADS   It is very rare to be able to identify precisely where a battalion action took place and even rarer also to have a clear account of what happened there. The situation becomes almost unique when the ground remains much the same as it was in 1914–18. Using Maps 7 and 8 you can be in just such a unique position.

Walk 700 yards north-east up the track from le Rutoir crossroads to the area of Point 33 on the recommended map. You are now where the 2nd Worcesters deployed for their attack on 26 September 1915.

By 26 September 7th Division was stuck in front of the Quarries. 2nd Worcesters, part of a temporary brigade under Colonel Carter of the King's Regiment, was ordered to attack the Quarries. (From where you are now they are immediately in front of a large coal heap due east – the heap was not there in 1915.) This is how the Regimental history tells the story:

'At 1 p.m. the Battalion filed into a big communication trench at Vermelles. This trench was a very long one and progress along it was difficult. The troops were carrying heavy loads and were hampered by wearing gas-masks, for several leaking gas-cylinders were lying in the trench. Crowds of wounded men were sheltering in the trench or making their way back, and other parties of all kinds impeded the advance. One by one the Worcestershire companies reached the forward lines, but not until 4.45 p.m. did the rearmost platoon get clear of the communication trench. Then the Battalion deployed for attack behind the original British front line. In front of them was a wide stretch of open ground – the former "No Man's Land" – on the far side of which was the old German front line, occupied by troops of the 7th Division. Still further forward on slightly rising ground a tangle of broken ground marked the near edge of the Quarries, the objective of the attack.

The Battalion deployed in four 'waves' – 'C' and 'D' Companies leading, 'A' and 'B' following, each company being formed in two lines. Colonel Lambton gave the signal, and the advance began.

With bayonets fixed, the companies of the 2nd Worcestershire swept forward across the open, wave after wave, in splendid order. The platoons came under a heavy fire as they reached the old German front line. That trench was found to be wide and deep, crowded with disorganised or wounded men of the 7th Division. . . . Colonel Lambton . . . coolly walked up and down the parapet under a heavy fire, directing the reorganisation of the attack. Major-General T. Capper, commanding the 7th Division, appeared in the trench and assisted in the direction of the fight . . . Colonel Lambton again signalled the advance. . . . The German rifles and machine-guns opened a devastating fire. Officers and men went down in rapid succession under a hail of bullets. On the left flank Major P. S. G. Wainman led his men forward, waving his stick till he fell riddled with bullets. Further to the right, General Capper himself rushed forward with one of the Worcestershire platoons, cheering them on until he was hit and fell mortally wounded. . . .

The leading groups reached a line of broken chalk, a half-dug trench within two hundred yards of the enemy's position. There they flung themselves down. . . [and] held their ground opposite the enemy's line during the remaining hours of daylight. . . . Night fell amid pouring rain, and it became possible to collect the wounded and count the loss. Of the 2nd Worcestershire nearly half had fallen – 13 officers and more than 300 N.C.O's and men. The 2nd-in-Command, all four Company Commanders, the Machine-Gun Officer, the Medical Officer and three out of the four Company-Sergeant-Majors were casualties. . . . All through the night the stretcher-bearers worked across the field of battle, searching for the wounded. . . . The Chaplain, the Rev. J. R. Stewart, earned general admiration by arriving in the front-line, leading a small party carrying cans of hot tea and jars of rum, which he personally distributed all along the line.'

General Capper is buried in Lillers Communal CWGC Cemetery. His grave stands alone near the gardener's shed.

Return to your car, continue along the Hulluch road to the first British cemetery on the right. Park.

ST MARY'S ADS CEMETERY   The attack along, inclusive and immediately north of this road up to the southern edge of the Hohenzollern Redoubt, was made by the 20th and 22nd Brigades of 7th Division. 20th Brigade had the area from the road to inclusive the German position known as Breslau Avenue (see Map 8). The leading battalions, the 2nd Gordon Highlanders and the 8th Devons, set off at 0630 in a cloud of their own gas. They were wearing smoke helmets, but these made it very difficult to breathe, and when they took them off to draw breath, many men were overcome by the gas. Despite heavy casualties from enemy artillery Gun Trench was taken and elements of both battalions reached the Lens–la Bassée road. (With the Devons in Gun Trench was the war poet William Noel Hodgson, who was to be killed on the Somme on 1 July 1916 after writing the prophetic poem, 'Before Action'. For his action at Loos Lt Hodgson was awarded the MC.)

The Advanced Dressing Station was set up during the battle and after the Armistice the cemetery was established on the same spot. Of the more than 1,760 burials in the cemetery (the majority from the battle of Loos) 90 per cent are unknown, evidence of the chaos that existed on the battlefield. One of them, reburied here in September 1919, was a lieutenant of the Irish Guards. In July 1992 the headstone marking his grave was changed to read 'Lieutenant John Kipling' when the CWGC believed that it had identified the body – on the grounds that Kipling was the only full lieutenant of the Irish Guards killed or missing in the Loos battle. This late identification was particularly ironic as his father, Rudyard Kipling, who sat on the committee of the Imperial War Graves Commission, spared no efforts to find his son's body, but in vain.

Continue along the D39 to the crossroads with the main la Bassée-Lens road (D947) and turn right. In due course the road begins to rise towards Loos-en-Gohelle and on the right is a minehead with winding gear. Stop.

In this area John Kipling was last seen on 27 September 1915 and the body that was eventually identified as his was found some 200 yards to your right.

PUITS 14   A *puit* (literally a well) is a minehead and the area was once dotted with them. Most had winding gear and this is a typical example. On the opposite side of the road is Bois Hugo. The hill immediately ahead is Hill 70. The area between here and Hill 70 was the secondary objective for the 44th and 46th Brigades of 15th Division who were attacking from the right starting beyond the built-up areas. As with 7th Division, the 15th Division was affected by our own gas remaining about our jumping-off trenches. To encourage the men to go forward Piper Laidlaw, of 7th KOSB, a leading battalion of the 46th Brigade, marched up and down the parapet playing his pipes until he was wounded, an action for which he was awarded a VC. It was also in this area that the Guards Division filled the gap left by the retreating 21st and 24th 'K' Divisions, one of the company commanders of the Irish Guards being Captain H. R. L. G. Alexander, later to become Lord Alexander of Tunis.

Continue on the D947 and over Hill 70 turning right, direction Béthune, at the main ring-road junction at the top. Take the first exit to the N43 Lens-Béthune road and turn right towards Béthune. The coal heaps to your left are the new multiple peaks of the Double Crassier.

THE DOUBLE CRASSIER The attack here came from left to right, due east as you drive, and was by the 140th and 141st Brigades of 47th Division. The gas worked well and on the extreme right of the attack German fire was attracted off target by the use of dummy figures – heads and shoulders pulled up and down by strings. In the 141st Brigade, the 1st/18th London (London Irish Rifles) Regiment which led the assault came on behind the gas and smoke cloud dribbling a football and by 0730 the trench line between the Double Crassier and the N43 had been taken. The Division advanced so well that elements penetrating into Loos village became mixed up with 15th Division north of the N43 and went on to the area of Hill 70 from where you have just come. On the first day of the battle, and mostly before 1000 hours, the 47th Division lost more then 1,200 officers and men.

Continue up the hill to the British cemetery on the crest. Stop, and be careful of the traffic.

DUD CORNER CWGC CEMETERY AND LOOS MEMORIAL During the battle of Loos many British shells that were fired were duds and on finding much unexploded shot lying around here the troops nicknamed it 'Dud Corner'. The memorial is virtually on the site of a German strongpoint (*stutzpunkte*) called the 'Lens Road Redoubt' captured by the 15th (Scottish) Division on the first day. The walls surrounding the cemetery record the names of almost 21,000 men with no known grave who fell in the battle of Loos 1915 and the later battles of the Lys, Estaires and Béthune. One of the names, now removed, was that of John Kipling (see above). Another is the 20-year-old, highly regarded war poet, Charles Hamilton Sorley, of the 7th Bn. the Suffolk Regiment. Three vc winners are commemorated, two from the Loos battle – Temporary Lt Colonel A. F. Douglas-Hamilton commanding 6th Cameronians for actions at Hill 70 on 25 and 26 September 1915 and Private G. Peachment of the 2nd KRRC for bravery near Hulluch on 25 September 1915 – and 2 Lt F. B. Wearne of the Essex Regiment for actions in 1917. A viewing platform on the north-west pier of the memorial offers a remarkable view over the battlefield, as does a position near the Cross of Sacrifice at the far end of the cemetery. The architect was Sir Herbert Baker.

There are some 1,800 burials in the cemetery, including two vcs – Captain A. M. Read of the 1st Northants for conspicuous bravery during the attack of 25 September 1915 near Hulluch, and Sergeant Harry Wells of the 2nd Royal Sussex for actions on the same day near le Rutoir.

Shortly before he died Rudyard Kipling left an endowment to fund the nightly sounding of the Last Post here, but no such ceremony takes place.

MAP 9	VERDUN – THE BATTLE AREA
	21 FEB – 18 DEC 1916

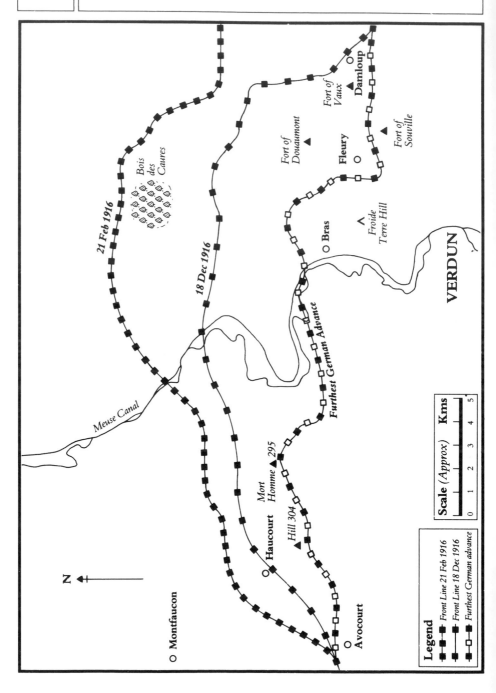

Bois des Caures

21 Feb 1916

18 Dec 1916

Fort of Vaux

Damloup

Fort of Douaumont

Fleury

Fort of Souville

Froide Terre Hill

O Bras

VERDUN

Furthest German Advance

Meuse Canal

Mort Homme ▲ 295

Hill 304

O Haucourt

O Avocourt

O Montfaucon

N ◄—

Scale (Approx)   Kms

0   1   2   3   4   5

Legend

▪▪ Front Line 21 Feb 1916

▪▪ Front Line 18 Dec 1916

□□ Furthest German advance

VERDUN
21 FEBRUARY–18 DECEMBER 1916

'Courage – On les aura!' ('Courage – We'll get them')
The last phrase of General Pétain's Order of the
Day to the defenders of Verdun on 10 April 1916

SUMMARY OF THE BATTLE

On 21 February 1916 the German 5th Army attacked the fortified French town of Verdun in an operation called *'Gericht'* – 'A place of execution'. The battle lasted for 10 months, but Verdun never fell. French casualties were estimated at 540,000, German at 430,000.

OPENING MOVES

The classic invasion route into France from the east crosses two rivers, first the Moselle, and then the Meuse. Above the Meuse to its east is a 1,500 ft high ridge and in its western shadow is Verdun. Attila came this way and destroyed the city, the Germans conquered it in the tenth century and France took it back in the sixteenth. In the late-seventeenth century the great French military architect Vauban included Verdun in his defensive scheme for the protection of France, but in the 1870 war Bismarck's armies, though they followed tradition and crossed the Moselle, by-passed Verdun and went on to Paris. Eventually Verdun fell to von Moltke the elder, the last great fortress to capitulate in the Franco-Prussian War. The well-trodden invasion path across the Meuse from Metz and between the two rivers is an area known as Alsace-Lorraine, which in the peace treaty of 1871 was ceded to Germany, leaving in every French heart the desire for revenge. Verdun thus became a border fortress town, the symbol of French *esprit* which, together with the lost provinces of Alsace and Lorraine, assumed a mystical significance dear to all Frenchmen. *'Ils ne passeront pas'* 'They shall not pass' was its slogan.

After 1871 France built up her defences to the east and north of Verdun adding three dozen forts in two lines, the largest of which was Fort Douaumont, less than five miles from the centre of Verdun. Yet in 1916, after eighteen months of war, Douaumont was virtually unmanned. Why?

The reason is a logical one. In 1914 when the Germans invaded Belgium their route took them directly onto the fortified towns of Liège and Namur, and although stirring defence by the garrisons delayed the invasion, the towns were first by-passed and then reduced by the German heavy artillery. Furthermore, the Schlieffen Plan was only hinged on Alsace-Lorraine, the main forward effort of the German invasion being well north through Belgium (see Map 1). General Joffre concluded from the failure of the Belgian forts to stop the enemy that Verdun no longer had value as a fortress, and this view was officially promulgated in a memorandum of 9 August 1915. In addition, since the German threat was concentrated elsewhere, the defence of Verdun was given low priority and invested in a command known as the 'RFV' – the Verdun Fortified Area – which relied upon a thin line of trenches partially manned by over-age reservists. Steadily Joffre disarmed the forts, moving some of their weapons elsewhere and downgrading the quality of the garrison. However, knowing the country's almost religious belief in the invincibility of Verdun, he issued optimistic and reassuring propaganda about its defences.

Not all French leaders were happy about what was happening in Verdun. General Herr, commanding the RFV, repeatedly warned Joffre that the defences were too weak, but the most effective and consistent complaints were made by Lt-Col. Emile Driant, a local political deputy. Joffre had taken offence at the steady increase in complaints against his policy at Verdun and ruled that no one in his command could directly approach their political representatives to express their views. Such actions were, he said 'calculated to disturb profoundly the spirit of discipline in the army.' Complaints had to be made to the next senior officer in the military hierarchy – with predictable results for the future career of the complainant. Driant, however as a Deputy himself, could maintain his political contacts. He had rejoined the colours at the outbreak of war and in 1916 commanded the 56th and 59th *Chasseurs à Pied* (infantry) based in the Bois des Caures, a wood in the centre of the western flank of the RFV (see Map 9). He wrote to the President of the Chamber of Deputies in August 1915 complaining about the state of the Verdun defences, 'The [German] sledge-hammer blow will be delivered on the line Verdun-Nancy. What moral effect would be created by the capture of one of these cities . . . if our first line is carried by a massive attack, our second line is inadequate and we are not succeeding in establishing it.' Gallieni, who had saved Paris and gone on to become Minister of Defence, learned of the letter and wrote to Joffre, 'Reports have come to me from various sources concerning the organisation of the front indicating that deficiencies exist in the conditions of the works at certain points. In regions of the Meurthe, Toul and Verdun notably, the line of trenches appears not to have been completed.' Joffre in his memoirs says, 'I confess that this letter impressed me disagreeably.' Four days later he sent a long reply to Gallieni repeating his oral mandate about soldiers not reporting to politicians and asking for the names of those whom Gallieni had described as 'various sources'. 'To sum up' wrote Joffre, 'I consider that nothing justifies the fears which, in the name of the Government, you express in your despatch.' However, Joffre did react to the situation and sent General de Castelnau to inspect the defences of Verdun. It was 20 January 1916, barely one month before the German hammer-blow would fall.

The German Chief of Staff, General Erich von Falkenhayn, was convinced that the heavily entrenched western front could not be broken, and in order to defeat France it was now a matter of breaking her will to fight. This could be done, he reasoned, by killing so many French soldiers that the nation would sue for peace. How then to kill enough Frenchmen to make his plan succeed without killing as many of his own men? His answer was artillery. If he could secretly assemble a huge array of guns and get the French army to stand in front of them he could shell it to death. How to make the French army rally to a particular place? Answer – threaten something that they value above all else, i.e. Verdun.

Thus the operation called 'A Place of Execution' was evolved and, during that same January that de Castelnau was inspecting Verdun, von Falkenhayn added to the already formidable artillery of the 5th Army. Into the narrow Verdun sector were brought over 500 heavy guns: 300 field guns, 150 giant mine throwers, 13 'Big Berthas' (420mm weapons that had been used against Liège) . . . the list went on and on. Three million shells were stockpiled and six new infantry divisions stood by. On 8 February Joffre and the French Council for National Defence met in Paris and agreed that 'a German offensive in the near future was unlikely'. Thirteen days later, on 21 February, the Germans attacked.

What Happened

At 0715 hours on 21 February the German artillery opened fire over a fifteen-mile front and at 1645 hours six infantry divisions advanced on a narrow six-mile corridor. They imagined that the advance would be a formality, that all French resistance would have been destroyed by the pounding of some 1,400 guns – a misconception repeated by the British six months later on the Somme. Shattered pillboxes, shapeless trenches and splintered stumps of trees in a moonscape of shellholes met the attackers, but so did French soldiers. In small disjointed actions the '*Poilus*' fought tenaciously, delaying the German advance so that only the front trench line was occupied before darkness fell.

On 22 February the attack widened. Lt Col. Driant and his men put up a valiant defence in the Bois des Caures. Driant was killed and of his 1,200 men only 100 got out of the wood that day. The French defences began to crumble and on 24 February Joffre sent for a new man to take over RFV – General Pétain. His staff rushed to the Hotel Terminus at the Gare du Nord in Paris where the 60-year-old Pétain was spending the night with his mistress. Pétain told them to wait until the morning, a decision that is game, set and match to Drake's insistence on playing bowls when confronted by the Spanish Armada.

On 25 February Fort Douaumont fell without firing a shot (cf. the Battlefield Tour – Fort Douaumont). Late that night Pétain arrived and immediately

MAP 10

VERDUN – 1916
The Battlefield Tour

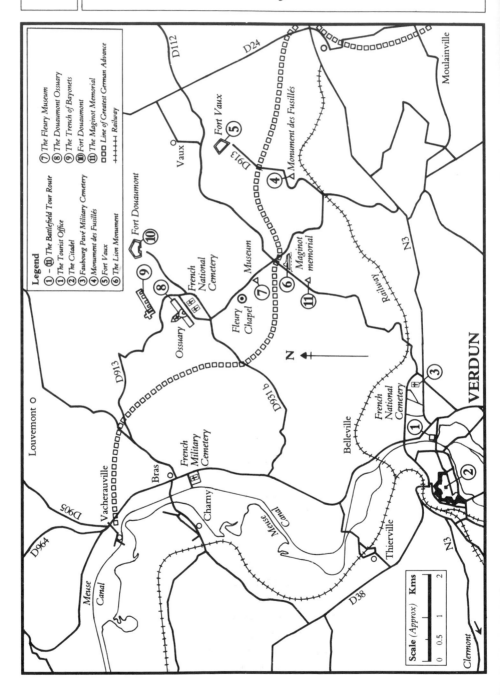

Legend

① – ⑪ The Battlefield Tour Route
① The Tourist Office
② The Citadel
③ Faubourg Pavé Military Cemetery
④ Monument des Fusillés
⑤ Fort Vaux
⑥ The Lion Monument
⑦ The Fleury Museum
⑧ The Douaumont Ossuary
⑨ The Trench of Bayonets
⑩ Fort Douaumont
⑪ The Maginot Memorial
□□□ Line of Greatest German Advance
+++++ Railway

reorganized the defence into four separate command and administrative areas and established the beginnings of the single-road supply system that became known as '*La Voie Sacrée*' ('The Sacred Way'). His positive, confident manner and precise orders steadied the French nerve and on 26 February Joffre concentrated all officers' minds by saying that he would court-martial anyone who ordered his men to withdraw.

In between short breathing spaces the German attacks continued. On 6 March the 5th Army attacked Mort Homme to the west of the Meuse and 9 April saw what was to be the last all-out offensive by the 5th Army. Pétain continued to exercise firm control and instituted a policy of immediate counter-attacks against what progressively had been 'nibbling' offensives by the Germans. At the same time, however, he pestered Joffre to send him more and more reinforcements, troops that Joffre could not spare, and on 1 May Joffre moved Pétain and replaced him with Nivelle. Nivelle opened the throttle on offensive spirit and although Mort Homme fell to the Germans at the end of May and Fort Vaux on 7 June, the German resolve was weakening. The beginning of the Somme Battle on 1 July drew German reserves away from Verdun and the last German assault took place on 11 July. On 29 August von Falkenhayn was replaced by von Hindenburg and Ludendorff. Between 24 October and 18 December 1916 General Nivelle's offensive recaptured Douaumont and Vaux. Just before Christmas 1916 the longest battle of the war was over.

THE BATTLEFIELD TOUR

The thorough student of military history could spend a week walking the battlefields around Verdun without exhausting all the marked footpaths. The less intense visitor can spend two full days following the road signs to places of military interest. The tour we propose does not pretend to be exhaustive. It offers the interested visitor a selection of important and relevant sites that match the commentaries and maps in this book and should lead to an overall under-standing of the issues at stake, the sacrifice of the French and the horrendous conditions in which the soldiers fought.

Total distance   20 miles

Total time   5 hours 30 minutes

Maps   IGN 10. Reims. Verdun 1:100:000 plus
                     IGN 11 Nancy. Metz. Luxembourg 1:100:000

The tour begins at the tourist office in Verdun and includes the town memorial and the Citadel before moving on past the military cemetery to Fort Vaux. After that comes the Memorial Museum at Fleury, followed by the Ossuary at Douaumont, The Trench of Bayonets, Douaumont Fort, the Maginot memorial and finally Verdun again.

Verdun is readily reached via the A4/E50 Autoroute de l'Est. Follow the tourist information signs to the office in the Place de la Nation near the Chaussée Gate and park.

THE TOURIST OFFICE   The Verdun battlefield is a major tourist attraction. That fact in no way undermines the reverence with which the sites and artefacts are maintained. There is no trace whatsoever of the false romance that attaches to the American Civil War battlefields so splendidly maintained by the American Parks Service, and who do not foster that romantic idealism. Simplistically it might be attributed to Margaret Mitchell, *Gone With the Wind*, Scarlett O'Hara and Rhett Butler. They have no counterparts in Verdun. In the tourist office they sometimes have on sale a Super 8mm film or video of the silent dramatization by Léon Poirier, *Verdun, Visions d'Histoire*. This is a skilful and effective mix of real footage and re-enactment that captures the true degradation of warfare overlaid with French mysticism. Also available is a good selection of guide and history books, many translated into English or by English authors, and a number of locally produced maps with English text that are essential for effective touring. During your visit check the opening times of the Citadel, the museums and forts on this itinerary, which vary from season to season. The tourist office, open most days at least from 1000–1200 and 1400–1630, takes life seriously enough in July and August to miss lunch and stay open all day. Its telephone number is 29 86 14 18. Annual commemorative ceremonies are held in Verdun in June, but the dates vary from year to year.

Immediately outside the office is a statue of General Sarrail who, while commanding the French 3rd Army defending Verdun in 1914, ignored Joffre's instructions to withdraw and thereby saved the town. Across the road are the bas relief statues of five soldiers, making a wall with their bodies to defend Verdun. This is the town memorial and beside it is a memorial tablet to General Mangin. Across the river is the Chaussée Gate, built in the fifteenth century and which is said to have been the inspiration for the badge of the US Corps of Engineers.

Using the tourist office map, make your way through Verdun to the Victory Monument, and thence to the Citadel.

THE VICTORY MONUMENT   Cut into the old wall of the town is a steep flight of 73 steps flanked by a pair of field guns captured on the Russian front. At the top is a 90 ft high column surmounted by a soldierly knight, inaugurated on 23 June 1929. At the base of the column is a small crypt in which is kept the Golden Book which records the names of all the soldiers who fought at Verdun. The monument is the focal point for the annual June commemorations.

THE CITADEL   Building began in 1624 and fifty years later Vauban added to it. In the late-nineteenth century nearly five miles of underground passages were built and during the First World War it had its own Commander and artillery defences. Today it houses a museum and offers both a film show and a slide presentation relating to life in the Citadel and the battles. It was in the Citadel that the French Unknown Soldier was chosen in the presence of André Maginot, and the scene is re-created in the room where it took place. An entrance fee is payable and it is advisable to wear a jacket inside as the temperature is always cold. Nearby outside are 16 large statues of famous French Generals of the Napoleonic, 1870 and First World War periods.

Drive out of Verdun on the N3 following signs to Champs des Batailles, direction Etain. Just before leaving the outskirts of Verdun there is a military cemetery on the left flying the Tricolore.

FAUBOURG PAVÉ MILITARY CEMETERY   There are some 5,000 burials here, together with a memorial to those executed by the Germans, erected in 1947. Below the cross in the centre are seven Unknown Warriors from among whom an eighth was chosen in the Citadel to lie under the Arc de Triomphe in Paris to symbolize the 1,700,000 Frenchmen who fell in the war. The traffic in the Champs Elysées leading to the Arc is stopped every evening to allow a procession to the grave of the Unknown Soldier where the Eternal Flame is rekindled.

Continue, following signs to the battlefields and then to Fort Vaux. Before reaching the latter, before a sharp bend on the right is a clearing in the trees and a memorial at the foot of a steep bank. If you miss it on the way in you can spot it on the way back from Fort Vaux.

MONUMENT TO LES FUSILLÉS DE TAVANNES   This commemorates sixteen members of the French Resistance who were brought here and shot by the Germans in 1944.

Continue and park at Fort Vaux

FORT VAUX   Building work began in 1881 and the basic fort was completed in three years, but around the turn of the century it was strengthened with 7 ft of steel reinforced concrete laid on top of a 5 ft thick shock barrier of sand. This was then covered with a thick layer of earth. The fort, surrounded by a moat, had its own water reservoir, kitchen and dormitories for a garrison of 250 men. The fort did not come under direct attack until March 1916, but during a bombardment by 420 mm Big Bertha artillery in February, the one-ton shells damaged the water reservoir, filled the moat with debris and destroyed the one 75 mm gun turret.

During May the garrison in the fort grew to 670 men, made up by stragglers from the battlefield and by June 2,000 shells per hour were falling on and around it. The Germans occupied the upper corridors, driving the defenders into the lower levels. There cordite fumes and concrete dust created by the explosions exacerbated the Poilus' thirst brought on by heat and lack of water. On 1 June water was down to 1 litre per man per day, on 4 June to ½ litre and on 5 June to zero. Major Raynal, the fort commander, sent out his last message by pigeon on 4 June and on 7 June at 0350 hours the fort surrendered. The Germans honoured the defenders and the German Crown Prince asked to meet Major Raynal.

There is a well-stocked book and souvenir shop and a guided, or sometimes self-guided (with an English script), tour around the interior of the fort, which takes about half an hour. There is an entrance fee. It is always chilly and damp inside. Take a sweater and watch out for the stuffed pigeon. It died after delivering its message and was awarded a medal.

Return past the Tavannes memorial, turn right at the road junction and follow signs to Fleury and Memorial Museum. On the way at a crossroads there is a recumbent stone lion on the left.

THE WOUNDED LION MONUMENT   The crossroads is called Chapelle Sainte-Fine and marks the site of a destroyed Chapel as well as the closest point to Verdun reached by the Germans (on 23 June 1916) who were attacking from your right.

Continue to the museum 200 yards further on and park in the car park

THE FLEURY MEMORIAL MUSEUM   In front of the museum, which was opened in 1967, is an array of artillery and a number of shells including a German 420 mm giant. There is also a speaking machine which, in English and other languages, tells the philosophy of remembrance behind the museum and the story of the destroyed village of Fleury which can be visited. It is behind the museum and is well-signed.

At the museum entrance (there is a fee) it is advisable to buy the English 'Souvenir Guidebook' which guides the visitor around the exhibits describing each display in turn. Since the booklet was produced there have been a number of additions to the museum, including continuous video displays and timed film shows. There is a large wall map which, at regular intervals, sets out to explain the battle with multi-lingual commentary, signs and coloured lights. It can be confusing. In the centre of the floor is a realistic reproduction of a battlefield, complete with debris, and overhead – and often overlooked – are a reconstructed, full-size Nieuport Bébé and a Fokker E111. There are further displays on the ground floor and it is advisable to allow up to one hour to examine everything thoroughly. The prescribed route takes you out through the book and souvenir shop. There are toilets.

A walk to the site of the village of Fleury, where small markers indicate where buildings once stood, is likely to take up to twenty minutes there and back, but it is a telling witness to the absolute destruction that took place here in 1916. At the end of the trail is a memorial chapel. The woods tend to attract mosquitos, so take precautions.

Return to your car and continue, following signs to Ossuaire. Park in the car park behind Douaumont Ossuary. There are coin operated toilets here.

DOUAUMONT OSSUARY   This dramatic and original building, with its art-deco overtones immediately demands the visitor's attention and reaction. Visible through small windows at ground level are the bones of 130,000 French and German soldiers whose remains were collected from around the battlefield. The ossuary, or mass grave, was begun in 1919 and transferred to the monument in 1927. The building was the idea of Monseigneur Ginistry, Bishop of Verdun, who raised money (some of it from the United States) for its construction. The foundation stone was laid in 1920 and the memorial was officially inaugurated on 7 April 1932. Below and in front of the building is the National Cemetery in which are buried 15,000 identified French soldiers, and the comfortable conformity and familiarity of the white crosses and red roses of the cemetery contrast with the uneasiness that most Anglo-Saxons feel when confronted by the Ossuary. On the 450 ft long façade are the names and coats of arms of the towns that contributed to the building and inside is a nave with eighteen alcoves, each corresponding to sectors of the battlefield where bones were found. Individual soldiers are commemorated on panels paid for by the families. In the centre of the building, opposite the entrance, is the Chapel, with four small, but beautiful stained-glass windows commemorating sacrifice, stretcher-bearers and field medical services. At one end of the nave is a vault in which a flame of remembrance is lit when services are held.

In the centre of the building is a 150-ft high tower which can be climbed for a small charge and on top of which is a lantern and a victory bell. Below (and approached from the car park) is a bookshop, and a comfortable theatre in which a most effective and moving 20-minute film, describing the life of the French soldier at Verdun and making a convincing plea for peace, can be seen. (There is an entrance fee.)

The whole mixture of visible bones, religious symbolism and commercial souvenirs, combined with the powerful architecture of the memorial, can disconcert the visitor. Perhaps that is a more appropriate reaction than a feeling of well-being, bearing in mind what took place here. It is said that if all the soldiers who were killed at Verdun tried to stand up there would not be room enough there for them to do so. *'Debout les Morts!'* 'Rise, the Dead' . . .

Return to your car and follow signs to 'Tranchée des baionettes'.

THE TRENCH OF BAYONETS This memorial commemorates an action of 23 June 1916 when two battalions of the 137th Infantry Regiment were buried alive in their trenches by German artillery fire. The story has it that a number of the Poilus, who were standing in their trench with fixed bayonets waiting to go over the top, died as they stood there and when the fighting stopped a row of bayonets remained visible above the filled-in trench. The mass grave was completed by the Germans and in 1919 the Colonel of the 137th erected a small wooden monument. George Rand, a wealthy American, hearing of the story, funded the building of the present memorial, towards the upkeep of which visitors are invited to contribute in a box inside the entrance. The simple, massive 'pharonic' style of the design emphasizes the significance of what is commemorated rather than the self-importance of the architecture. The bayonets are the object of souvenir hunters and may or not be in evidence.

Return uphill towards Fort Douaumont, following the signs.

FORT DOUAUMONT If you didn't climb on top of the Fort Vaux, you should climb onto Douaumont. You may be able to make out Fort Vaux (look for the Tricolore to the south-east) and the Fleury museum (to the south-west) and by using the sketch maps in this book you can now get a good idea of the size and shape of the battlefield.

The fort was built in 1885 and like Vaux was improved up to 1914. Following the failure of the Belgian forts to stop the German invasion, Douaumont was stripped of its garrison, though its main guns remained. On 25 February 1916, four days after the battle opened, a patrol of the 24th Brandenburgers entered the fort unopposed and captured it together with its garrison of about a dozen. Just how this happened is not clear. Some accounts say that the garrision was asleep, but that seems unlikely at 1600 hours in the middle of a battle. Other reports say that the Germans had disguised themselves in red uniforms as French Zouaves.

Fighting around the fort continued and at the end of May the French got into the northern part but were driven out. It was not until General Mangin's offensive of 24 October that the fort was recaptured and held despite strong German counter-attacks.

There is a souvenir bookshop in the fort and a tour, often self-guided like Vaux, which can also be chilly, even in mid-summer. There is an entrance fee. The workings of the fort's 75 mm and 155 mm gun platforms can be seen and are familiar to those who have visited the Maginot Line. (The conference that led to the building of the Maginot Line was held in Verdun after the war.) On 8 May 1917 a grenade store inside the fort exploded and 679 German soldiers were killed and are buried in the fort in a walled gallery where today there is a memorial chapel.

Return to your car, drive past the Fleury Museum and at the lion crossroads turn right towards Verdun. On the way you pass the Maginot Memorial on the left.

MAGINOT MEMORIAL André Maginot, like Lt Col. Driant, was a local Deputy and enlisted at the outbreak of war. On 9 November 1914 Sgt Maginot was wounded and disabled. In 1916 he returned to Parliament and became Minister for War when, influenced by the fact that the fortress of Verdun had proven invincible, he supported the building of a defensive wall of forts to guard against a future war. His efforts in raising government money to build the system caused it to be named 'The Maginot Line'. The memorial was erected by his friends and consists of a shield in front of which is a bronze group of soldiers sculpted by Gaston Broquet. The memorial was pictured on fund-raising posters just before the Second World War.

Return to Verdun – a city now dedicated to Peace, not War.

THE SOMME
1 JULY 1916–17 NOVEMBER 1916

'The general conduct of the war has been entrusted to
incompetent men – there the trouble lies.'
King Albert of the Belgians, 5 December 1916

SUMMARY OF THE BATTLE

On 1 July 1916 a volunteer British army attacked entrenched German positions
in the Department of the Somme in France. Over-reliance on the destruction of
enemy defences by preparatory artillery bombardment led to almost 60,000
British casualties on the first day and more than 400,000 before the fighting
ended on 17 November 1916. The maximum advance made in all that time was
6½ miles. Total German casualties are estimated to have been about the same as
the British.

OPENING MOVES

Few campaigns of recent history provoke such emotive British opinions as 'The
Battle of the Somme'. Those who study the First World War tend to fall into two
main camps: those who are anti-Haig and those who are pro-Haig. But there are
those who move from one opinion to the other, according to the quality of
debate. Was the C-in-C a dependable rock, whose calm confidence inspired all,
whose far-seeing eye led us to final victory and who deserved the honours later
heaped upon him? Or was he an unimaginative, insensitive product of the social
and military caste system that knew no better: a weak man pretending to be
strong, who should have been sacked? Doubtless the arguments will continue
and more space than is available here is needed for a fair consideration, but there
are some immovable elements: for instance the misjudgement concerning the
artillery's effect upon the German wire and the appalling casualties on 1 July
1916. Those casualties, while not sought for by the French, may well have been
hoped for by them. At the end of 1915 the French and British planned for a joint
offensive on the Somme, with the French playing the major role. Masterminded
by Joffre, the plan was (as far as Joffre was concerned) to kill more Germans than
their pool of manpower could afford. But when the German assault at Verdun
drew French forces away from the Somme, the British found themselves with
the major role, providing sixteen divisions on the first day to the French five.

| MAP 11 | **THE SOMME – 1 JULY 1916** |
| | *The British Plan of Attack* |

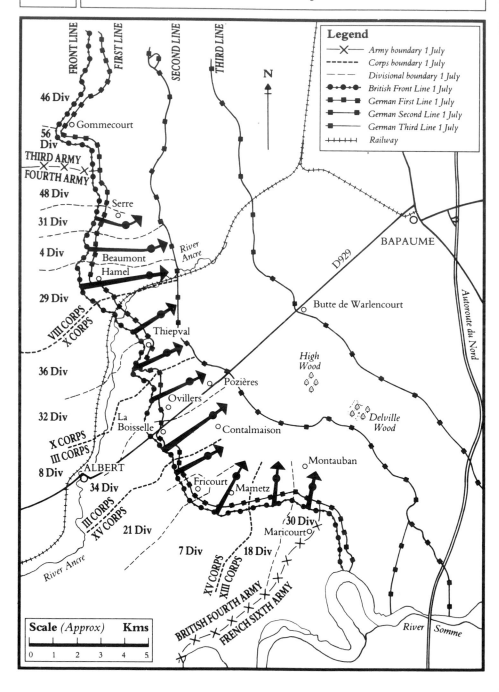

Legend
- ✕ Army boundary 1 July
- - - - Corps boundary 1 July
- – – Divisional boundary 1 July
- ●–●–● British Front Line 1 July
- ■–■–■ German First Line 1 July
- ■–■ German Second Line 1 July
- ■ German Third Line 1 July
- ┼┼┼┼ Railway

N

FRONT LINE
FIRST LINE
SECOND LINE
THIRD LINE

46 Div
○ Gommecourt
56 Div
THIRD ARMY ✕ ✕ ✕
FOURTH ARMY
48 Div
Serre
31 Div ○
4 Div
Beaumont
Hamel
River Ancre
29 Div
VIII CORPS
X CORPS
Thiepval
36 Div
Pozières ○
Ovillers ○
32 Div
La Boisselle ○
X CORPS
III CORPS
8 Div
ALBERT
34 Div
III CORPS
XV CORPS
21 Div
7 Div
River Ancre
Fricourt ○
Mametz ○
Contalmaison ○
Montauban ○
30 Div
Maricourt ○
18 Div
XV CORPS
XIII CORPS
BRITISH FOURTH ARMY
FRENCH SIXTH ARMY

BAPAUME ○
D929
Autoroute du Nord
Butte de Warlencourt ○
High Wood
Delville Wood

River Somme

Scale *(Approx)* **Kms**
0 1 2 3 4 5

It was to be the first joint battle in which the British played the major role and in the opinion of some French politicians, not before time. There was a growing feeling that the British were not pulling their weight and a bloody conflict would stick Britain firmly to the 'Cause'. It was to be the first major battle for Kitchener's Army following their rush to the recruiting stations in the early days of the war.

It was also to be the first battle fought by General Haig as C-in-C. There was a great deal riding on the outcome of the Battle of the Somme. The British plan was based upon a steady 14-mile-wide infantry assault, from Serre in the north to Maricourt in the south, with a diversionary attack at Gommecourt above Serre (see Map 11). 100,000 soldiers were to go over the top at the end of a savage artillery bombardment. Behind the infantry – men of the Fourth Army, commanded by General Rawlinson – waited two cavalry divisions under General Gough. Their role was to exploit success.

What Happened

The battle may be divided into five parts:

Part 1 The First Day   1 July
Part 2 The Next Few Days   2 July +
Part 3 The Night Attack/The Woods   14 July +
Part 4 The Tank Attack   15 Sept
Part 5 The Last Attack   13 Nov

PART 1   THE FIRST DAY: 1 JULY   At 0728 hours, seventeen mines were blown under the German line. Two minutes later 60,000 British soldiers, laden down with packs, gas mask, rifle and bayonet, 200 rounds of ammunition, grenades, empty sandbags, spade and water bottles, clambered out of their trenches from Serre to Maricourt and formed into lines 14 miles long. As the lines moved forward in waves, so the artillery barrage lifted off the enemy front line.

From that moment onwards it was a life or death race, but the Tommies didn't know it. They hadn't been 'entered'. Their instructions were to move forward, side by side, at a steady walk across No Man's Land. It would be safe, they were told, because the artillery barrage would have destroyed all enemy opposition. But the Germans were not destroyed. They and their machine guns had sheltered in deep dugouts, and when the barrage lifted, they climbed out, dragging their weapons with them.

The Germans won the 'race' easily. They set up their machine guns before the Tommies could get to their trenches to stop them, and cut down the ripe corn of British youth in their thousands. As the day grew into hot summer, another 40,000 men were sent in, adding more names to the casualty lists. Battalions disappeared in the bloody chaos of battle, bodies in their hundreds lay around the muddy shell holes that pocked the battlefield.

And to what end this leeching of the nation's best blood? North of the Albert-

Bapaume road, on a front of almost 9 miles, there were no realistic gains at nightfall. VIII, X, and III Corps had failed. Between la Boisselle and Fricourt there was a small penetration of about half a mile on one flank and the capture of Mametz village on the other by XV Corps. Further south, though, there was some success. XIII Corps attacking beside the French took all of its main objectives, from Pommiers Redoubt east of Mametz to just short of Dublin Redoubt north of Maricourt.

The French, south of the Somme, did extremely well. Attacking at 0930 hours they took all of their objectives. 'They had more heavy guns than we did', cried the British generals, or 'The opposition wasn't as tough', or 'The Germans didn't expect to be attacked by the French'. But whatever the reasons for the poor British performance in the north they had had some success in the south – on the right flank, beside the French.

PART 2   THE NEXT FEW DAYS: 2 JULY +   Other than the negative one of not calling off the attack, no General Command decisions were made concerning the overall conduct of the second day's battle. It was as if all the planning had been concerned with 1 July and that the staffs were surprised by the appearance of 2 July. Twenty-eight years later, on 7 June 1944, the day after D-Day, a similar culture enveloped the actions of the British 3rd Division in Normandy. Aggressive actions were mostly initiated at Corps level while Haig and Rawlinson figured out what policy they ought to follow. Eventually, after bloody preparation by the 38th (Welsh) Division at Mametz Wood, they decided to attack on the right flank, but by then the Germans had had two weeks to recover.

PART 3   THE NIGHT ATTACK/THE WOODS: 14 JULY +   On the XIII Corps front, like fat goalposts, lay the woods of Bazentin le Petit on the left and Delville on the right. Behind and between them, hunched on the skyline, was the dark goalkeeper of High Wood. Rawlinson planned to go straight for the goal. Perhaps the infantry general's memory had been jogged by finding one of his old junior officer's notebooks in which the word 'surprise' had been written as a principle of attack, because, uncharacteristically, he set out to surprise the Germans and not in one, but in two, ways.

First, despite Haig's opposition, he moved his assault forces up to their start line in Caterpillar Valley at night. Second, after just a five-minute dawn barrage instead of the conventional prolonged bombardment, he launched his attack. At 0325 hours, twenty thousand men moved forward. On the left were 7th and 21st Divisions of XV Corps and on the right 3rd and 9th Divisions of XIII Corps. The effect was dramatic. Five miles of the German second line were over-run. On the left Bazentin-le-Petit Wood was taken. On the right began the horrendous six-day struggle for Delville Wood. Today the South African memorial and museum in the wood commemorate the bitter fighting.

But in the centre, 7th Division punched through to High Wood and with them were two squadrons of cavalry. Perhaps here was an opportunity for a major breakthrough at last. Not since 1914 had mounted cavalry charged on the Western Front but, when they did, the Dragoons and the Deccan Horse were alone. The main force of the cavalry divisions, gathered south of Albert, knew nothing about the attack. The moment passed, the Germans recovered, counter-attacked and regained the wood.

There followed two months of local fighting under the prompting of Joffre, but, without significant success to offer, the C-in-C began to attract increasing criticism. Something had to be done to preserve his image, to win a victory – or both.

It was: with a secret weapon – the tank.

PART 4   THE TANK ATTACK: 15 SEPTEMBER   Still very new and liable to break down, 32 tanks out of the 49 shipped to France in August assembled near Trônes Wood on the night of 14 September for dispersal along the front, and the following morning at 0620 hours, following a three-day bombardment, eighteen took part in the battle with XV Corps. Their effect was sensational. The Germans, on seeing the monsters, were stunned and then terrified. Nine tanks moved forward with the leading infantry, nine 'mopped up' behind. Barely over three hours later, the left hand division of XV Corps followed a solitary tank up the main street of Flers and through the German third line. Then Courcelette, too, fell to an infantry/tank advance.

The day's gains were the greatest since the battle began. But there were too few tanks and, after the initial shock success, the fighting once again degenerated into a bull-headed contest. The opportunity that had existed to use the tank to obtain a major strategic result had gone. Many felt that it had been squandered. Yet the tank had allowed 4th Army to advance and the dominating fortress of Thiepval finally fell on 26 September, helped, it was said, 'by the appearance of 3 tanks'. At last the British were on the crest of the Thiepval-Pozières-High Wood ridge. But Beaumont Hamel in the north still held out.

PART 5   THE LAST ATTACK: 13 NOVEMBER   At the northern end of the battlefield, 7 divisions of the Reserve (5th) Army assaulted at 0545 hours on 13 November. Bad weather had caused seven postponements since the original date of 24 October. V Corps was north of the River Ancre and II Corps was south. The preparatory bombardment had been carefully monitored to see that the enemy wire had been cut, but this eminent practicality was offset by the stationing of the cavalry behind the line to exploit success. Apart from the overwhelming evidence of past battle experience that should have made such an idea absurd, the weather's effect on the ground alone should have rendered it unthinkable. The generals were as firmly stuck for ideas as any Tommy, up to his waist in Somme mud, was stuck for movement.

The attack went in with a shield of early morning dark and fog, the troops moving tactically from cover to cover. Beaumont Hamel and the infamous Y Ravine were taken by the 51st Highland Division and their kilted Highlander

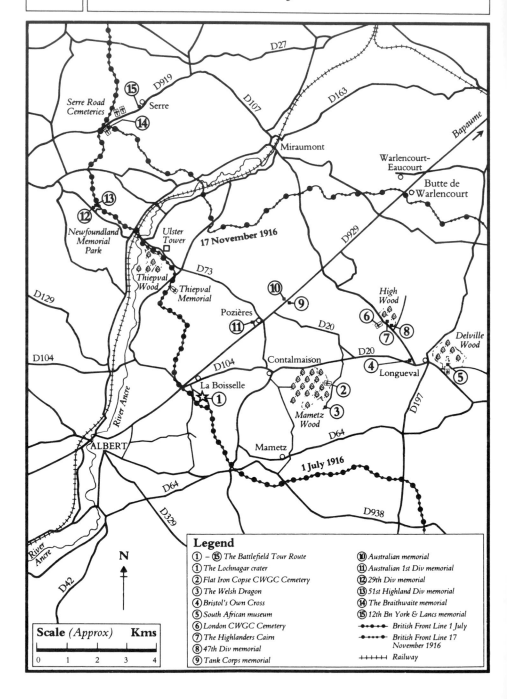

MAP 12

THE SOMME
The Battlefield Tour

Legend

① – ⑮ *The Battlefield Tour Route*
① *The Lochnagar crater*
② *Flat Iron Copse CWGC Cemetery*
③ *The Welsh Dragon*
④ *Bristol's Own Cross*
⑤ *South African museum*
⑥ *London CWGC Cemetery*
⑦ *The Highlanders Cairn*
⑧ *47th Div memorial*
⑨ *Tank Corps memorial*
⑩ *Australian memorial*
⑪ *Australian 1st Div memorial*
⑫ *29th Div memorial*
⑬ *51st Highland Div memorial*
⑭ *The Braithwaite memorial*
⑮ *12th Bn York & Lancs memorial*
●━●━● *British Front Line 1 July*
●┄●┄● *British Front Line 17 November 1916*
┼┼┼┼ *Railway*

Scale *(Approx)* **Kms**
0   1   2   3   4

memorial stands there today in memory of that achievement. Fred Farrell, the official artist attached to the Divisional HQ, sketched in detail the taking of the main German position at Y Ravine, identifying the men involved. The drawing is included in a collection published by T. C. and E. C. Jack in 1920. Fighting went on for several more days, and 7,000 prisoners were taken – though Serre did not fall. But at last enough was enough. The attack was stopped and the Battle of the Somme was over.

THE BATTLEFIELD TOUR

There are more than 100 sites of particular interest to be seen on the Somme battlefield of 1916 – excluding those associated with the Kaiser's Offensive of 1918. With a motor car a reasonably detailed tour can be made in three days using our *Holts' Battlefield Guides: The Somme*, book and our *Battle Map of the Somme*. Here we have selected those places whose names or memorials feature in the top dozen requests made to us over the years (see Map 12).

The tour begins in Albert and moves north-east and anti-clockwise via the mine crater at la Boisselle, the South African memorial and Museum at Delville Wood, Mametz Wood, High Wood, the tank memorial at Pozières, Pozières itself and the largest Commonwealth War Graves Commission memorial in the world at Thiepval. The next stop is the Ulster Tower followed by the preserved battlefield and Newfoundland memorials at Beaumont Hamel, ending at Serre, barely 30 minutes from Arras.

Total distance   22 miles
Total time   5 hours
Maps   IGN 4 Arras/Laon 1:100,000

Drive to the church in Albert which is surmounted by a golden figure holding aloft a baby. Stop.

ALBERT   Fierce fighting around Albert began in the early months of the war, the first enemy shelling being on 29 September 1914. By October 1916, when the Somme offensive had pushed the German guns out of range, the town was a pile of red rubble. On 26 March 1918, during their final offensive, Albert was taken by the Germans and re-taken by the British on 22 August, the East Surreys entering the town at bayonet point. Albert was a major administration and control centre for the Somme offensive, and it was from here that the first Press message was sent announcing the start of the 'Big Push'.

The golden figure above you is the Virgin Mary holding aloft the baby Jesus. It stands on top of the basilique of Notre-Dame des Brébières. Before the war thousands of pilgrims came annually to see the black Madonna inside the church which, legend says, had been discovered locally by a shepherd in the Middle Ages (hence the church's name, from *brébis*, the word for ewe). In January 1915, German shelling toppled the golden Madonna on the steeple to an angle below horizontal, but it did not fall. Visible to soldiers of both sides for many miles around, the statue gave rise to two legends. The British and French believed that the war would end on the day that the statue fell (it is said that the Allied Staff sent engineers up the steeple at night to shore it up to prevent raising false hopes). The Germans believed that whoever knocked down the Madonna would lose the war. Neither prediction came to pass. During the German occupation from March to August 1918 the British shelled Albert and knocked down the Golden Virgin. The figure was never found and today's statue is a replica. The townspeople strongly resisted the suggestion to remount it in its wartime leaning position. The basilique was rebuilt to the original design. Most of the town (notably the station) was rebuilt in the 1920s in the distinct 'art–deco' style then in vogue. The idea to declare it a *zone rouge* (too dangerous to rebuild, like some of the battlefields around Verdun) was also strongly resisted by the inhabitants of Albert. Under the church is an excellent museum.

Three hundred yards uphill is the Town Hall, by the main entrance of which is a plaque commemorating the more than 60,000 casualties suffered by the Machine Gun Corps during the war.

Drive north-east out of Albert on the D929 towards Bapaume. This road was the axis of the British attack on 1 July 1916.

Continue up and down over the hill (known as the Tara-Usna line) to the crossroads in la Boisselle. This was the British front line and there is a memorial seat to the Tynesiders on the right. (Those who are fortunate enough to possess a copy of John Masefield's classic *The Old Front Line* will find many of its descriptions still valid from this point onwards.)

Fork right on the D104 past the seat and turn right at the next junction and follow signs to la Grande Mine.

LA BOISSELLE/LOCHNAGAR CRATER The land containing the crater was purchased in 1978 and is maintained privately, by Englishman Richard Dunning, as a personal memorial to all those who fought in the Battle of the Somme and in particular to those, of both sides, killed in the crater. Other memorials have subsequently been erected there. One is a stone in memory of Tom Easton, a private in the 2nd Bn of the Tyneside Scottish. Another is a memorial seat on which the plaque simply states, 'Donated by friends who visit in memory of friends who remain.' Mr Dunning has also raised a simple 12-ft high cross made from church timber originating on Tyneside. If readers wish to commemorate an individual or unit, he is willing to discuss the placing of a small plate on the cross, or a rose bush. He may be contacted on 0483 67871. On 1 July each year at 0728 a simple memorial gathering takes place at the crater under the auspices of the Lochnagar Memorial Fund and the Sue Ryder Foundation. Donations to the Fund may be made to Account No. 32626584, c/o National Westminster Bank, 185 Sloane Street, London SW1X 9QS.

Mine warfare had been carried on in this area well before July 1916 and there were many craters in No Man's Land. In June, along the Western Front as a whole, the British had blown 101 mines and the Germans 126. In this area some of the shafts dug, from which tunnels then reached out to the enemy line, were over 100 ft deep with tunnels at up to four levels.

When dug, the mine here was known as Lochnagar, and had been started by 185th Tunnelling Company in December 1915. It was finished by 179th Tunnelling Company and packed with two charges of 24,000 and 36,000 lb of ammonal. Seventeen British mines, including Lochnagar, were exploded at 0728 hours along the front on 1 July and the circular crater here measured 300 ft across and was 90 ft deep. Debris rose 4,000 ft into the air and, as it settled the attack began. It failed. The attacking battalions of Tyneside Scottish followed by the Tyneside Irish were reduced to small parties of survivors.

Following the failure of the attack by the Tynesiders of 34th Division, the 10th Worcesters were ordered to move up from beside Albert to make an assault at dawn on 2 July. So chaotic were conditions in the communication trenches that the battalion got lost, and the attack did not go in until 3 July. The Worcesters took the crater area and the village, Private F. G. Turrall winning a VC in the process, but the battalion lost a third of its fighting strength and the Commanding Officer was killed.

Return to the village and take the D104 to Contalmaison and there follow signs to Bazentin and Longueval. Just before the D104 meets the D20 follow signs to 'Flat Iron Copse CWGC Cemetery' down a track to the right.

FLAT IRON COPSE CWGC CEMETERY The cemetery was begun by the 3rd and 7th Divisions on 14 July 1916 as they cleared Mametz Wood after its capture by 38th (the wood is immediately behind the rear wall of the cemetery). There are over 1,500 burials, including two pairs of brothers, each serving with the RWF. Corporal Thomas Hardwidge of the 15th RWF was injured on 11 July and when his brother L/Cpl Henry Hardwidge went to give him water they were both shot and killed. Four days earlier, on 7 July, the Tregaskis brothers, Leonard and Arthur, both Lieutenants in the 16th RWF, were killed under similar circumstances. A particularly notable burial is that of Sgt Edward Dwyer, VC of the 1st Battalion, East Surreys. Dwyer received his award for 'conspicuous bravery and devotion to duty at Hill 60 [in the Ypres Salient] on 20th April 1915' and when back in Britain gave lectures to help the recruiting effort. In the 1980s Pavilion Records of Sussex produced a remarkable pair of records, GEMM 3033/4, which feature original recordings from the 1914–18 period. Track 2, side 2 of the first record is a monologue by Sgt Dwyer, most probably the only contemporary recording of a First World War VC.

Continue down the track which follows the eastern edge of Mametz Wood until you reach the magnificent red Welsh dragon at the south-eastern corner.

THE WELSH AT MAMETZ To a first approximation the dragon faces the wood as did the attacking Welsh. On the morning of 7 July 1916, one week after the first day of the Battle of the Somme, two British divisions began a pincer attack on Mametz Wood, a German stronghold held by the Prussian Guard. The two divisions were the 17th, attacking from the west, and the 38th (Welsh) attacking from the east. The attack was a failure. German machine guns, apparently unaffected by the preparatory artillery bombardment, inflicted heavy casualties upon the attackers, approaching across the open ground. Battlefield communication broke down and a covering smokescreen failed to appear. At the end of the day neither division had even reached the wood, let alone captured it. Three days later, just after 0400 hours on 10 July the two divisions were ordered in again. The main thrust this time was towards the southern face of the wood by the Welsh – a frontal assault. The leading battalions were the 13th, 14th and 16th RWF and despite the hail of German small arms fire they made it to the wood. The struggle became increasingly bitter in the thick undergrowth beneath the splintered trunks. More and more Welsh battalions were committed to the struggle until almost the whole division was in among the trees. The bloody contest, often bitter hand-to-hand fighting, continued for two days until, on the night of 11 July, the Germans withdrew.

The cost to the 38th (Welsh) Division, proudly raised by Lloyd George and inadequately officered by his cronies and protégées, was high – some 4,000 men were killed or wounded. Although they did capture the wood they came under severe criticism for having taken five days to do so and in 1919 Lt Col. J. H. Boraston, co-author of *Sir Douglas Haig's Command*, effectively accused them of a lack of determination which prevented a significant Fourth Army advance on the Somme. The extraordinarily high proportion of literate, articulate writers serving with the RWF chronicle the division's side of the story. Lt Wyn Griffith, author of *Up to Mametz*, served with the 15th Bn RWF and fought in the wood, his young brother, a dispatch runner, being killed when Griffith sent him out with a message in a desperate attempt to stop our own barrage which was falling on the Welsh. Private David Jones chronicles the epic struggle in what is probably the war's most original work of literature – the poem 'In Parenthesis'. Robert Graves and Frank Richards, both of the 2nd Bn, describe the horror of mopping up in the wood a few days after the attack and Siegfried Sassoon watched it go in from Pommiers Redoubt. Inspired by their accounts, Colin Hughes wrote the definitive account of the raising of the division and the attack on the wood in *Mametz* (Orion Press, 1982).

The exuberant and emotional Welsh dragon memorial, designed by sculptor-in-iron David Peterson, was raised mostly through the tireless fund-raising and organizational efforts of Cardiff Western Front Association member Harry Evans and his wife Pat. It was unveiled on 11 July 1987 and although not an 'official' national memorial, is the focal point of Welsh remembrance on the Western Front.

Return to the D104 and continue on the D20 in the direction of Longueval. Stop at the memorial cross at the junction with the D107 just before Longueval.

BRISTOL'S OWN CROSS This memorial was raised by British and French volunteers under the leadership of Dean Marks, a technician with Dupont UK. Inspired by an old photograph showing Bristol veterans standing beside a cross on the Somme, Dean investigated and found that the cross in the picture had disappeared during the Second World War. He determined to replace it and helped by friends, members of the Western Front Association, Bristol Civil Authorities and others, he set to work. In the 70th Anniversary year of the Battle of the Somme his two-year-old daughter Amy, his father Roy, the Mayor of Longueval plus a party of helpers put up the new cross. It stands where the 12th Battalion Gloucestershire Regiment set off to battle and commemorates those who fell around Longueval and Guillemont between July and September 1916.

Continue to Longueval village and there follow signs to the South African Memorial, Delville Wood.

DELVILLE WOOD There are two separate memorials here. On the right of the road is Delville Wood Cemetery, Longueval, which was made after the Armistice. There are over 5,200 burials and almost two-thirds are unknown. One grave of note is that of Sergeant Albert Gill, KRRC, who won a posthumous VC when rallying his platoon by standing up in full view of the enemy, 151 graves are those of South Africans. On the left of the road is Delville Wood itself, the South African National Memorial and behind it the museum built in 1985–6. The memorial (unveiled by the widow of General Louis Botha on 10 October 1926) is topped by a sculpture of Castor and Pollux clasping hands. The sculpture, designed by Alfred Turner, symbolizes the unity of the English- and Afrikaans-speaking peoples of South Africa. A replica overlooks Pretoria from the terrace of the Government Buildings designed, as was the memorial, by Sir Herbert Baker, ARA. The museum is a beautifully designed building with delicately engraved glass windows around an inner courtyard and dramatic bas reliefs in bronze depicting the bitter days of fighting for the wood. In the large car park there are clean toilets and a shop serving snacks which also has an exceptional range of First World War books, postcards and collectables. Open October–March 0900–1600. April–September 0900–1800. Closed Mondays.

The battle for the wood was a complex one and is well told in the museum and in booklets available there. The South African Brigade was attached to 9th Scottish Division, and when the latter took Longueval village on 14 July, the Springboks were given the task of taking the wood. At dawn on 15 July the assault began with a fearsome artillery duel. Five days of hand-to-hand fighting followed. It rained every other day and enemy artillery fire reached rates exceeding 400 shells a minute. The landscape was a tangled mess of broken tree stumps, huge shell holes, mud and water overlaid with bodies of soldiers of both sides (many of whom still lie in the wood). Though the South Africans were told, and tried, to take the wood 'at all costs', they couldn't quite do it, and when they were relieved by 26 Brigade on 20 July only 143 men of the original 3,150 came out of the trenches. It was not until 25 August 1916 that 14 (Light) Division finally overcame all enemy resistance in the wood.

A great uncle of one of the authors survived being buried alive by a shell for several days, though he never fully recovered from the horrific experience. Lord Moran, later to become Churchill's doctor, but then serving with the 1st Bn the Royal Fusiliers in the trenches immediately south of Delville Wood during the battle, described in his book, *The Anatomy of Courage*, the burials of some of his men. 'Shells were bursting all around and in the black smoke men were digging. Muffled appeals for help, very faint and distant, came out of the earth and maddened the men who dug harder than ever, and some throwing their spades away, burrowed feverishly with their hands like terriers. It was difficult to get the earth away from one place where they said someone was buried without piling it where others were digging also. We were getting in each other's way. We were afraid too of injuring those buried heads with the shovels and always through our minds went the thought that it might be too late. Then there was a terrific noise, everything vanished for a moment, and when I could see Dyson and the two men working beside him had disappeared. They were buried.' Following the Gulf War there was considerable debate about 'friendly fire'. The Royal Fusiliers had been under friendly fire during this incident.

In the 1918 battles the Germans over-ran the area on 24 March and 38th (Welsh) Division retook the wood on 28 August.

Return to Longueval village and branch off the D20 on the D107 signed to Martinpuich and Courcelette. At the first British cemetery on the left stop.

LONDON CEMETERY AND EXTENSION AND MEMORIALS The original cemetery was begun in September 1916 by the burial of 47 men 'in a large shell hole' by 47th Division, and was later enlarged by the addition of other graves to make a total of 101. That area is immediately to the left of the main entrance. The cemetery was further extended after the Armistice and is the third largest on the Somme, containing over 3,330 graves of which more than 3,100 are unknown. There is a 1939–45 plot in the cemetery too.

Death makes no political distinction and just as Herbert Asquith, Liberal Statesman and Prime Minister until December 1916, lost a son (Raymond) on the Somme, so did Arthur Henderson, leader of the Labour Party at this time (who was to win the Nobel Peace Prize in 1934). Captain David Henderson of the Middlesex Regiment, attached to 19th London Battalion, was killed in High Wood on 15 September 1916, age 27, and is buried here.

The wood across the road from the cemetery is High Wood and two memorials are readily visited by walking back along the road.

THE GLASGOW HIGHLANDERS' CAIRN The cairn commemorates the unsuccessful attack of 9th (Glasgow Highlanders) Battalion, Highland Light Infantry of 15 July 1916. Privately erected by Alex Aitken, whose book *Courage Past* deals with the attack, it was inaugurated in November 1972. 192 stones brought by

Alex from Culloden individually commemorate each man killed and form a cairn 5 ft 7 in tall, the minimum recruiting height for the battalion. The square stone on top was a Glasgow paving stone. The Gaelic inscription reads, 'Just here, Children of the Gael went down shoulder to shoulder on 15 July 1916.'

47TH LONDON DIVISION MEMORIAL   The stone porch surrounding a cross commemorates the action of the Division on 15 September 1916. It was 47th Division that finally took High Wood and one of the assault formations was 1st Battalion, Prince of Wales' Own Civil Service Rifles. They were told that they were to attack at 0550 hours on 15 September and that they would be supported by two tanks instead of having an artillery barrage. At zero hour the tanks had not arrived and the attack went in without them – and without artillery support – resulting in many casualties. The unit history records, 'Meanwhile the tanks had not shown up though one of them later on, after nearly smashing up Battalion Headquarters, got stuck in a communication trench and materially interfered with the removal of the wounded. Its pilot got out and going into Battalion Headquarters asked the Commanding Officer where High Wood was.' The CO's reply is not recorded.

Continue through Martinpuich to the D929 Albert to Bapaume road and turn left. Continue to the tall wireless mast before Pozières and stop by the gate and memorial on the left. Beware the traffic.

THE TANK CORPS MEMORIAL   It was at the battle of Flers–Courcelette, Part 4 of the Somme offensive, that tanks went into action for the first time. This obelisk, with its four superb miniature tanks, is a memorial to the fallen of the Corps, and its fence is constructed from tank 6 pounder gun barrels and early driving chains. This point was one of several where the tanks mustered ready for the attack after assembling behind Trônes Wood on the night of 14 September.

Walk across the road to the other memorial.

POZIÈRES MILL AUSTRALIAN MEMORIAL   The ruins of the old windmill can still be seen sticking out of the mound of earth. This was the high point of the Pozières Ridge, so bitterly and bloodily fought for by the Australians. Over the month of August when Haig, pushed by Joffre, was indulging in piecemeal attacks, it was the three Australian divisions that hammered towards the high ground of the ridge along the Albert–Bapaume road (the one along which you are driving). In 45 days the Australians launched 19 attacks and lost 23,000 officers and men. The site was bought by the Australian War Memorial Board and the inscription here reads, 'The ruin of Pozières windmill which lies here was the centre of the struggle in this part of the Somme Battlefields in July and August 1916. It was captured on 4 August by Australian troops who fell more thickly on this ridge than on any other battlefield of the war.' Ten days after the Aussies left the Somme the tank made its debut.

Continue down the hill past the Pozières crossroads for about 200 yards and turn right along a small road signed to the 1st Australian Divisional Memorial.

THE 1ST AUSTRALIAN DIVISION MEMORIAL   The village was captured on 24 July 1916 by the 1st Australian Division and the British 48th Division, the main German trench defended by the 117th Division being along the line of this small road. Across the road opposite the memorial is a German bunker known as Gibraltar.

Continue to the T junction by the church, turn left and follow the road to the Thiepval Memorial.

THIEPVAL ANGLO–FRENCH MEMORIAL   The structure is both a battle memorial and a memorial. As the former it commemorates the 1916 Anglo-French offensive on the Somme and as the latter it carries the names of over 73,000 British and South African men (the Australians, Canadians, Indians, Newfoundlanders and New Zealanders are commemorated on their own national memorials or elsewhere) who have no known grave and who fell on the Somme between July 1915 and 20 March 1918. 141 ft high it was designed by Sir Edwin Lutyens and has 16 piers on whose faces the names of the Missing are inscribed. It stands on a concrete raft 10 ft thick built 19 ft below ground and is the largest British war memorial in the world. It was unveiled on 31 July 1932 by HRH the Prince of Wales in the presence of the President of the French Republic. During the 1980s it had to be refaced owing to deterioration of the original bricks chosen by Lutyens. Behind the memorial is a small Anglo-French cemetery, which symbolizes the joint nature of the war. Its construction was paid for equally by both governments and 300 dead of each nation are buried there, the French graves marked by crosses, the British by their traditional headstones.

This area was captured by the 18th Division on 27 September 1916 in Part 4 of the Somme Battle and a memorial to them stands at the road junction behind Thiepval. There is another in Trônes Wood. Thiepval fell to the Germans again on 25 March 1918 and was recaptured by the 17th and 38th (Welsh) Divisions on 24 August 1918.

The 73,000 names include musicians (like Lt George Butterworth, MC, of the DLI) and poets (like Lt T. M. Kettle of the Dublin Fusiliers). It is worth looking in the registers for your own family name – many visitors have been surprised to discover a forgotten relative on the memorial.

Drive to Thiepval crossroads by the church and take the D73 signed to the Ulster tower. Stop at the tower.

THE ULSTER TOWER   This is a replica of the tower known as Helen's Tower on the estate of the Marquis of Dufferin and Ava at Clandboye in County Down where the 36th (Ulster) Division trained before coming to France. There is a small chapel on the ground floor and excellent views over the Ancre Valley from the top, During the summer an Ulsterman curator is resident in the tower. In 1990 it was rededicated by Princess Alice, Duchess of Gloucester, and refurbished by young people of the Farset organization which encourages cross-community relationships in west Belfast.

Stand on the road with your back to the entrance gates. Straight ahead at 12 o'clock is Thiepval Wood (now shown on modern French maps as Authuille Wood). At 9 o'clock is Connaught Cemetery and beyond it the Thiepval Memorial. At 2 o'clock on the horizon is Beaumont Hamel Memorial Park.

On 1 July the Ulsters walked, and then charged, from the forward edge of Thiepval Wood, across the road, up past where the Tower stands and on to the crest and beyond. They were the only soldiers north of the Albert–Bapaume road to pierce the German lines. Some say their achievement was due to a mixture of Irish individualism, alcoholic bravura and religious fervour. It was also the emotive anniversary of the Battle of the Boyne. Whatever the reason, it was a magnificent feat of arms. Within an hour and a half, five lines of German trenches had been overwhelmed. Some small parties of 8th and 9th Royal Irish Rifles penetrated the German second line, but unsupported by advances on their left or right, shelled by their own artillery, exposed to enemy machine guns on their flanks and subject to fierce counter-attacks, they were forced to withdraw at the end of the day. Fourteen hours after the assault began the lines finished virtually where they started, but the Irish, unlike most, had won the race at 0730. If the rest of the 4th Army had advanced at the same speed it is certain that the outcome on 1 July would have been totally different. Four vcs were won by Ulstermen that day: by Capt. Eric Bell of the 9th Bn, Royal Inniskilling Fusiliers, Lt Geoffrey Cather, 9th Bn Royal Irish Fusiliers; Pte William (Billy) McFadzean, 14th Bn Royal Irish Rifles and Pte Robert Quigg of the 12th Bn, Royal Irish Rifles.

Continue down the hill, over the River Ancre and the railway. (To the right is Ancre cwgc Cemetery. In it are buried some of the men of the Royal Naval Division killed in November 1916 and remembered by A. P. Herbert in his poem 'Beaucourt Revisited', e.g. Vere Harmsworth, son of the newspaper magnate. To the left is the area described by Edmund Blunden in 'The Ancre at Hamel: Afterwards') *Turn left, following signs up the hill to the Newfoundland Memorial Park. Stop at the entrance. Walk into the park.*

NEWFOUNDLAND MEMORIAL PARK The park covers 84 acres and was purchased by the Government of what was then Newfoundland as a memorial to their soldiers and sailors killed in the Great War. It was officially opened by Earl Haig on 7 June 1925. There are a number of memorials and cemeteries in the park, as well as preserved trench lines which have been maintained in their original shape. The park Superintendent normally lives in the house to the right from April to November.

The attack on 1 July was in the direction in which you are walking. The assault division was the 29th. The first brigade to go in, the 87th was cut down and the 8th was ordered up. One assault formation was the 1st Battalion of the Royal Newfoundland Regiment. They made their attack across the area of the park you are now entering. It lasted less than half an hour.

Every officer who went forward was either killed or wounded. Of the 801 that went into action, only 68 members of the regiment were unwounded, probably the highest casualty count for any regimental unit on 1 July.

The first memorial to be seen is that to 29th Division, its distinctive red badge displayed on a stone cairn, which is on the left of the path a few metres from the entrance. Then almost immediately on the left is the bronze box containing the Visitors' Book and a plaque on the right carrying a verse by John Oxenham. Further on is the striking figure of a Caribou, the emblem of the Newfoundland Regiment (there are three others in France – at Gueudecourt, Masnières and Monchy-le-Preux). A path leads to a parapet around the Caribou on which are orientation arrows identifying various parts of the battlefield, including the three British cemeteries in the park: Hawthorn Ridge No. 2, Y Ravine and Hunters – a circular cemetery which had originally been a large shell hole. At the bottom of the mound on which the Caribou stands are three bronze plaques on which are named 591 officers and men of the Royal Newfoundland Regiment, 114 of the Newfoundland Royal Naval Reserve and 115 of the Newfoundland Mercantile Marine who lost their lives during the war and have no known grave.

Also visible are the 'Danger Tree', a twisted skeleton of an original trunk which marks the spot where casualties were heaviest on 1 July (about halfway to Y Ravine) and in the distance at the bottom of the slope, the kilted Highlander of the 51st Highland Division bearing the Gaelic inscription, 'Friends are Good on the Day of the Battle'. It stands on a platform of Aberdeen granite and commemorates the action of the Division in taking Beaumont Hamel and the natural feature of Y Ravine (a main German support position then riddled with tunnels) on 13 November during Part 5 of the Somme Battle. The figure is some 35 m from the Ravine (about 20 m deep) and between them is a Celtic memorial cross.

Continue to Auchonvillers, turning right and then left to join the D919. Turn right towards Arras and stop at the first British cemetery on the right.

SERRE ROAD CWGC CEMETERY NO. 2 This cemetery is one of three named Serre Road. They were begun by V Corps in the spring of 1917, over-run by the Germans in March 1918 and retaken in August. Here are over 7,100 burials, including some Germans. At the Serre end of the cemetery, outside the wall by the roadside, is a private memorial to Lieutenant V. A. Braithwaite, MC, of the SLI, a regular officer who had served in Gallipoli and who was killed on the first day of the Somme battle, along with his Commanding Officer, Adjutant and fourteen other officers in the 1st Battalion. Their attack had been made along the line of the road, and to its right, against the German stronghold known as Quadrilateral Redoubt, which was on the site of the cemetery. Beside winning the MC, Braithwaite had twice been mentioned in dispatches. His son fought as a Company Commander with the Regiment in the Normandy campaign in 1944. Also killed that day was Brigadier General C. B. Prowse, GOC 11th Infantry

Brigade, the Somersets' Brigade. He too had once been in the 1st Battalion. A little further on, on the left of the road, is the French National Cemetery which contains more than 800 graves of men from two infantry regiments – the 243rd and the 327th, both raised in Lille. It was constructed in 1921 and opposite, on the right of the road, is a memorial chapel. Next to the French Cemetery is Serre Road No. 1.

SERRE ROAD NO. 1 CWGC CEMETERY This was begun in May 1917 by V Corps but was enlarged after the Armistice by concentration of over 2,000 graves from other parts of the Somme battlefield. There are some 2,100 burials, including 71 French soldiers. On 1 July 1916 it was the Leeds and Bradford Pals who attacked here, i.e. the 15th, 16th and 18th West Yorks. On the other side of the road are signs to the Redan Ridge cemeteries, Waggon Road and Munich Trench, while 100 yards further on to the left are signed Luke Copse, Railway Hollow, Queen's and Serre Road No. 3. Among the latter group is the Sheffield Battalion Memorial. Just before entering the village of Serre is the memorial to the 12th Battalion, Yorks and Lancs, on the left. The road continues to Arras.

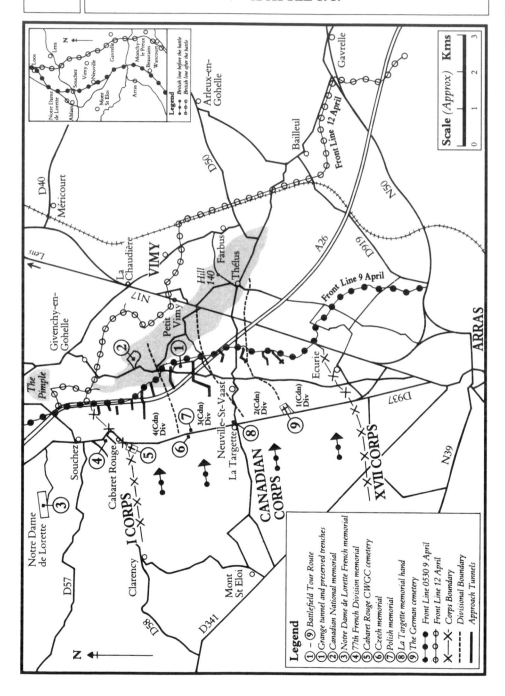

| MAP 13 | VIMY RIDGE 9 – 12 APRIL 1917 |

Legend
- ①–⑨ Battlefield Tour Route
- ① Grange tunnel and preserved trenches
- ② Canadian National memorial
- ③ Notre Dame de Lorette French memorial
- ④ 77th French Division memorial
- ⑤ Cabaret Rouge CWGC cemetery
- ⑥ Czech memorial
- ⑦ Polish memorial
- ⑧ La Targette memorial hand
- ⑨ The German cemetery
- ●—● Front Line 0530 9 April
- ○—○ Front Line 12 April
- ✕—✕ Corps Boundary
- – – – Divisional Boundary
- ——— Approach Tunnels

Scale (Approx) Kms

VIMY RIDGE
9–12 APRIL 1917

'In the morning, tired and back from night duty, we
lay down with the words, "Now let us put the
blankets over our heads and sleep." Suddenly there
was heavy drumfire. We jumped up, all tiredness
gone, for our country and our lives were at stake.'
A German Fusilier's memory of 9 April 1917 on Vimy Ridge

'Within forty minutes of the opening of the battle,
practically the whole of the German front line
system on the front attacked had been stormed and taken.'
Sir Douglas Haig's Dispatches.

A SUMMARY OF THE BATTLE

On 9 April 1917 the Canadian Corps attacked what was probably the strongest
of German defensive positions in northern France. They rehearsed their assault
and used miles of tunnels to approach the enemy lines. By midday only the
highest point of the ridge, Hill 145, remained in German hands and that fell the
following day. German casualties were about 20,000, the Canadian losses were
half that. Four VCs were won.

OPENING MOVES

Vimy Ridge forms part of the front that was known as the 'Arras Sector'. This
ran from Lens in the north to Beaurains in the south. Arras itself was never
occupied by the Germans and a salient bulged east from the city into enemy
territory throughout the war.

The front formed in October 1914, at which time the Germans took Vimy
Ridge. In May 1915 the French mounted an attack towards Vimy with their
seasoned 10th Army and gained the crest of the ridge, but were unable to
consolidate their positions. In September 1915 as part of the Artois Offensive, of
which the British attack at Loos was the northern prong, the 10th Army again
set their faces towards the ridge, but German counter-attacks drove them back.

Trench warfare, which had begun late in 1914, now became the order of the
day and the French and Germans adopted a 'live and let live' policy. The Arras

83

front became what was known as a 'quiet sector'. In March 1916 the British took over the Arras front from the French 10th Army which had lost a reported 130,000 men in trying to take the ridge. In late autumn the Canadians came north from the Somme to relieve the British and settled for a cold winter of strengthening defences. At the end of the year, at Chantilly, the British and French agreed to continue their policy of joint offensives, a decision unaffected by the replacement of Joffre by Nivelle on 31 December. Nivelle, the new broom, proclaimed the need for an offensive of 'violence, brutality and rapidity', and told all and sundry that his plan would end the war by breaking through the German lines. As a preliminary to his assault, planned to begin on the Aisne mid–April 1917, the British were tasked to attack on the Arras sector with their First and Third Armies, drawing German forces away from the Aisne.

The British preparation was very thorough and included the use of tunnels to bring troops forward to the front line without being observed or shot at. Arras itself has two major cave systems dating back to the seventeenth century and in the eastern suburbs these were enlarged and connected to a series of tunnels by special Tunnelling Companies – particularly by the New Zealanders. Twenty-five large caves were excavated with room for 11,000 troops and electric light, running water and ventilation systems were installed. In order to bring forward the vast amount of supplies of ammunition and stores needed, standard and narrow gauge railways were built and plank roads laid. A very deliberate policy of achieving air superiority was maintained by offensive flying, particularly in the days immediately prior to the attack. Although this resulted in heavy casualties, with 28 British aircraft losses to the Germans' 15, it allowed the British artillery the freedom to register their guns effectively. Three weeks before the assault the artillery began to bombard the German wire. Heavy artillery concentrated on the rear areas, on headquarters and on communications. As the day of the attack approached, the intensity of shelling increased by night and day and at intervals along the front gas discharges were made. The total frontage of the attack was just on 15 miles from Vimy Ridge to Croisilles south-east of Arras. The southern half was entrusted to the Third Army under Allenby and the northern half to the 1st Army under General Horne. The assault on what General Haig called 'an important tactical feature, possession of which I considered necessary', was delegated to General Julian Byng's Canadian Corps, part of 1st Army. The feature was Vimy Ridge.

WHAT HAPPENED

At 0530 on 9 April 1917 in driving sleet the British armies emerged from their tunnels and trenches and advanced behind a rolling barrage. It was Ludendorff's 52nd birthday. What a present! He was not in the best of spirits anyway, having heard that three days earlier America had declared war on Germany. He had observed all the careful preparations and had expected the British attack, indeed he had anticipated it with confidence, but the force of the assault broke through the German positions, in places to their third lines, and Vimy Ridge was effectively lost soon after midday. It took two days of counter-attacks and movement of reserves to stem the possibility of a British breakthrough, but in the week before Nivelle's offensive on the Aisne, the First Army (in effect the Canadians) took 4,000 prisoners and 54 guns while in the south the Third Army took 7,000 prisoners and 112 guns. The penetration made and held was estimated by Ludendorff to have been '12 to 15 kilometres wide and 6 or more kilometres deep'. Ten days after the attack began, there were almost twice as many infantry opposite the British as there had been at the start. Haig's men had done what had been asked of them – 'take some German forces away from the Aisne'.

The aerial combat over Vimy during this month of April 1917 was so costly to the British that they dubbed it 'Bloody April'. During those 30 days Rittmeister Baron Manfred von Richthofen increased his 'score' from 31 to 50, despite 'Boom' Trenchard putting 754 planes into the air to the Germans' 264. But the Germans were flying over their own territory and their Albatross D111 triplanes were superior to the allied Spads and FEs – both in speed and manoeuvrability. One of the Red Baron's opponents that month was Captain William Avery Bishop, DSO, DFC, who won his MC on 7 April 1917 for shooting down a German balloon, and who later in 1917 was awarded the VC 'for most conspicuous bravery, determination and skill'.

THE BATTLEFIELD TOUR

The tour starts at the Canadian Memorial Park at Vimy Ridge then continues via Souchez to the French National Memorial at Notre Dame de Lorette on through Cabaret Rouge to the Czech and Polish memorials. Next comes la Targette with its unique memorial and German cemetery and the tour ends in Arras.

Total distance   25 miles
Total time   4 hours 45 minutes
Maps   IGN 1:25,000 2406 Est Arras plus 2405 Est Lens

A ready route to Vimy is via exit 7, 'Arras Centre', from the A26–E17 autoroute. In any event the memorial park is well signed from the N17 Arras–Lens road. Once inside the park turn left at the T junction, follow signs to the trenches (tranchées) and stop in the car park.

VIMY PRESERVED TRENCHES AND TUNNELS   There is a visitor reception centre, usually open from April to September, which is readily seen, and well-presented booklets and pamphlets on what happened here are usually available and there are clean toilets nearby. There is a tunnel system which may be entered, but for security reasons only in groups accompanied by guides. Application to join a group can be made at the reception. There is no charge. The guides are usually bilingual Canadian students on vacation who have been specially recruited and trained by the Canadian Government. A trip into the tunnel, which begins near the Canadian flag, generally lasts about 25 minutes and should not be taken by anyone who is at all claustrophobic. It is cold underground and often wet and slippery.

Beyond the tunnel, clearly signed, are the preserved trench lines formed with concrete sandbags. Work on preserving this area began in the late 1920s and was still going on in 1936 when the Vimy Memorial (your next stop) was unveiled. The first trenches are the Canadian line, and sniper posts, firesteps and duckboards are plain to see. Just over the top of the Canadian parapet is one of the features that makes Vimy so extraordinary – a huge mine crater.

When the British took over this 'quiet sector' from the French, peace gave way to conflict. Fighting patrols were sent out to take enemy prisoners, raids were launched, 'nuisance' bombardments began and underground too the warfare intensified. Tunnel after tunnel was driven under the enemy trenches, packed with explosives and fired. Huge craters resulted with identifying codenames: 'Irish', 'Montreal', 'Love', 'Grange' . . .. The crater immediately beyond the Canadian line is 'Grange' (and it is the Grange tunnel through which one walks underground). The effectiveness of the mine warfare is evident in a report from the German 163rd Regiment. 'The continual mine explosions in the end got on the nerves of the men. One stood in the front line defenceless and powerless against these fearful mine explosions.'

Both sides attempted to sabotage each other's mining by burrowing under the other's galleries and blowing them up. Miners had to stop and listen at regular intervals for the sound of enemy digging and then make fine judgements about just where the other's tunnel was and what he was about to do. The tension must have been heart-stopping. Dark cramped conditions, foul air to breathe, hot and probably wet too, trapped mole-like underground – it needed special qualities just to remain sane. Tunnels were frequently dug at different levels. Near Souchez (you drive through the area later) mining went on at 110 ft and 60 ft down, and some tunnels were over 1,000 yards long. One, called 'Goodman', was more than 1,800 yards. Grange tunnel was a sophisticated tunnel 800 yards long with side-bays for headquarters, signal offices, water points, etc. and standing room. It was meant for the movement of troops. Six miles or more of such tunnels were dug before the battle. Tunnels to be used solely as a means of reaching the enemy lines in order to place explosives under them were frequently crawling-size only. There is yet another surprise in store because just across the crater, on the opposite lip, are the German trenches.

It was a remarkable feat for the Canadians to do so well here. The whole attack had been rehearsed day after day at unit level on a full-scale replica behind the front. Short, reachable objectives were marked on maps as lines – black, red, blue and brown, attacking formations only moving on or through as each line was established. The Canadians went in ten battalions abreast, fighting, for the first time as a national contingent, and working steadily forward from objective to objective. The 4th Division was delayed briefly at Point 145 but that position was taken during the afternoon. The Grange position was defended by companies of the Germans 261st Reserve Regiment of the 79th Reserve Division. When the fighting was over the 261st Regiment had lost 86 killed, 199 wounded and 451 missing – a total of 736 men. The Canadian assault here was made by 7th Brigade of the 3rd Division and alongside to the north 111th Brigade of the 4th Division. One of the Canadians waiting in the Grange tunnel at 0530 hours described the sound of the opening barrage as 'like water on a tin roof in a heavy thunderstorm'. Around the Grange crater area there are many other craters and paths lead off into the wood of Canadian pine, each tree said to represent a soldier's life lost on the ridge.

Drive from the car park and follow signs to the Memorial car park where there are toilets and an orientation map.

CANADIAN NATIONAL MEMORIAL. POINT 145 This is the rear of the memorial which is reached along a narrow stone path. The guardians who look after the 250 acres of the park, given by France 'In perpetuity' to Canada, are armed with whistles which you quickly discover if you step off the cream stone road. At one time in the 1930s it was even forbidden to take photographs! When the Canadians decided to erect a national memorial here to replace the divisional memorials placed after the battle, they invited competitive designs and 160 were submitted. The winner, who said that the design came to him in a dream, was Walter Seymour Allward, a Toronto sculptor. The two tall pylons symbolize Canada and France and between them at the front, carved from a single 30-ton block of stone, is a figure of Canada mourning for her dead. Below the figure is a sarcophagus carrying a helmet and laurels and a Latin subscription commem- orating the 60,000 Canadians who died during the Great War. On the wall of the memorial are the names of 11,285 Canadian soldiers who were killed in France and who have no known grave. The 15-ft high memorial stands on Point 145, the highest point of Vimy Ridge. The base was formed from 12,000 tons of concrete and masonry and 6,000 tons of Dalmatian stone was used for the pylons and the figures, of which there are twenty, all 12 ft high. Construction began in 1925 and Allward's aim was, he said, to produce 'a structure which would endure, in an exposed position, for a thousand years – indeed, for all time'.

When you drive off you have to follow the one way circuit. Try to stop below the memorial for a brief view of what was designed as the front.

When the memorial was unveiled on 26 July 1936 (it took four years longer to build than at first estimated) it was in the presence of King Edward VIII, his only overseas official engagement as King. Also present was M. Victor Maistriau, the Burgomaster of Mons, which had been liberated by the Canadian Corps on 11 November 1918. He carried with him the personal flag of Lt Colonel Sir Arthur

Currie who had commanded the Corps. The General had presented his flag to the town and it now hangs in the museum. The area between where you are hovering and the memorial was filled with pilgrims, of whom 8,000 had come from Canada.

Also in the park are memorials to the 3rd Canadian Division and a Moroccan Division and three CWGC cemeteries – Givenchy Road, Zouave Valley and Canadian No. 2.

Drive back to the N17 and turn left towards Lens. After a mile turn left on the D51 and navigate through Givenchy and under the motorway to the D937. Turn right through busy traffic and continue north out of Souchez. Follow signs to Notre Dame de Lorette and park at the south-east end of the cemetery (by the toilets).

FRENCH NATIONAL MEMORIAL AND CEMETERY, NOTRE DAME DE LORETTE
This hill and Vimy Ridge, which is to the south-east and separated from it by the motorway are adjacent features. On a clear day Vimy Ridge, Arras to the south and the battlefield of Loos to the north-east are all clearly visible.

The hill, which is 165 m above sea level, had its first chapel in 1727 which was enlarged to a church in 1870. During the 'Race to the Sea' in 1914 the Germans took part of the hill, pushing the French lines to about 100 yards west of the present basilique. In 1915 there were three major actions around Notre Dame de Lorette. On 9 May the 21st Division and the 33rd Division under General Pétain attacked to the south of the hill as part of a 10th Army offensive and gains were made everywhere, but the feature was not cleared. On 16 June the same formations attacked again, but any gains they had made were wiped out by German counter-attacks on 13 July, although in both actions the Moroccan Division had distinguished itself by its bravery and élan. The attack of 25 September 1915 was more successful. The village of Souchez, through which you have driven, was taken by the French 13th and 70th Divisions and Cabaret Rouge (where you go later) was cleared by the 77th Division. This part of the feature was also taken but the plateau of Vimy Ridge remained in German hands and stayed with them until the Canadian assault of 9 April 1917, almost two years later.

On 12 September 1920 the Association of Notre Dame de Lorette was founded, with the aim of building a cemetery, an ossuary, a symbolic lighthouse and a chapel in order to commemorate those who died. The Association has almost 3,000 members and the memorial area was officially recognized as a National Monument in 1963. The cemetery contains 19,000 identified burials and six mass graves containing more than 16,000 soldiers, all arranged around a clear central area in which is the tower and the basilique. The tower, designed by Maître L. Cordonnier, is 205 ft high and has 200 stairs and 5 floors. At the top is a 3,000 candlepower light that rotates at 5 times per minute and when shining can be seen for more than 40 miles. In the crypt of the tower are an unknown soldier from the Second World War (16 July 1950), the ashes of people deported to concentration camps (25 April 1955), an unknown soldier from Indo–China (16 October 1977) and an unknown soldier from North Africa (8 June 1980). The first stone was laid on 19 June 1921 by Marshal Pétain and the tower was inaugurated on 2 August 1925 by President Painlevé. To enter the tower there is a nominal charge which goes towards the upkeep of the memorial. On the first floor is a small museum which was opened in 1964 and it is possible to climb to the top and to look out over the battlefield. The basilique, or chapel, was consecrated on 26 May 1927 in the presence of Marshal Pétain and has inside, on the left, a statue of Monseigneur Julien, the founder of the Association and on the right a statue of Notre Dame de Lorette. The stained-glass windows commemorate famous historical events.

Outside and almost opposite to the cemetery entrance is an orientation table, put up in 1975. Standing with your back to the cemetery, and looking out over the plain below, the ruined tower of the Abbey at Mont St Eloi can be seen, left as a reminder of the First World War, as was the ruined steeple of the church at nearby Ablain-St-Nazaire. On the esplanade between the tower and the chapel is a bronze Croix de Guerre which supports the eternal flame. The first grave on the left as you enter the cemetery is that of General Barbot of 77th (French) Division who was killed on 10 May 1915, just after his division had left Souchez – you pass the divisional memorial later. On the far side of the cemetery from where you are parked (you can drive round to it if you wish) is a building offering refreshments. Next to it is an excellent museum, recreating the life of the soldier on the Artois front, with many interesting dioramas with sound effects, and collections of artefacts, which should not be missed. There is an entrance fee.

The memorial area should be open every day, from 1000 to 1230 and 1400 to 1900, but these times may vary, especially in winter.

Drive back to the D937 and turn right towards Arras. A number of memorials and cemeteries will be passed, including the following (see Map 13):

77TH (FRENCH) DIVISION MEMORIAL   This is on the right side as the road rises leaving Souchez village and shows a victory figure and a French soldier wearing a beret. It commemorates the period from October 1914 to February 1915 when the division was in the Souchez sector.

CABARET ROUGE CWGC CEMETERY, SOUCHEZ   This was started by the British 47th Division in March 1916 and used by fighting units including the Canadian Corps until September 1918. It was enlarged after the Armistice. There are over 7,000 burials and 60 special memorials. Between the wars pilgrims to the cemetery were able to refresh themselves at a nearby café called 'The Better 'Ole' after Bairnsfather's famous cartoon. The French writer, Henri Barbusse, author of *Le Feu* (Under Fire) served in this area in 1915. In his diary he recorded his impressions of Cabaret Rouge. Never have I seen such total devastation of a village. Here, nothing with any shape left, not even a stretch of wall, a railing, a doorway left standing. It might have been a dirty, boggy wasteland near a town whose inhabitants had, through the years, been tipping on it their debris, rubbish, rubble from demolished buildings and scrap iron. In the foreground, the fog, the unearthly scene of massacred trees.

THE CZECH MEMORIAL, NEUVILLE ST VAAST   The Czechs joined the French Foreign Legion in Paris in 1914, forming part of the 2nd Regiment of Infantry. Together with the Moroccans they fought in the May 1915 Artois offensive as part of the French 10th Army taking this area but with heavy casualties. The memorial particularly refers to the 9 May 1915 attack on the German strong-point at Hill 140 (Thélus Mill) just north of Thélus village (see Map 13). They went over the top from this area and although they took the hill, they had 80 per cent casualties. The memorial was erected in 1925 and behind it are graves from the First and Second World Wars, plus a memorial shelter put up in May 1968. Looking across the road, to the left of the Polish memorial, the tops of the pylons of the Vimy Canadian memorial can be seen on the skyline.

THE POLISH MEMORIAL, NEUVILLE ST VAAST   This is on the opposite side of the road to the Czech memorial and commemorates the part played by the Poles, probably as members of the Foreign Legion in the Artois campaign. They too attacked Hill 140 on 9 May 1915. The memorial was inaugurated on 9 May 1935, twenty years after the attack.

Continue to the crossroads in the centre of la Targette village. Stop on the left.

THE LA TARGETTE HAND MEMORIAL   This striking village memorial of a huge hand and wrist (which bears an identification tag with the name of the village upon it) emerges from broken soil to hold aloft the flame of life – a concept explored in John McCrae's poem, 'In Flanders Fields', and in the sculpture on the Vimy memorial. It was completed on 20 October 1932. The village was utterly destroyed, mostly during French mining activities in May 1916.

Continue on the D937 to the well-signed 'Deutsche Friedhof' on the left.

THE GERMAN CEMETERY, NEUVILLE ST VAAST   This is the site of the heavily defended German position known as 'the Labyrinth'. It has been graphically described by two famous writers of the First World War. One was Henri Barbusse – a comparatively elderly (forty-one when he enlisted in 1914) socialist – some would say communist – whose uncompromisingly subjective book *Le Feu* drew heavily on his experiences of attacks like the desperate one against the Labryinth. The book was controversial because of its brutality, but it had a profound influence on the realism of Sassoon and Owen when they read it at Craiglockhart. The other writer, also to become controversial – for his supposed Nazi sympathies in the 1930s – was Henry Williamson, who described it in the account of his return to the battlefields after the war, *The Wet Flanders Plain*, as the scene of some of the most terrible fighting during the first two years of the war . . . an underground fortress with access to scores of ferro-concrete blockhouses, [each] held machine-guns under steel cupolas which resisted destruction by all but the heaviest shells . . .. Here a maze of trenches were protected by belts of unpenetrable barbed wire. The Labyrinth spread over thirty acres of chalk . . . like the web of an immense spider.' In 1915, following almost continuous fighting for Vimy Ridge thousands of shredded French and colonial uniforms lay on the barbed wire above heaps of bones and skulls. Williamson was appalled by the number of black crosses marking the German graves, concentrated from many areas nearby, that confronted him in 1924. These original crosses remained until the early 1960s when improvement work began. Today there are 37,000 burials here, as well as over 8,000 in one mass grave. In the entrance is a stone block on which is a bas-relief map showing all the cemeteries in this area, including Lens. Opposite is a farm known as la Maison Blanche, the original of which gave its name to this sector.

Continue to Arras and park if possible near the railway station.

ARRAS Opposite the railway station on the central area is the Arras war memorial, which shows scars from the Second World War. All around the square are numerous cafés and beyond the war memorial, in the Boulevard de Strasbourg, is the local tourist office, from which a town map may be obtained. The town has been a centre of trade and population since ancient times. It was fortified by Vauban who built the citadel. It was briefly overrun by the Germans in September 1914 but then held by the French until March 1916 and then the British until the end of the war. Two places of particular military interest should be visited: the Town Hall and the Arras CWGC memorial and cemetery.

L'HÔTEL DE VILLE (TOWN HALL) This is a five minute walk from the station area (follow signs to 'Les Places', or you may even park under the Grand' Place). Through it is access to the *'Boves'* – the caves and tunnels dating from the fourteenth century that were enlarged and extended during the 1914–18 war. There is a small charge to enter and the Town Hall is usually open from 0900 to 1200 and 1500 to 1700, Monday to Friday. The Boves may be visited on Saturday mornings and Sunday afternoons.

THE FAUBOURG D'AMIENS CWGC CEMETERY AND MEMORIALS TO THE MISSING This is on the Arras ring road, just south of the junction with the N25 to Doullens. Despite the name, it is the Arras memorial. It takes the form of a wall carrying almost 36,000 names of the missing of the battles around Arras. On it are the names of the First World War poet Capt. T. P. Cameron Wilson of the Sherwood Foresters, Lt Geoffrey Thurlow of the same regiment – one of Vera Brittain's coterie of friends, and Captain Charles McKay and Private David Sutherland of the Seaforths. David was the subject of Lt. E. A. Mackintosh's poem, 'In Memoriam', which describes his death during a trench raid on 16 May 1916 in which McKay also took part. The wall encloses the cemetery, begun in March 1916, and which contains 2,700 burials. At the back are separate small rows for Hindus, Mohammedans and Sikhs. Just within the entrance wall, in a space once occupied by the grave of French soldiers, is the Royal Flying Corps

Memorial. It takes the form of a column surmounted by a globe. The flight of doves encircling the globe is following the path of the sun on 11 November 1918. It carries the names of all RNAS, RFC and RAF personnel missing on the Western Front, including Major Lanoe Hawker, VC and Major E. ('Mick') Mannock, VC.

MUR DES FUSILLÉS Outside the memorial the *'Mur des Fusillés'* is signed along an unmade path. A 15-minute walk (cars can be drive up it with care) leads to a poignant area where between July 1941 and July 1944 the Germans shot over 200 Frenchmen, including some liberated in the 'Operation Jericho' Amiens prison raid of 1944. A concrete marker indicates the execution post and memorial plaques commemorate those who were killed. Entry to the area is controlled by a gate which closes at dusk.

THIRD YPRES
7 JUNE–10 NOVEMBER 1917

'Rain has turned everything into a quagmire and the
shell holes are full of water. Duckboards are
everywhere leading to the front line, but Jerry has these
well taped and frequently shells them or sprays them
with indirect machine-gun fire . . .. Guns of all calibres
are everywhere, in places wheel to wheel. The debris of
war is lying about. Broken guns, limbers, horses
blown to blazes. But very few human bodies, for they
have all been swallowed up in the mud and water of
this horrible sector. It seems madness on the part of
Higher Authority to expect any advance over this
indescribable morasse.'
The diary of a Sergeant in the Somerset Light Infantry

SUMMARY OF THE BATTLE

On 7 June 1917 the British attacked and captured the Messines Ridge, a
dominant feature that extended northwards to the German-held Passchendaele
Ridge. On 31 July, the British attacked again and floundered in mud and rain in
an assault that earned General Haig the title of 'Butcher' and won the Passchendaele Ridge after 16 weeks' fighting. British losses were over 300,000 and
German losses, never published, variously estimated between 65,000 and
260,000.

OPENING MOVES

Early in May 1917, following the bloody failure of Nivelle's attack on the
Chemin des Dames, the French Army began to mutiny until sixteen Army
Corps were involved. On 15 May, General Pétain, 'the saviour of Verdun', took
Nivelle's place and, by a mixture of personal visits to front line units and
summary courts martial, including executions, set about restoring discipline.
Richard M. Watt, in his book *Dare Call it Treason*, supposes that at least 100,000
men actively mutinied and even the official figures admit that between May and
October 1917 23,385 men were found guilty of offences. Yet, extraordinarily,
the news of the mutinies did not become general knowledge.

MAP 14	THIRD YPRES
	7 June – 10 November 1917

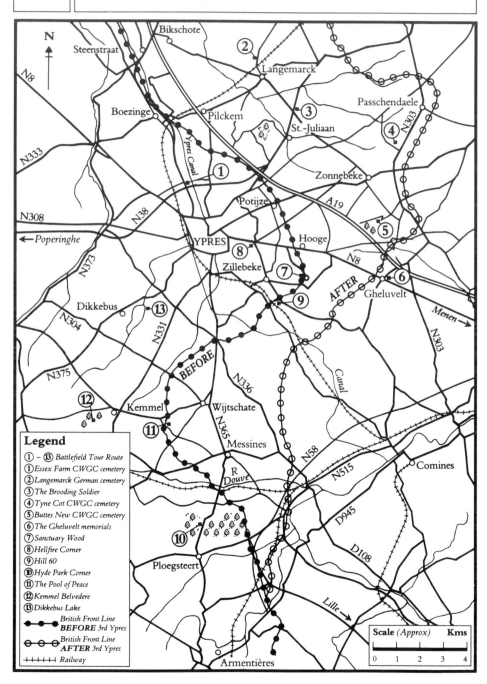

N

Bikschote

Steenstraat

N8

②

Langemarck

Boezinge

Pilckem

③

St.-Juliaan

Passchendaele

④ N303

N333

Ypres Canal

①

N308

N38

Zonnebeke

A19

Potijze

⑤

Poperinghe →

YPRES

Hooge

⑧

N8

⑥

Zillebeke

⑦

AFTER

Gheluvelt

Menen →

N373

⑨

N303

Dikkebus

⑬

N304

N331

BEFORE

N336

Canal

N375

⑫

Kemmel

Wijtschate

⑪

N365

Messines

N58

Comines

N515

R Douve

N515

⑩

D945

Ploegsteert

D108

Lille →

Armentières

Legend

① – ⑬ *Battlefield Tour Route*
① *Essex Farm CWGC cemetery*
② *Langemarck German cemetery*
③ *The Brooding Soldier*
④ *Tyne Cot CWGC cemetery*
⑤ *Buttes New CWGC cemetery*
⑥ *The Gheluvelt memorials*
⑦ *Sanctuary Wood*
⑧ *Hellfire Corner*
⑨ *Hill 60*
⑩ *Hyde Park Corner*
⑪ *The Pool of Peace*
⑫ *Kemmel Belvedere*
⑬ *Dikkebus Lake*

●–●–● *British Front Line* **BEFORE** *3rd Ypres*
○–○–○ *British Front Line* **AFTER** *3rd Ypres*
+++++ *Railway*

Scale *(Approx)* Kms
0 1 2 3 4

Haig therefore realized that the French would have to be left out of any immediate British plans for an offensive and later asserted that Pétain actually asked him to maintain British attacks on the Germans in order to relieve pressure on the French. Haig had fought his first battle as C-in-C the previous year on the Somme and opinions were sharply divided about its outcome – whether it had been a strategic success in the casualties inflicted upon the Germans, or a costly failure because of our own losses. Nevertheless, Haig was still determined to prove himself as a commander. His conviction that the only way to win the war was by frontal assault remained undimmed. If he wanted to win the war alone he had to hurry, because on 6 April 1917 America had declared war on Germany and soon her soldiers would arrive to swing the balance against the Germans.

Thus to 'help' the French, to prove himself and his men, and to do it before the Americans arrived, he set about planning an attack. First though, he had to persuade a reluctant War Committee that an attack was both needed and would have positive results. The War Cabinet, which had to sanction the C-in-C's plans, was led by the Prime Minister, Lloyd George, who was very unhappy at the long British casualty lists for which he held Haig personally responsible. Haig promised that his campaign would be a limited one and proposed that it should be in Flanders in order to capture the German U-Boat bases on the Belgian coast, said by the Admiralty to be the source of the submarine offensive. In fact the U-Boats were coming from Germany and the Belgian theory surprised many people, including the chief of Haig's intelligence staff who later said, 'No one really believed this rather amazing view.' However, Haig found it useful and when he maintained that 'if the fighting was kept up at its present intensity for six months, Germany would be at the end of her available manpower', the War Committee reluctantly agreed to his plans.

First of all the C-in-C wanted to gain a foothold at the southern end of the Ypres Salient, around a village called Messines. It was to be a remarkably successful battle that by its very success may have doomed General Gough's Fifth Army to the seemingly endless slog up the slope to Passchendaele.

WHAT HAPPENED

The high ground at the southern end of the Salient had been occupied by the Germans since the British shortened their lines at the end of Second Ypres. The Messines-Wijtschate area was of particular value to the Germans because from there they could enfilade much of the British trench system. The task of dislodging them was given to General Plumer's Second Army. Plumer had already been preparing for an assault for over a year by tunnelling under the German lines and placing 19 huge mines in a ten-mile arc from near Hill 60 via Spanbroekmolen to Ploegsteert Wood. There were over four miles of tunnels and more than a million pounds of high explosives. The attack was planned in great detail and models of the German positions used so that formations down to company level could be quite clear what their objectives were, and those objectives were limited and precise.

At 0310 on 7 June 1917, the mines exploded following more than two weeks bombardment by over 2,000 guns. X (British) Corps and II (Anzac) Corps advanced, assisted by 72 tanks and with complete air superiority. By the end of the day the first objectives were all taken. The 36th (Ulster) Division and the 16th (Irish) Division took Wijschate and Messines fell to the New Zealanders.

So far so good. So now on to the Passchendaele Ridge while the momentum of success was still warm? No. Now a six-week delay while preparations were made for the next attack. Why wasn't the Messines attack delayed until it could be followed immediately by the second phase? Were the French in such desperate straights that we *had* to grasp the German's attention in June? Perhaps. Perhaps too we needed to assemble and to reposition our artillery, something not done in a few hours, but the delay was fateful. It saw out the good weather and gave the Germans time to put the finishing touches to their new scheme of defence – defence in depth. Gone now were the old linear lines. Now trenches ran backwards and forwards in great depth and within the grid so formed were disconnected strongpoints and concrete pillboxes. The manning philosophy had changed too. The ground was covered by mutually supporting machine guns and forward positions were lightly held with reserves well back and concentrated ready for counter-attack. On top of all that the Germans introduced mustard gas.

The preliminary bombardment began on 22 July 1917. Over 3,000 guns hurled almost five tons of shells at every yard of the front. Ten days later, at 0350 hours on 31 July, twelve divisions advanced on an 11-mile front in pouring rain. North of Ypres advances of two miles were made, the Pilckem Ridge was recaptured, but further south and around the Menen Road the attack quickly stuck. The preliminary bombardment had totally destroyed the water table and the rain could not run away. Shell holes filled to overflowing with water and the earth turned into a thick glutinous mud, stinking and foul with the decay of dead horses and thousands of corpses. The mud reached out and sucked under any unwary soldier who left the duckboard path. Gough advised Haig that the attack should be stopped, but the C-in-C, falsely buoyant from the success at Messines, perhaps, or determined to demonstrate what Clausewitz called the 'maintenance of the Aim', i.e. steadfastness of purpose, pressed on, through battle after battle and casualty after casualty.

The Official History records the following battles:

Messines	7 – 14 June
Pilckem	31 July – 2 Aug.
Langemarck	16 – 18 Aug.
Menen Road	20 – 25 Sept.
Polygon Wood	26 Sept. – 3 Oct.

Broodseinde	4 Oct.
Poelcapelle	9 Oct.
First Passchendaele	12 Oct.
Second Passchendaele	26 Oct. – 10 Nov.

In the first week of November, 16 weeks after the second phase began, the 1st and 2nd Canadian Divisions occupied the shapeless ruins of Passchendaele village. The mud and blood bath was over. It is said that Lt-Gen. Sir Launcelot Kiggell, Haig's Chief of Staff, visited the battlefield for the first time just after the fighting was over (a terrible indictment in itself) and when he saw the foul swamp in which it had been fought burst into tears saying, 'Good God! Did we really send men to fight in this?'

THE BATTLEFIELD TOUR

Although three battles of Ypres are normally identified and treated separately as historical bites, it is not possible to tour them in isolation. Therefore the battlefield tour described here is a tour of the Ypres Salient and encompasses all three battles. To tour the Salient in a comprehensive manner requires at least three days and travellers with that amount of time are referred to our guide book *Holts' Battlefield Guides: The Ypres Salient*. In constructing this tour we have drawn upon many years of experience of the place-names and events most familiar to visitors and, bearing these in mind, have selected as suggested stops only those place where there is something quite obvious to see (see Map 14).

The tour begins at the Cloth Hall Museum in Ypres, St George's Memorial Church and the Menen Gate Memorial. It then moves north and clockwise via Essex Farm, Langemarck German cemetery, the Canadian Brooding Soldier memorial, Tyne Cot British cemetery (Passchendaele), Polygon Wood and Gheluvelt. Next is the Sanctuary Wood Museum and preserved trenches followed by Hellfire Corner, Hill 60, Hyde Park Corner, the Pool of Peace, Kemmel Hill and Dikkbus Lake. If possible travellers should return to the Menen Gate by 2000 hours (any and every day of the year) for the Last Post ceremony.

Total distance	46 miles
Total time	5 hours
Maps	Best of all are the Carte de Belgique 1:25,000 Nos. 20/5-6, 28/1–2, 28/3–4, and 28/5-6. The Carte de Belgique No. 28 IEPER 1:50,000 is coloured and covers the whole area and shows the road changes, including the motorway up to 1979. IGN 2 Lille/Dunkerque 1:100,000 covers the area. Don't attempt this tour without a good map and beware of the confusion created by the disparate Flemish and French versions of the same place name, e.g. Mesen and Messines, Ieper and Ypres, Rijsel and Lille.

Drive into the centre of Ypres and park in the Grand'Place (Main Square) in front of the large cathedral-like building. This is the Cloth Hall. The actual Cathedral (St Martin's) is behind it. At the eastern end of the Cloth Hall are the tourist office and war museum. Visit the tourist office for up to date information, tourist literature and maps and general directions to St George's Church and the Menen Gate. Then visit the war museum past the Second World War mine.

YPRES SALIENT MUSEUM, CLOTH HALL This is, in our opinion, amongst the finest local war museums in the world. It began in the Butter Market building in Ypres after the war, exhibiting only artefacts found in the Salient. It moved to the ground floor of this building and then in the mid-1980s to its present location. The museum still mainly consists of items directly associated with the Salient, many of which have been donated by veterans or their families returning over the years. An item of particular interest is the Roman numeral V which used to be on the face of the original clock on the Cloth hall before it was destroyed. The numeral was returned to Ypres in 1983 by the daughter of the dare-devil cavalry officer who 'captured it' by scaling the ruined clock tower, Captain Sydney Kemp, MC, who also won the French Croix de Guerre. He took it home to his mother who at one time lent it to the Imperial War Museum for exhibition. It was returned to the family and remained with them until Capt. Kemp's daughter (who had never seen her father who was killed later in the war) brought it back. The museum curator Albert Beke arranged a small ceremony for the occasion. Other numerals from the clock made similar journeys to and back from the UK and are also displayed here. One Roman numeral 'I' did not return. It is set into the village war memorial at Westwell Manor near Burford.

At the entrance is a recreation of a section of trench line which can be entered and at the far end of the museum a lifesize scene of a horse struggling to escape from the Flanders mud which dramatically brings home the horror of that war. In between are dozens of fascinating small exhibits, including some of Sir Douglas Haig's personal possessions. The photographs in particular reward study as they graphically illustrate the total devastation of the town and the surrounding countryside as well as the life of 'Tommy' in the Salient. Most are the work of the photographer Anthony of Ypres. They are images to be stored in the mind to be released during the tour of the battlefield.

The museum has a selection of books and postcards for sale and is open every day 0930–1215 and 1330–1730 from 1 April–31 October. Otherwise it is open Sundays only (and all day on 11 November) 1000–1200 and 1400–1800. There is a small entrance fee.

Leave the museum on foot via the archway to the left of the exit and continue left around the building (in which, incidentally, there are good public toilets) to the main entrance to the cathedral. St George's Church is on the opposite side of the road to the cathedral.

ST GEORGE'S MEMORIAL CHURCH The idea of having a British memorial church or chapel in Ypres was raised formally as early as 1920 when the Church Army appealed for donations to establish a building fund. In 1924 Sir John French, who had taken the title Earl of Ypres, added his voice to the call and the foundation stone was laid on Sunday, 24 July 1927. Sir John had died in 1925 (and is buried in a neglected plot in the churchyard at the village where he was born – Ripple in Kent) and leadership of the Appeal Committee passed to Lord Plumer. On 24 March 1929 the church was dedicated by the Right Reverend Bishop of Fulham. At that time the British community in Ypres, mostly employees of the then Imperial War Graves Commission and their dependents, numbered about 500 and as a tribute to the 342 old Etonians who fell in the Salient the College provided the 'British School'. In his letter to the old Etonians asking for donations, Provost M. R. James said that the project would commem- orate 'the unforgotten friends of youth'. The school building is next door to the church and is now used by the Royal British Legion as a club house. Both the club and the church are supported by the Legion and the 'Friends of St George's Church' who have a regular newsletter. Services are held every Sunday and on 11 November each year the congregation is swelled by hundreds of people from all over Britain and spills into the nearby theatre or the Cloth Hall.

Every item in the church is a memorial, from the beautiful stained-glass windows to the chairs, on each of which is a brass plate naming the missing loved one. On one choir stall 'Dick' Collick is remembered. Dick came to Ypres in 1924 with the Imperial War Graves Commission and married a local girl, becoming Church Warden Emeritus in 1985. It was he who instructed the Belgian buglers in playing the Last Post 'English style' when the nightly ceremonies began. On the south wall of the church is a bust of Sir John French and on either side of it memorials to Field Marshal Montgomery and Sir Winston Churchill who both served in the Salient. New memorials continue to be erected, for the church now commemorates the fallen of both World Wars. A few minutes contemplation in this home of memory brings gentle pride in the solid beliefs of the men who fought for King and Country and there is sadness too that so many had to suffer, both on the battlefield and left alone at home. It is right to remember the sacrifice and the penalties and here it can be done without pomp or circumstance. The church is usually open. If not, make enquiries at the Tourist Office. There are usually postcards available on a table beside the door, a visitors' book to be signed and a collection box. The church depends on donations. Please help. The Legion Club is generally open in the evenings and will always give a warm welcome to visitors.

Return past the Cloth Hall museum and walk up the Menen Road to the Menen Gate.

THE MENEN GATE BRITISH MEMORIAL Winston Churchill said of Ypres, 'A more sacred place for the British race does not exist in the world', and proposed that the town be left in ruins as an eternal memorial to the million men who fought in the Salient. The townspeople had other ideas and began to rebuild their homes, and it was agreed that on the site of an old Vauban gateway from Ypres on the road to Menen, the road taken by tens of thousands of British soldiers on their way to the trenches, a memorial arch should be constructed. Work under Sir Reginald Blomfield began in 1923 and great difficulties were experienced with water and sand, which were solved only by constructing a huge concrete platform reaching 36 ft into the ground. The material used was French limestone and the arch is 80 ft high, 135 ft long and 104 ft wide. It was unveiled on 24 July 1927 by Field Marshal Plumer (the same day that he laid the foundation stone of St George's Church) in the presence of the King of the Belgians and many thousands of veterans and relatives of the Fallen. The whole ceremony was transmitted by wireless by the BBC. The Last Post was sounded at the Gate for the first time and one of the buglers was Dick Collick. Carved over all the walls of the great gate, inside, up the stairs and around the top on each side over-looking the ramparts are the names of almost 55,000 soldiers who fell in the Salient between the beginning of the war and 15 August 1917. They simply disappeared.

In his address Lord Plumer said, 'It can be said of each one in whose honour we are assembled here today, "he is not missing, he is here".'

Among the thousands of names are those of seven of the forty VC winners buried or commemorated in the Salient. The supreme award for bravery has many strong associations with the Salient. At Hill 60 the first VC for a TA officer was won by 2nd Lt G. H. Woolley on 21/22 April 1915. He survived and was ordained in 1920. Lt A. Martin-Leake, RAMC won a bar to his South African VC for conspicuous gallantry near Zonnebeke in the Salient in 1914. Capt. Noel Chavasse won a bar to his already-held First World War VC for services in the Salient in 1917. He is buried in Brandhoek. The first Salient award was that to Drummer William Kenny of the Gordon Highlanders for action at Gheluvelt on 29 October 1914 and the last to L/Cpl Edward Seaman of the 2nd Bn Inniskilling Fusilliers for bravery on 29 September 1918 at Passchendaele. Seaman has no known grave and is commemorated at Tyne Cot. Kenny survived the war.

On the town side at the top of the arch is a sarcophagus, while looking down the Menen Road is a British lion sculpted by Sir Reid Dick RA. Under each is an inscription by Kipling (after whom the street to the left beyond the arch is named):

TO THE ARMIES OF THE BRITISH EMPIRE WHO STOOD HERE

FROM 1914 TO 1918

AND TO THOSE OF THEIR DEAD

WHO HAVE NO KNOWN GRAVE

and over the arch to the southern staircase, also by Kipling, is:

IN MAJOREM DEI GLORIAM

HERE ARE RECORDED NAMES

OF OFFICERS AND MEN WHO FELL
IN YPRES SALIENT, BUT TO WHOM
THE FORTUNE OF WAR DENIED
THE KNOWN AND HONOURED BURIAL
GIVEN TO THEIR COMRADES IN DEATH

On a cold, dark winter's night listening to the Last Post played under the Gate, the visitor feels in the spine the apprehension of those men who passed this way to war. An anonymous poem tells their story in simple lines:

'What are you guarding Man-At-Arms?
Why do you watch and wait?'
'I guard the graves', said the Man-At-Arms,
'I guard the graves by Flanders Farms,
Where the dead will rise at my call to arms,
And march to the Menin Gate.'

'When do they march then, Man-at-Arms?
Cold is the hour and late.'
'They march tonight,' said the Man–at-Arms,
'With the moon on the Menin Gate,
They march when the midnight bids them to,
With their rifles slung and their pipes aglow,
Along the roads – the roads they know,
The roads to the Menin Gate.'

'What are they singing, Man-at-Arms,
As they march to the Menin Gate?'
'The marching songs,' said the Man-at-Arms,
'That let them laugh at Fate;
No more will the night be cold for them,
For the last tattoo has rolled for them;
And their souls will sing as of old, for them,
As they march to the Menin Gate.'

At ground level in the pillars are the brass boxes containing the details of those commemorated, first in regimental order and then by name. The ramparts should be visited above the Gate, access being via the stairways in the centre. It is possible to walk around the beautifully renovated ramparts to the Lille (Rijsel) Gate.

Return to your car and leave the Square via Diksmuidsestraat following signs to Diksmuide. On the outskirts of Ypres, immediately after passing a motorway-type road bridge, there is a British war cemetery on the right. Stop.

ESSEX FARM CWGC CEMETERY   (see maps 4, 6 and 14) The cemetery lies beside the Yser Canal which runs north from Ypres to Diksmuide. At the back of the cemetery is a memorial obelisk to 49th (West Riding) Division. There are over

1,000 UK graves and those of five German prisoners. To the left between a private house and the canal are some concrete bunkers which were used as a dressing station from 1915 to 1918 and during Third Ypres casualties from the 38th (Welsh) Division and 51st (Highland) Division were treated there. At the roadside is a memorial plaque to Col. John McCrae, author of the poem, 'In Flanders Fields', which was written at this spot and first published in *Punch* in December 1915. McCrae was born in Guelph, Ontario, in a limestone cottage now preserved as a museum and garden of remembrance. He began writing poetry while in his teens and following his BA in 1894 went on to medical school, getting his second degree in 1898. After time as an intern and then resident, he joined a Guelph artillery battery and served for a year in South Africa during the Boer War. In 1904 McCrae, a major by then, resigned his commission and concentrated on medicine, both running his own practice and lecturing. At the outbreak of the First World War McCrae, like 45,000 other Canadians, volunteered to join up before August was out and by April 1915 he was here in the Ypres Salient as a medical officer. In a letter home to his mother he wrote, 'For seventeen days and seventeen nights none of us have had our clothes off, nor our boots even, except occasionally.' It was the period following the German gas attack of 22 April.

On the day before he wrote his famous poem, one of McCrae's closest friends was killed and buried beneath a temporary wooden cross in ground where poppies were blooming. Saddened by the death of his friend and horrified by the suffering he had seen, McCrae took a pencil and began, 'In Flanders Fields the poppies blow . . ..' The three short verses that followed became one of the, if not *the* best-known poems of the war and was a major contributing factor to the emergence of the poppy as the symbol of remembrance. Sadly McCrae fell ill with pneumonia in January 1918, contracted meningitis and died on the 28th. He was buried with full military honours in Wimereux CWGC Cemetery just north of Boulogne.

Continue north to the village of Boesinghe. There turn right across the canal road and continue through the village of Pilckem (the road runs along the Pilckem Ridge) to Langemarck crossroads (traffic lights). Turn left and follow the signs to the 'Deutsche Soldaten Friedhof'.

LANGEMARCK GERMAN CEMETERY This area was captured by the British 20th (Light) Division on 16 August during the Third Ypres offensive of 1917. It had been defended by the French in 1914 and lost on 22 April 1915 (Second Ypres) during the gas attack. In continuing operations in October 1917 the 4th Bn Worcester Regiment were ordered to push further north from here. On the evening of 7 October the battalion had marched out from Ypres following the route you have driven, turned right at Boesinghe and along the Pilckem Ridge via duckboards to the front line at the northern end of the cemetery. They were in position by dawn on 8 October and spent the day preparing for their assault.

At 0500 hours on 9 October the quartermaster brought up tea for everyone and at 0530 hours they went over the top. After less than 500 yards they were held up by machine-gun fire coming from one of the many blockhouses the Germans had built. The Regimental history tells what happened next:

'One of the concrete blockhouses in front of the line had not been struck by the shells, and its machine-gun swept the line of the labouring troops with burst after burst of fire. Officers and men were shot down or were driven to shelter in the shell-holes. Musketry was useless against the concrete walls, and messages were sent back for trench-mortars to deal with the block-house. But before the mortars could be brought up the fire of the machine-gun suddenly stopped. A minute later every man within sight was on his feet cheering and laughing, for stumbling through the mud towards the British line came a little crowd of enemy with hands raised in surrender, and behind them came a solitary British soldier, labouring along under the weight of a machine-gun – *their* machine-gun. The cheering grew as he was recognised: 'Dancox', the troops shouted, 'Good old Dancox!'

Private Frederick George Dancox, a solid old soldier, had served with the battalion throughout the war. For that day he had been detailed as one of a party of 'moppers-up', intended to deal with isolated enemy strongholds such as that block-house. The mud and the enemy's fire had broken up his party, and Dancox found himself out in front alone. Nothing daunted, he proceeded to attack the block-house single-handed. To approach its machine gun from the front was impossible. Behind and about the block-house our own shells were bursting. Carefully working round from shell-hole to shell-hole, Dancox ran the gauntlet of the bursting shells and reached the back wall of the block-house unobserved. With a grenade in his hand he walked through the doorway at the back of the block-house into the midst of the enemy. Surprised and terrified the machine-gunner surrendered. Holding his grenade ready to throw, Private Dancox backed out of the block-house, beckoning the Germans to follow. Once outside, he ordered his prisoners off to our lines. Then, when he had seen them started on their way, he went again into the block-house and dismounted the machine-gun. He carried the weapon back in triumph, and fired it himself throughout the rest of the day in great good humour and amid the laughing congratulations of all around. For this example of cool bravery, Private Dancox was subsequently awarded the vc.

The cemetery is maintained by the *Volksbund Deutsche Kriegsgräber fürsorge* – the German People's Organization for the Care of War Graves – and is the only German cemetery in the Salient. When the war was over the Belgian people, quite naturally, were not inclined to give the Germans ground in which to bury their dead, who lay in 678 different locations. In 1925 the maintenance of German graves in Flanders was regularized by a convention between Germany and Belgium and concentration of the graves began. In 1954 there was another international convention, and since that time, mostly between the years 1956 and 1958, the eighteen remaining German War Cemeteries were amalgamated into four: Langemarck, Menen, Vladslo and Hooglede. As the bodies were exhumed, all those that could be identified were reburied in marked graves, sometimes several inscribed on one tombstone to symbolize comradeship in death and because there simply was not enough land to bury each individually. The unknowns were buried in a mass grave. Most of the landscaping work was completed between 1970 and 1972, much of it by international students working voluntarily during their vacations, although detailed work at Langemarck was not completed until the late 1980s.

Langemarck is one of the largest German cemeteries in Belgium, with 44,292 bodies, and has an impressive entrance with two chambers, one with the names of the missing carved in oak, and the other bearing a relief map showing the past and present German cemetries in Belgium and containing the Visitors' book and Cemetery Register. The cemetery is planed with oak trees, the symbol of German strength, and in the communal grave rest the remains of 25,000 soldiers – half of whose names are known. The four impressive sculptures which over-look the cemetery were executed by Professor Emil Krieger and around the mass grave are the Regimental insignia of the student brigades who fought in this area. In the north wall of the cemetery are the remains of some massive German block–houses, doubtless similar to the one that Private Dancox captured.

Drive back to Langemarck traffic lights and continue straight over to the next crossroads at which there is a tall memorial column.

THE BROODING SOLDIER MEMORIAL This remarkable, dramatic memorial, represents a soldier standing with 'arms reversed', the traditional stance at a funeral. When the Canadian government decided to erect memorials in Europe to their war dead, they initiated a competition to find the most appropriate design. This was the runner-up. The winning design was erected on Vimy Ridge. The architect here was Chapman Clemesha, from Regina, who had fought in the war and had been wounded. The 35-ft high central column of Vosges stone rises out of a circular pavement on which are marked direction indicators to other parts of the battlefield. The bowed helmeted head was carved in Brussels. At the back of the memorial is the bronze box containing the visitors' book. The inscription on the column in French and in English reads. 'This column marks the battlefield where 18,000 Canadians on the British left withstood the first German gas attacks the 22nd–24th April 1915. Two thousand fell and lie here buried.' 'Here buried' does not literally mean on this spot, but over the battlefield. The memorial was unveiled on 8 July 1912 by the Duke of Connaught in the presence of Marshal Foch. The Canadian cedars are trimmed to represent shells.

The German gas attack launched in the afternoon of 22 April 1915 caught the Allies by surprise, but it ought not to have done, as this letter from a Canadian soldier stationed but a hundred yards from here, testifies. It is dated 16 April, 6 days before the attack. 'We are on a long salient here, near the apex, with German trenches on three sides of us, so we have a pretty jolly time both day and night . . .. Last night we got ready to receive a German attack. Divisional headquarters notified us that the Germans intended to attack with tubes of poison gas, but it didn't materialise . . ..'

The French Colonial troops on the left side of the allied line broke before the 22 April attack and the Canadians, with British county regiment reinforcements – the Buffs, Middlesex, York and Lancs, Leicesters – moved into the gap and held both that attack and the second on 25 April. The soldiers had no gas masks but discovered that, by soaking handkerchiefs in water and stuffing them into their mouths, they could get some relief. This road junction is also known as Vancouver Corner and Kerselaar.

Continue past the Brooding Soldier towards Zonnebeke. After 100 yards there is small road/track left which may be signed route '14–18' and if taken will eventually lead to Tyne Cot cemetery and will en route offer a good view of the battlefield of 1917. However, the less adventurous should continue past the turning to the village of Zonnebeke.

This is readily identified by three tall chimneys of the Van Biervliet brickworks in which a huge underground redoubt (the Bremen, part of the *Bayern Stellung*) was uncovered in the 1980s and can be visited by arrangement. Enquiries should be made at the Streeksmuseum in the village (the museum has an excellent First World War section) next to the Tourist Office.

At the road junction with the church turn left and at the next crossroads left again signed 'Passchendaele'. The road now runs along the top of the Passchendaele Ridge and after about 1,000 yards a small sign left indicates the turning to Tyne Cot.

TYNE COT CWGC CEMETERY On this forward slope of the Passchendaele Ridge are both the largest British war cemetery in the world and a memorial wall designed by Sir Herbert Baker on which are commemorated the almost 35,000 soldiers missing with no known grave for whom room could not be found on the Menen Gate, i.e. those killed after 15 August 1917. The local name for this area is Nieumolen, but British soldiers of the Northumberland Fusiliers, seeing on the ridge square shapes which they thought resembled Tyneside cottages called it 'Tyne Cot'. In actual fact the square shapes were the new German pillboxes and inside the cemetery on each side of the central path two of them can still be seen, now surrounded by poplar trees and at the end of the path is the Cross of Sacrifice which has been built on top of a third pillbox.

In 1922 King George V and Queen Mary toured the battlefields and memorials of Belgium and France on what became known as 'the King's Pilgrimage'. They travelled by train accompanied by Major General Sir Fabian Ware, Vice-Chairman of the Imperial War Graves Commission and its inspiration, and a small entourage. At selected stops the King was met by motor cars and driven to his visits. Thus his train stopped at Zonnebeke railway station and he drove here just as you have done. An official booklet of the Pilgrimage was published to which Rudyard Kipling contributed a specially written poem. All profits from the sale of the book were distributed to organizations helping the bereaved to visit loved one's graves. It records the King's visit here thus: 'Tyne Cot he saw for the first time this May afternoon. He understood how appalling was the task that his soldiers faced there and turning to the great pillbox which still stands in the middle of the cemetery he said that it should never be moved, it should always remain as a monument to the heroes whose graves stood thickly around. From its roof he gazed sadly over the sea of wooden crosses, a 'massed multitude of silent witnesses to the desolation of war'. It is indeed fitting that this should form, as it will, the foundation for the great Cross of Sacrifice shortly to be built up as a central memorial in this cemetery.'

Today at the base of the cross a small patch of that original block-house can still be seen, contained within a bronze wreath, while on the far side of the cross, between it and the memorial wall, is a higgledy piggledy collection of some 300 graves. These are the original battle burials left where they were found after the Armistice. They included some German graves. The other, almost 12,000, graves which stand in parade ground order, were brought in from all the surrounding area. The majority of them are unidentified, being exhumed from the engulfing Flanders mud. The register for the cemetery is in a box under the entrance porch and the registers for the memorial wall are in the left-hand loggia. It is a sobering experience to look for one's own name in the registers and many a visitor has discovered the details of an unknown relative.

Looking back from the cross to the entrance, the chimneys of Zonnebeke should be visible well to the left and to their right on the near horizon the spires of the Cloth Hall can be seen on a clear day. The battle of Third Ypres surged up to here for three months from the direction of Ypres, the Germans holding this ridge, defending it with pill-boxes, machine-guns, barbed wire and mustard gas. It was an Empire battle, the graves bearing witness to the team effort – some 8,900 from the UK, 1,350 from Australia, almost 1,000 from Canada and over 500 from New Zealand.

It was not until the end of October 1917 that the village and the ridge were taken, much of the latter in this area by the Australians and the empty village by the Canadians. In an action on 12 October the Australian 34th Infantry Battalion attacked two German pillboxes 400 yards north of here and was held down by heavy machine-gun fire. Captain Clarence Jeffries organized and led a bombing party against one of the pillboxes, taking 35 prisoners and capturing four machine guns. He then led a successful attack on another machine-gun emplacement and while attempting yet another he was killed. Born in Wallsend, New South Wales on 26 October 1894, Jeffries joined the militia at the age of fourteen, and was promoted to Captain four months before his death in the action which won him the vc. He and five other vcs are buried or commemorated here. This is truly a 'Silent City', each headstone representing not just a life lost, but a family bereaved and generations unborn. Standing beside the white sentinels on this new peaceful hillside in Flanders, it is difficult to believe that all the suffering was worthwhile – and yet, simply to be able to stand here is a privilege won and paid for by many thousands who lost everything they had, including their name, and whose headstone reads only 'A Soldier of the Great War Known Unto God' – a phrase chosen by Kipling.

Return to the ridge and go back to Zonnebeke, passing the church at the T junction you encountered earlier from the Brooding Soldier. Some 300 yards later as the road bends right there are signs left to Polygon Wood cemetery and Buttes New British cemetery. Follow them and go first into the cemetery on the left.

BUTTES NEW BRITISH CWGC CEMETERY This area is 1½ miles due north of Gheluvelt (the next stop on the itinerary) where the Worcesters distinguished themselves in 1914. You are at the north-eastern end of the wood which in November 1914 (First Ypres) was held by 1st Kings with just 450 men and 6 officers strung along the 1 mile long southern edge and two companies of the Black Watch in the south-west corner.

On 11 November 1914, the Prussian Guard made a determined attack in massed strength along the axis of the Menen Road moving east to west, Their efforts to break through this wood were stopped by dogged resistance by the Kings and the Black Watch. By the end of the day only one Black Watch officer was unwounded. His name was Captain Fortune! The 1st Kings had originally entered the wood during the first week in November and were told to hold it at all costs. They came under shell-fire almost immediately and that, combined with heavy rain, turned the ground into a quagmire. Trenches, such as they were, were knee deep in water and it was impossible to get warm because a fire straightaway brought down German artillery. Hand pumps were used both to draw water and to clear the trenches, and it is claimed that it was a 'squeaking pump' in the wood that inspired the Bairnsfather cartoon entitled 'The Fatalist'. It shows a soldier operating a pump at night and has the sub-caption, 'I'm sure they'll 'ear this damn thing squeakin'. Yet despite their discomfort, the casualties which mounted steadily and being outnumbered, the Kings held on to the wood that day and for a further four days until they were relieved. Following the German gains made after the gas attacks of April 1915 (Second Ypres) the wood became enfiladed from Pilckem Ridge and on 3 May it was evacuated. One of the withdrawing battalions was the 2nd Kings. During 3rd Ypres the wood again featured in a named battle – the 'Battle of Polygon Wood', 26 September to 3 October 1917, and the Germans had constructed a number of pillboxes in it. At one end is a high mound which is an old musketry butte, first used before 1870, and it had been thoroughly tunnelled for defensive positions.

The offensive opened at 0550 on 26 September being a rolling barrage with seven divisions in line on a 6–mile front. In the centre were the Australian 4th and 5th Divisions attacking west to east. The wood here and the butte were the objectives of the 14th Australian Brigade, the Australian line stretching north from here to Zonnebeke (from where you have just come).

The barrage was overwhelming. Immediately behind the Australians were the 2nd RWF and Private Frank Richards recalled the experience: I entered one pillbox during the day and found 18 dead Germans inside. There was not a mark on one of them. One of our heavy shells had made a direct hit on top of it and they were killed by concussion, but very little damage had been done to the pillbox. They were all constructed with reinforced concrete and shells could explode all round them but the flying pieces would never penetrate the concrete. There were small windows in the sides and by jumping in and out of the shell holes attacking troops could get within bombing [grenade] range. If a bomb was thrown through one of the windows the pillbox was as good as captured.

By the end of the day the wood was taken but the two Australian divisions had 5,500 casualties.

On top of the butte is a memorial to the Australian 5th Division and below are over 2,000 headstones of the Butte cemetery. This was made after the Armistice by concentrating graves from the Zonnebeke area, almost all of them from 1917. More than four-fifths are unknown, a testimony to the savagery of the fighting. At the far end of the cemetery is a Memorial Wall to the officers and men of New Zealand who fell in this area and have no known graves. It has its own register.

The small cemetery opposite Buttes is Polygon Wood cemetery, begun in August 1917 in the front line, which has some 100 burials, mostly of New Zealanders. There was at one time a German cemetery at the back of it, but the graves have been moved, probably to Langemarck.

Continue along the side of the wood in your car following signs to Ypres or to Veldhoek until you reach the road bridge over the motorway.

BLACK WATCH CORNER   This is where the two companies of the regiment put up such a fine stand in November 1914, as did the 2nd Bn RWF in September 1917 (as graphically described by Captain J. C. Dunn, DSC, MC and Bar, DCM in his book *The War the Infantry Knew 1914–1919*).

Continue over the motorway immediately forking left to Veldhoek and on until you meet the Menen Road. Turn left towards Menen and drive to Gheluvelt crossroads. Park below the windmill.

THE GHELUVELT MEMORIALS   At the foot of the windmill are memorials to the 1st South Wales Borderers and to the 2nd Bn Worcestershire Regiment which commemorate a famous action of 31 October 1914. The German attacks astride the Menen Road towards Ypres began on 29 October 1914, urged on by the Kaiser, certain that he would soon address his victorious army from the

Cloth Hall in Ypres. So confident was the Kaiser that he moved nearer to the front line in order to be on the spot for the triumphal entry into the town. The German Order of the Day read, 'The break through will be of decisive importance. We must, and therefore will, conquer, settle for ever the centuries long struggle, end the war, and strike the decisive blow against our most detested enemy. We will finish with the British, Indians, Canadians, Moroccans and other trash, feeble adversaries who surrender in mass if they are attacked with vigour.'

The Germans, in overwhelming strength, pushed hard against the thin line of defenders. This area was the responsibility of the British 1st Division under General Lomax. At midday on 31 October Gheluvelt fell and shortly afterwards Lomax was killed by a shell in his headquarters at Hooge (nearer to Ypres). The game was in the balance. General Haig, the Corps Commander, was somewhere along the Menen Road at this time, but unaware of the true tactical situation. However, he did issue orders to the effect that if his Corps could not hold on where it was, it should fall back to a line just in front of Ypres. Meanwhile local commanders took matters into their own hands. The commander of the Menen Road front was Brigadier-General C. FitzClarence, late of the Irish Guards, who had won a VC as a Captain in the Boer War at Mafeking for 'extraordinary spirit and fearlessness'.

A counter-attack by the 1st South Wales Borderers had made the Germans pause just past Gheluvelt and at 1300 on 31 October FitzClarence called upon the Worcesters, gathered at the southern end of Polygon Wood, to regain the village. The Worcesters were actually part of 2nd Division, but General Lomax had arranged that in an emergency they could be detached to 1st Division. They had been in continuous action for ten days and were down to about 500 men, little more than half of their original strength. Major Hankey, commanding the Worcesters, sent one company to cover the Menen Road itself, lined up his three remaining companies side by side, fixed bayonets and doubled across the open ground between Polygon and the village. Just short of the village was Gheluvelt Château and here the Worcesters found gallant remnants of the South Wales Borderers still hanging on.

Together they pushed forward to the village, now burning furiously and under bombardment from both German and British artillery. Brigadier FitzClarence decided to withdraw to a firmer position and at 1800 the Worcesters and Borders began a move backward to Veldhoek (where you joined the Menen Road). The German tide had been stopped, but it had cost the Worcesters dear – 187 of the 500 had been killed or wounded. The chase across the open field with bayonets may have saved Ypres, may have saved the BEF, may have saved the war. The British Commander-in-Chief, Sir John French, said that the moment of the counter-attack was 'the worst half-hour of my life'. Sadly, on 12 November, less than two weeks later, Brigadier FitzClarence was killed. His body was never found and he is commemorated on the Menen Gate.

Drive along the Menen Road towards Ypres and pass the Bellewaerde fun park on the right followed immediately by Hooge Chapel which has been converted into a First World War museum. Shortly after, at the bottom of the hill, is a sign pointing left to 'Hill 60 and Sanctuary Wood.' Drive up the road, 'Canadalaan' or 'Maple Avenue' and park at the museum.

SANCTUARY WOOD   The wood in which the museum is sited is on the forward slopes (Ypres side) of the last ridge before the town. At the top of the road is Hill 62, where a Canadian memorial in the form of a small garden and Stone of Remembrance commemorates the Dominions' efforts in the Salient and in particular the presence in 1914 of the first Canadian troops – Princess Patricia's Light Infantry – to fight against the Germans. During the First Ypres battle the wood still had trees, not yet destroyed by artillery, and it housed a few reserves, medical facilities and dozens of stragglers. Brigadier General Bulfin, of 2nd Division, ordered that the stragglers be left 'in sanctuary' until he instructed what should be done with them – and the wood got its name.

The museum here is owned by Jacques Schier. During the First World War his grandfather lived with his parents in Poperinghe where they kept a café and so heard many stories from the soldiers about what it was like to serve in the Salient. In 1919 he came back to the family home, from which they had been evacuated following the gas attack of 1915, to find that everything had been destroyed. The ground was covered in trenches, shell holes and barbed wire, and there was no sign of their home. Grandfather Schier built himself a small house and acted as a guide to the increasing numbers of soldiers and relatives who came to see the battlefields and saved enough money to buy the land upon which the museum stands today. He left the land as it was, with its scars of war, until 1934 when he built the present house and museum to house his family. In 1939 his son (Jacques' father) was called up into the Belgian army and sent to guard the Albert Canal. Realizing that the Germans were bound to break through he sent a telegram to his wife telling her to hide all the exhibits that they had collected for the museum. Jacques' mother and two of her brothers carried everything into the cellar and covered the entrance with concrete. During the German occupation, officers and soldiers were regular visitors to the museum and Goering himself came to see it. When asked what happened to the exhibits, they were told that the British had stolen them! Once the war was over the family built up the museum again and it opened to visitors in 1947, since when it had steadily improved its exhibits and facilities. Coffee, beer and snacks can be had, as well as a cheerful welcome and even toilets. There are two parts to the Sanctuary Wood Museum – the building and the preserved trenches. The building houses the bar and bookstall, with various military souvenirs on sale, and a museum for which there is a small entrance fee. The souvenirs are not exclusively from the First World War, although many of the artefacts on sale were actually found in the Salient. It is always sensible to be cautious about remnants of bullets and shells and collectors should *never* pick up anything on the battlefield itself. People are still occasionally killed or maimed by First World War explosives. Every year farmers plough up what is called the Iron Harvest and the Belgian Army collects it at regular intervals and blows it up in controlled explosions.

In the museum there is a musty air which curiously adds to the impact of the items on show. Curling, faded photographs mix with rusty hardware. Here and there a recent addition gleams with oil, but the heart of the collection is the dozen or so 3D wooden viewing cabinets. They are a *must*. Each one has different glass slides that when viewed with persistence focus dramatically into sharp 3 dimensions. Here in this atmospheric environment is the true horror of war – dead horses, bodies in trees, heads and legs in trenches and, everywhere, mud, mud, mud. The history of the pictures is obscure. Jacques maintains that they are Belgian, others say that they were once owned by the Imperial War Museum and disposed of during a clean-out in the 1950s. There are similar, if not identical, cabinets and slides at the Armistice Carriage Museum at Compiègne and in a stationer's shop in Verdun. They may well be of French origin. At the back of the museum, past hardware so rusty that is difficult to see how it keeps heart and soul together, are the trenches. They are original in the way that George Washington's axe, with three new heads and two new handles, is original. Yet they follow the shape and nature of the original trenches, which were designed to twist and turn so that invaders were always isolated in a short length of trench and could not set up machine guns to mow down the defenders in lines. They smell, but not with the stench of death that hung over the Salient for four long years. They are damp, probably with water underfoot, and in the middle is a concrete tunnel, passable to the wellie brigade. It defies the imagination to conjure up a picture of trenches in strips up to a mile or more wide joined in chicken-wire patterns and stretching from the North Sea to Switzerland – but that was how it was.

Return by car to the CWGC cemetery on your left.

SANCTUARY WOOD CWGC CEMETERY   The cemetery was built around one of three battle cemeteries which were established here in 1915 following Second Ypres and contains almost 2,000 graves of which over 1,200 are unknown. One grave of particular note is that of Lt. Gilbert Talbot, after whom padre Tubby Clayton named the rest house in Poperinghe – Talbot House, or 'Toc H', as the army signallers called it. The Toc H movement survives today, a Christian organization devoted to developing the international spirit of youth through care and co-operation. The 'old house' as it is known, in Poperinghe, is maintained much as it was during the war, with original pictures and artefacts. It is an ideal base for touring the Salient. Visitors are always welcome and comfortable and economical accommodation is available there for those who are happy to cater for themselves. Tel: 01032 57 333228. Near to Talbot's grave is that of Hauptmann Hans Roser, who was the observer in an Albatross of Field Flying Section 3 which on 25 July 1915 was shot down by a Bristol Scout piloted by Captain Lanoe Hawker. Many British soldiers watched the action, including, it is said, General Plumer. Hawker won the vc for his victories that day.

Continue to the Menen Road, turn left and drive to the first crossroads, where there is a memorial marker in the centre of the right hand junction. Stop.

HELLFIRE CORNER   Ypres was in effect under siege for almost four years and German artillery could choose its targets with care. A crossroads is a good target. Firstly it is readily found on a map and the distance to it from the guns can be measured exactly, so that the weapons can be precisely aimed. In addition targets concentrate at a crossroads with traffic coming from four possible directions and so at any sign of movement German observers on the ridge could tell their pre-set guns to fire with a good chance of hitting something. Add to the road crossing a railway line and the area becomes a most attractive target to enemy gunners – and there was a railway here. The old rail route is followed by the N37 to Zonnebeke.

In summer great clouds of dust often gave away the movement of men and materials and, to reduce the likelihood of being spotted, canvas screens were frequently erected on the enemy side of roads. (Sir William Orpen, RA was sent to France in April 1917 as an official war artist and after a visit to the Somme he drew a picture called *The Great Camouflage, Combles*, which shows such screens. The picture is in the Imperial War Museum.) Such traffic junctions were places to be avoided at best and to be crossed at speed at the worst. They gave new meaning to the phrase, 'the quick or the dead'.

The memorial is a 'Demarcation Stone', marking the closest point to Ypres along the Menen Road that the Germans reached and held for more than 24 hours. There are 12 stones around Ypres and originally some 240 stones along the whole front from the North Sea to Switzerland, their position decided by the General Staff under Marshal Pétain to mark the greatest German advance. The helmet on top of the stone varied according to whose sector the stone was in – Belgian, French or British – and the design was approved by the touring clubs of France and Belgium. On three faces, in French, Flemish and English, were the words, 'Here the invader was brought to a standstill 1918' and on the top the location was given – thus here, 'Hellfire Corner'.

This stone has had a chequered history, having been attacked by motor vehicles a number of times. Its present location was set up in the 1990s. During the Second World War the Germans defaced many of the stones by chiselling out the message about the invader.

The relationship between the sites you have visited is clearly demonstrated by this extract from the history of the Worcestershire Regiment covering the period of Third Ypres – 'On 13 June 1917 the 1st Bn marched into Ypres and found quarters in the old barracks. Next night they went up to the front line. After dark the platoons marched forward in succession through the Menen Gate and along the Menen Road to Hellfire Corner and then by covered ways to the front trenches. The line taken over by the battalion included the trenches in Sanctuary Wood immediately south of the road – trenches which the 3rd Bn had known well in 1915.'

Drive left at Hellfire Corner, i.e. go south, and continue through the village of Zillebeke, turning left at the junction after the church following signs to Zandvoorte, but before reaching it turn right following signs to Hill 60. Stop at the museum.

HILL **60** AND ITS MEMORIALS   Between the wars this was the most visited part of the Ypres battlefield and until the late 1950s rows of trenches similar to those at Sanctuary Wood, but sandbagged, could be seen. The museum was at that time run by an Englishman, but when he left the trenches filled in (although their outlines can still be traced) and the area became what you see today – a crumpled mound with memorials (both on the mound itself and beside the road 200 yards on from where you now are), small craters, a blockhouse and across the road a museum. This has a reasonably well preserved collection of weapons and hardware and is run by a cousin of Jacques Schier. There is a small entrance charge and the opening hours are irregular. There is a bar to revive the weary.

The 'Hill' was formed by the spoil taken from the cutting through which the railway runs (200 yards further up the road) and gets its name because the resultant feature is 60 metres above sea level and forms an extension to the Messines Ridge. The French lost the Hill to the Germans in 1914 and when the British took over from them following the race to the sea it was then decided that the feature must be retaken. Much of the fighting here was underground and it was probably here that the first British mine of the war was blown by Lt White, RE on 17 February 1915 – though the tunnelling had actually been taken over from the French. It was decided that a major mining operation should be undertaken and the job was given to 173rd Tunnelling Company, RE. Work began early in March 1915 and three tunnels were begun towards the German line about 50 yards away, a pit having first been dug some 16 ft deep. Almost immediately the miners came upon dead bodies and quick-lime was brought up to cover them and the bodies were dragged out. Many more bodies would be uncovered in the months ahead and the smell of quick-lime hung over the hill for four years. Digging had often to be done by 'clay kicking'. That is where a man lies on his back in the tunnel and pushes metal plates attached to his heels into the tunnel face ahead of him and by bending his knees brings the soil towards him. It was hot, unpleasant and dangerous work. Apart from the constant threat that the tunnel would collapse and bury the miners alive, there was the possibility of poison gas and not least that the enemy might break into the tunnel or explode a mine of his own below it. By the time that the digging was finished the tunnels stretched more than 100 yards, and dragging the ninety-four 100 lb bags of gunpowder to the mineheads, winching them down the shafts and then manoeuvring them along the tunnels was a Herculean task. On 15 April all the charges were ready and on 17 April at 1905 hours the mine was fired.

The explosion built up over 10 seconds throwing volcano–like debris nearly 300 ft high and for 300 yards all around. Simultaneously British, French and Belgian guns opened an artillery barrage and encouraged by regimental buglers the Royal West Kents fixed bayonets and charged the dazed Germans of the 172nd Infantry Regiment, killing about 150 for only seven casualties of their own. The Hill was won.

Three days later Lt Geoffrey Harold Woolley won the first Territorial Army VC in resisting a German counter-attack. His citation reads, For most conspicuous bravery on Hill 60 during the night of 20th–21st April 1915. Although the only officer on the hill at the time, and with very few men, he successfully resisted all attacks on his trench and continued throwing bombs and encouraging his men till relieved. His trench during all the time was being heavily shelled and bombed, and was subjected to heavy machine-gun fire by the enemy. Woolley was a member of the 9th London Regiment, Queen Victoria's Rifles who had, with the Royal West Kents and King's Own Scottish Borderers, taken part in the initial assault on 17 April. The Queen Victoria's, the 14th Light Division and the 1st Tunnelling Company have memorials on the Hill. Underground warfare went on here for another 10 months until the beginning of Third Ypres. Many of the men who worked and fought in those black corridors in the clay died there and are there still. Hill 60 is a cemetery.

Continue over the railway and turn right towards Ypres. The next stop is Hyde Park Corner CWGC cemetery on the main road south from Ypres to Armentières. You can either now continue on this road until it meets the Armentières road just outside Ypres or take the second left and follow signs to Voormezele, once again in due course reaching the Armentières road. In either case then drive south towards Armentières and on reaching a large cylindrical memorial on the right hand side, with a cemetery opposite. Stop.

HYDE PARK CORNER (ROYAL BERKS) CWGC CEMETERY Beyond the small cemetery to the east of the road is Ploegsteert Wood, known to the Tommies as 'Plugstreet'. The critical fighting for possession of the wood took place in 1914, between mid-October and the beginning of November and was known as the Battle of Armentières. It ran, therefore, concurrently with First Ypres and this point, Ploegsteert, marked the bottom end of the Salient. The wood is about 2,000 yards wide east to west and 1,000 yards north to south, and although the enemy made excursions into the eastern edge of the wood it was never lost. A fine bayonet charge by 1st Somersets ('their first in France', as the Regimental History puts it, although they were in fact in Belgium) stopped one German attack on the village of le Gheer at the south-east corner of the wood.

Among the regiments that served in the wood in those early days was the 1st

Bn the Warwickshire Regiment and one of their machine-gun officers was Lt Bruce Bairnsfather. To relieve the awful monotony of mud, cold and destruction, Bairnsfather, an artist by training, began to draw cartoons on the walls of cottages, on ration boxes, on anything that came to hand and from his experience in the trenches came the most famous series of drawings of the entire war – 'Fragments from France' – and its most famous soldier character – 'Old Bill'. Just north of the wood is the small village of St Yvon and it was in the cellar of a ruined house there that Bruce drew his first 'Fragment.' His sense of humour brought relief to his own men and soon to tens of thousands of others as his cartoons were published weekly in *'The Bystander'* magazine. It was needed relief. Conditions in the wood were abominable. The Somersets history records, 'On 25 October . . . the trenches were absolute quagmires . . . the water and mud were ankle deep in the front lines; by the beginning of November the trenches in places were knee-deep in slime and filth. The stench from dead bodies often partially buried in the soggy, slimy ground, just as they had fallen, was awful. Unwashed, caked with mud, clothes sodden . . . aching with rheumatism and the early symptoms of trench feet, verminous and generally in a deplorable condition [the British soldier] held the line with a degree of staunchness, determination and cheerfulness of spirit never surpassed in the whole glorious history of the Army'.

The rotunda across the road is known as the Ploegsteert Memorial to the Missing and is guarded by two lions, one baring his teeth. It was designed by H. Charlton Bradshaw and the sculptor was Sir Gilbert Ledward. Inside the walls are inscribed the names of nearly 11,500 men, missing with no known grave following the battles of Armentières, 1914; Aubers Ridge, Loos and Fromelles, 1915; Estaires, 1916; and Hazebrouck, Scherpenberg and Outtersteene, 1918. It was inaugurated on 7 June 1931 by the Duke of Brabant. The graves around the memorial are in the Hyde Park Corner Cemetery Extension which was begun in June 1916, the original cemetery being on the opposite side of the road. It had been started during Second Ypres by the 1st/4th Royal Berkshires.

One of the burials in the smaller cemetery over the road is that of Private Albert Edward French who, in the 1980s was the subject of a BBC radio documentary entitled, 'He shouldn't have been there, should he?' His story came to light when his letters home to his sister Mabel were found. Albert had been an apprentice engineer at Wolverton railway works in Buckinghamshire when he left to enlist in October 1915. His father found out what had happened and tried to stop it, but Albert had already taken the King's shilling. On 15 June 1916 Albert was killed. He was 16 years old.

Drive back north towards Ypres noting the squat shape of Messines church on the ridge as you cross it.

It is said that Corporal Adolph Hitler sheltered in the crypt of the old church during his service in the Salient. He drew a number of water colours while he was here and these were later published by his photographer Heinrich Hoffmann. They show a draughtsman–like talent far in excess of what might be expected of the 'housepainter' that British Second World War propaganda claimed him to be. There is a small war museum in the Town Hall.

In the village of Wijtschate ('Whitesheet', according to the Tommies) turn left and follow the road around the bandstand and square heading for Kemmel and about halfway there look out for a green CWGC sign to the left to Lone Tree cemetery. Turn up the track and on the left before the cemetery is the 'Pool of Peace'.

SPANBROEKMOLEN. THE POOL OF PEACE The opening of Third Ypres was to be the capture of Messines Ridge. It was proposed to surprise the enemy by exploding a series of huge mines under his front line trenches and then overwhelming him by a rapid advance. One of the largest mines exploded here.

The digging of the initial shaft began in December 1915 about 500 yards away towards Kemmel Hill which should be visible to the west. At a depth of 60 ft the miners began to tunnel towards here, the German front line. British and Canadian tunnellers worked on the digging and by June 1916 at a length of 1717 ft the tunnel had been dug and the charges placed – 91,000 lb of ammonal. It was not until 7 June 1917 that everything was ready, nineteen mines placed in a huge arc from the area of Sanctuary Wood in the north out to Spanbroekmolen and then back around Ploegsteert Wood in the south. At 0310 the mines were fired – this one 15 seconds late. Sadly, a number of men from the 36th Ulster Division who had the task of taking this area left their trenches too soon and were killed by falling debris. They are buried in Lone Tree Cemetery a little further up the track. The noise of the explosion was said to have been heard in England and the ground for miles around heaved and shuddered as if awakening from a deep sleep.

Sir Philip Gibbs, the war correspondent described the scene thus, Suddenly at dawn, as a signal for all of our guns to open fire, there rose out of the dark ridge of Messines and 'Whitesheet' and that ill-famed Hill 60, enormous volumes of scarlet flame from nineteen separate mines, throwing up high towers of earth and smoke all lighted by the flame, spilling over into fountains of fierce colour, so that all the countryside was illuminated by red light, hellishly. The ground shook as though in an earthquake, as indeed it was, so that many of our soldiers waiting for the assault were thrown to the ground. The German troops were stunned, dazed and horror-stricken if they were not killed outright. Many of them lay dead in the great craters opened by the mines.

Two mines, which had been prepared somewhere near Ploegsteert Wood were in the event not used because they were considered to be outside the area finally chosen for the attack. They were never used and their location was forgotten. On the night of 17 June 1955 during a violent thunderstorm, one of the mines (at "Le Pélérin) exploded. Fortunately no one was hurt. But there is still one out there somewhere waiting to go off. Tread softly!

Lord Wakefield, who had bought the 'Old House' in Poperinghe for Toc H, bought this crater too in 1930 and it has been left to mellow as a 'Pool of Peace'.

Return to the tarmac road and turn left following signs to Kemmel Hill or Kemmelberg and park by the café next to the Belvedere (tower).

KEMMEL HILL   The story of Kemmel and the German capture of it during the last big attack in April 1918 varies according to the language in which it is told. The British say that the French lost Kemmel and that we had to get it back again. The French say that the British and the Portuguese collapsed south of Armentières and let the Germans right in to the southern slopes of the hill. The mutual distrust of Frenchmen and Englishmen is solidly justified in each account of the other's activities, a trait evident in the campaign against Saddam Hussein in 1991. What is certain here is that the Germans did capture the hill, but were so exhausted by their efforts that they were unable to advance further. On 17 April 1918, eight German divisions attacked Kemmel. Earlier, on 7 April, the British had evacuated Armentières following a bombardment by 40,000 gas shells and the Germans pressed steadily northwards so that by 14 April the line ran from Kemmel along the road you have driven (past the Pool of Peace) to Wijtschate. On 16 April a force commanded by the British 9th Division and supported by the French 28th Division was scheduled to make an attack. The French did not turn up (shades of Arras in 1940) and the following day the British held off the German attack of the 17th. Between 18 and 20 April Kemmel was handed over to the French and on 25 April the Germans attacked the French behind a heavy gas barrage. One British account says disparagingly, 'The fact that the French on both flanks of the hill gave way almost at once is sometimes attributed to their use of an insufficient gas mask.' The French say that the Germans captured the hill only after a bombardment heavier than that at Verdun and that it was the heroic defence of the Poilus that prevented the enemy from going any further. Whatever the truth, if such a commodity exists in warfare, the hill was torn apart, stripped of every living thing to the bare earth and the French lost almost 11,000 men between 16 and 25 April.

It is possible to climb the Belvedere for a small charge which is paid in the café or, in the summer, at a kiosk outside. On a clear day the whole battlefield can be seen from the white church spires in Armentières to the Cloth Hall in Ypres. The squat church at Messines is a useful landmark and is visible on most days to the south-east.

Continue over the top of Kemmel, first passing an obelisk with a winged female figure at the base.

FRENCH MEMORIAL   This 'Winged Victory' is a memorial to the French soldiers who fell on Belgian soil and in particular to those who fell from 15–29 April 1915. It was unveiled in 1932. The 45-ft high column was originally capped by a Poilu's helmet but when repairs were made to the column following a lighting strike the helmet was not replaced.

Continue down the hill to a small French cemetery enclosure on the left.

FRENCH OSSUARY This is the resting place of over 5,000 Poilus who were killed in the fighting on the hills. In the centre, standing over the mass graves, is a small pyramid crowned by the French cockerel, symbol of the Republic. On the pyramid a plaque reads, 'In the ossuary lie the remains of 5,294 unknown French officers, NCOs and soldiers who died for their country on Belgian soil.'

Continue downhill to the junction with the next tarmac road and turn very sharply right back to Kemmel. At the T junction short and west of Kemmel crossroads, turn left towards Reningelst and at the next main crossroads turn right towards Dikkebus and Ypres. On leaving Dikkebus village look out for a large sign right to 'Dikkebusse Vijver'. Follow it as far as you can go and stop.

DIKKEBUS LAKE In almost every conversation with a veteran of the fighting in the Salient the name of 'Dickybush' would crop up. It was a designated rest area with huts and tents ringing the lake (artificial) but even so it wasn't out of range of the bigger calibre guns or of air raids. Kemmel and Dickybush, however, were relatively quiet until the German push of 1918 and although Kemmel fell, Dickybush did not. Kemmel Hill should be visible across the far side of the lake and the traveller can find more comfortable rest today than did Tommy as the restaurant serves excellent food (eels are its speciality). There are few memories of the war here, just shells supporting the chain-link fence beside the lake and evidence of that military genius Vauban in the watchtower beside the car park.

Return to Ypres and arrive at the Menen Gate 10 minutes before 2000 hours in order to be in a good position for the Last Post Ceremony.

THE LAST POST CEREMONY This is where the echoes still remain, under the Menen Gate at 2000 hours every evening when the call of the Last Post rings out under the impressive arch. Just before 2000 hours two policemen arrive, stop the traffic and stand guard at each end of the gate. The buglers, just two in civilian clothes on most nights, or as many as six in uniform on special occasions, stand at the side of the road by the north-east pillar and, as the Cloth Hall clock strikes eight, they march together into the centre of the road, face the town and play the Last Post. Sometimes there may be very few people present. When the authors first visited the Salient, over two decades ago, they were often the only people listening to the buglers. In recent years the tide of remembrance has been growing and very rarely now, except perhaps in mid-winter, will there be less than a couple of dozen listeners, and often there are a hundred or more. However many are gathered together for the ceremony the emotion is overwhelming, because within the grasp of the arch are all those names of the missing (Siegfried Sassoon called them 'intolerably nameless names') – ordinary men now being remembered by a simple, ordinary ceremony that is extraordinary in its power to move.

It is the very simplicity of the occasion that makes it poignant, the absence of martial organization. Here are people gathered together in an orderly and respectful manner to remember, not because they have been told to do so but because they wish to do so. Even the school parties that attend are gathered into the atmosphere. Now and again a particular regiment may bring a colour party to the occasion, a Legion branch or school cadet force may come, and so the ceremony may be extended by the laying of wreaths, the recitation of Binyon's words of Exhortation, the playing of the Reveille. There are, too, the growing number of conducted battlefield tours groups, but each bows to the Gate's tradition (it is not appropriate to applaud). This is not a ceremony extolling the glories of war. This is remembrance, acknowledgement of a debt by those that remain to those who sacrificed, together with the hope that knowledge of war's legacies might increase the hope of future peace. Ypres has linked itself to Verdun as a 'City of Peace'. May there be many more to follow.

When the ceremony is over, do thank the buglers. They are dedicated people from the local fire brigades and Commonwealth War Graves gardeners. They take it in turns to play the nightly ceremony and they are proud and long-serving. Daniel Demey has been playing for well over thirty years and two others – Antoon Verschoot and Albert Verkouter – are not far behind. Marciel Verschoot is relatively new compared with them, but the youngest are the twins, Rik and Dirk Vandekerchkove – they are so alike that we joke they cannot tell each other apart. The ceremonies are co-ordinated by the Last Post Committee whose dedicated Chairman is Mr Guy Gruwez and the idea for the ceremony was that of Pierre Vandenbroembussche, Commissioner of Police in 1927. From 1 May 1929 the Last Post was sounded every morning until interrupted by the Second World War, when the ceremony was continued at Brookwood cemetery near Pirbright. Twenty-four hours after the liberation of Ypres in September 1944 by the Poles the ceremony recommenced. The silver bugles used were presented to the Committee on 16 September 1928 by British Legionnaires living in Belgium at a ceremony under the Menen Gate attended by the British ambassador. On 11 November 1959 Lt Col. John Whitaker who had served in the First World War presented two silver trumpets to the Committee and some eighteen months later two more silver trumpets were presented by Edward Lancaster, Honorary Colonel of the 44th Canadian Field Regiment. However, the Belgian buglers (who still play in the style imparted by Dick Collick) did not find the trumpets easy to play and so they are rarely used. On 8 October 1960 the Last Post was played for the 10,000th time. On 12 July 1992, the 75th Anniversary year of the Battle of Passchendaele, the 65th anniversary of the Menen Gate was celebrated, once more by the presentation of new bugles.

MAP 15 | WHAT WE GAINED AND LOST AT CAMBRAI
20 November 1917 – 6 December 1917

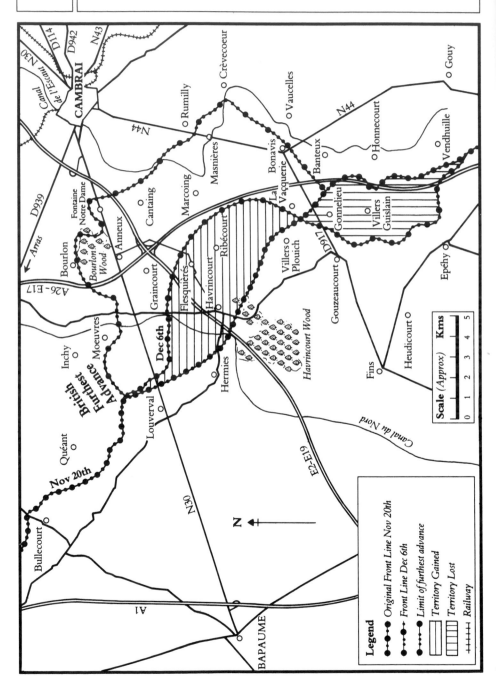

Legend
- Original Front Line Nov 20th
- Front Line Dec 6th
- Limit of furthest advance
- Territory Gained
- Territory Lost
- Railway

CAMBRAI
20 NOVEMBER–6 DECEMBER 1917

'A tank, like a warship, is nothing more than a moving
fortress . . . the idea was so simple that by many it was
not seen and when observed by a man of the 'Haig'
type of mind, its potentialities became so terrifying that
his one idea was to scrap it.'
Major General J. F. C. Fuller, The Army In My Time

'The infantry, tanks and artillery working in
combination were to endeavour to break through all
the enemy's lines of defence on the first day. If this
were successfully accomplished . . . cavalry were then
to be passed through.'
Sir Douglas Haig's Dispatches

'And what was the cavalry doing? Why carrying out
the regular tactics for advancing by stages into an
enemy's country . . .. No wonder they were late . . ..
The cavalry squadrons were only just crossing No
Man's Land and it was nearly 2 p.m. just six hours after
the barbed wire entanglements had been cleared for
them.'
Tankmen Stephen Foot, Three Lives

SUMMARY OF THE BATTLE
On 20 November 1917 the British 3rd Army launched a surprise attack on
General Marwitz's German 2nd Army using a total of almost 400 tanks. It was
the first mass use of tanks in history. On the first day a 6-mile-wide hole was
punched in the Hindenburg Line south-west of Cambrai. Two weeks later the
British were back almost where they started. Casualties on each side were about
equal at 40,000.

OPENING MOVES
In December 1915 Winston Churchill wrote a paper on how the new British
secret weapon, the tank, was to be used. In February 1916, Colonel Ernest

Swinton, who had originated the tank idea, expanded on Churchill's paper. The core of Swinton's argument was that the tank should not be used until it could be employed en masse. Despite this, General Haig used the tank in small numbers during the Battle of the Somme in 1916 and the opportunity to overcome the enemy through the surprise use of the new weapon was lost. Yet the tank proved that it had arrived to stay and a Tank Corps was formed that set about defining the role of the new arm, its tactics and operating procedures.

At Tank Corps Headquarters in France in August 1917, Colonel J. F. C. Fuller (later Major General), seeing how the Passchendaele offensive was bogging down in the mud of the Ypres Salient, proposed that an attempt to take St Quentin should be made, using large numbers of tanks. After discussion his idea was amended to be 'a tank raid south of Cambrai'; and this won the approval of General Byng whose command (Third Army) included the Cambrai area. However, Haig's staff felt that it was important to concentrate upon the Ypres offensive and the Cambrai 'raid' was turned down. Nevertheless Byng and the Tank Corps continued to press the idea, upgrading their proposal; from a one-day operation which had no intent to capture ground to a large-scale offensive which included the capture of Cambrai. By mid-October the Passchendaele offensive was looking ever more like a costly failure and perhaps GHQ saw in Fuller's idea the possibility of the redemption of British prestige. In any event the plan was then accepted. General Byng allocated the opening phase of the battle to two corps. III Corps on the right had the 6th, 12th, 20th and 29th Divisions plus the 2nd and 3rd Tank Brigades. IV Corps had the 36th (Ulster), 51st (Highland) and 62nd (West Riding) Division, 1st Cavalry Division and the 1st Tank Brigade. The Third Army Commander set out three main aims for the offensive:

1.   to break through the Hindenburg Line between the Escaut Canal and the Canal du Nord;
2.   to capture Cambrai and Bourlon Wood;
3.   to exploit towards Valenciennes.

On 19 November, the day before the battle was due to begin, Brigadier-General Hugh Elles commanding the Tank Corps issued Special Order No. 6. It contained five paragraphs. The first and last were:

'1. Tomorrow the Tank Corps will have the chance for which it has been waiting for many months – to operate on good going in the van of the battle.

5. I propose leading the attack of the centre division.'

Between 200 and 300 tanks would lead with him.

WHAT HAPPENED

At 0620 hours on Tuesday, 20 November 1917 the British guns opened fire and simultaneously the tanks led off into No Man's Land followed by the infantry. In front of the 6th Division was General Elles in his tank, 'Hilda', flying the green, red and brown battle standard of the Tank Corps. The Germans were taken completely by surprise. Tanks trailing grapples drove through the enemy wire tearing wide holes in it for the infantry to pour through. Other tanks carrying huge 2 ton bundles of wood called fascines, dropped them into the German trenches to form bridges over which they and others could drive. The effect of so many of the metal monsters looming up, seemingly unstoppable through the early-morning mist, was too much for many of the defenders who turned and ran.

On the first day III Corps achieved all of its initial tasks, breaching the Hindenburg Line between Crèvecoeur and Bonavis (see Map 15) and moving up to the St Quentin Canal. It also forced crossings over the canal at Masnières and Marcoing and it was across these that the 2nd and 5th Cavalry Divisions were planned to advance and sweep round and behind Cambrai. General Elles's 'Hilda', however, had come to grief before Ribecourt and he had to return to his HQ. Of the two assault divisions of IV Corps, the 62nd (West Riding) made excellent progress aided by its support force, 36th (Ulster) Division. Havrincourt, Graincourt and Anneux were taken and by the end of the day 186th Brigade had reached the Bapaum-Cambrai road (N30). At Flesquières, however, the other assault division the 51st (Highland) was stopped dead (see Map 16).

Due to poor communications and the stationing of the main cavalry forces too far in the rear on the first day, the six-mile-wide and five-mile-deep hole in the German lines remained unexploited. Flesquières was taken on the 21st and so was Fontaine Notre Dame, but Bourlon Wood became a scene of bloody conflict. Little further advance was made that day. General Haig had initially limited the offensive to 48 hours. The time was now up. What to do: carry on the attacks or consolidate the gains and be satisfied? General Haig knew that he had no reserves to exploit any success with because they were either stuck at Passchendaele (where less ground had been gained in three months than in one day at Cambrai), or had gone to help the Italians after Caporetto. Hope must have sprung eternal in the C-in-C's breast because he continued the attack, which developed into a slogging match, particularly around the dominating feature of Bourlon.

Most unsportingly the Germans counter-attacked in force. Just after dawn on 30 November, following a short 'hurricane' bombardment with gas and smoke shells they attacked with infantry moving in small groups and bypassing centres of resistance which were left to low-flying aircraft and close support artillery. It was a technique that had been developed in Russia by General Oskar von Hutier and which had been used to such effect at Caporetto. It was now the British turn to be surprised, and they were. After a week of hanging on grimly the British fell back to a 'winter line' on 6 December. The Cambrai adventure was over (see Map 15).

On 14 December 1917 GHQ issued a note saying that the BEF would cease

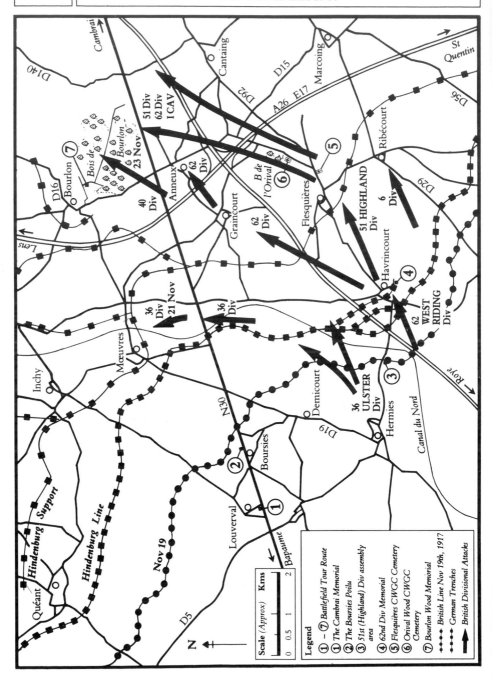

aggressive operations and take 'a defensive posture'. Perhaps the scale of casualties was beginning to tell on the C–in–C, or perhaps he had one eye on the Prime Minister, Lloyd George, whom he knew had half a mind to sack him if he lost many more men.

THE BATTLEFIELD TOUR

The tour begins in Bapaume and first visits the Cambrai memorial. Thereafter it traverses the IV Corps area visiting Boursies, Havrincourt, Flesquières CWGC Cemetery, Orival Wood CWGC Cemetery and the memorials at Bourlon. It ends in Cambrai.

Total distance   25 miles
Total time   3 hours 30 minutes
Map   IGN. 4. Laon/Arras 1:100,000

Take the N30 north-east out of Bapaume and after 5 miles stop at the British cemetery on the left hand side.

THE LOUVERVAL MEMORIAL AND CWGC CEMETERY   The memorial is also known as 'The Cambrai Memorial' since it records the names of over 7,000 men of the 3rd Army who are missing and have no known grave. They fell mostly in the fighting that followed the dramatic advances of the first day. The names are inscribed on a semi–circular wall which has a cloistered walk and amongst the names are Private Frederick George Dancox, VC, who won his award near Langemarck in October 1917 (see Third Ypres) and the Queripel brothers of the Channel Island's Militia (Captain Lionel Queripel of the same family would win a posthumous VC at Arnhem in 1944). There is also Lt Gavin Patrick Bowes Lyon, 3rd Bn Grenadier Guards, a cousin of Queen Elizabeth, the Queen Mother. (Her brother, Fergus, is commemorated at Dud Corner, Loos.) On the end walls of the memorials are fine bas relief panels by C. S. Jagger, RA showing graphic cameo details of life in the trenches. The memorial itself was designed by H. Charlton Bradshaw and stands in the same grounds as the cemetery which was begun in April 1917. Among the 118 known burials (there are six unknown) is Surgeon F. P. Pocock who took part in the Zeebrugge Raid in April 1918 on the ferry boat 'Iris' and was killed here five months later.

The road along which you have travelled was a main forward axis of the British assault. The preparations for the attack were carried out in the greatest secrecy with all forward area movements taking place at night. Some one thousand guns were brought up and camouflaged, their sights being set without preliminary ranging fire. The tanks were brought up on 36 special trains to a Corps collecting area near Bray sur Somme and then moved to just behind their associated battalions. One at a time battalions were withdrawn to practice infantry/tank co-operation tactics.

The final moves to the front were made on the night of 17 November. The tanks moved slowly in low gear to keep the noise down, following white tapes and the glowing cigarette tips of battalion guides, while aircraft flew overhead to mask the activity.

Continue along the Cambrai road to the village of Boursies. Almost at the bottom of the hill into the village is a war memorial on the left. Stop.

BOURSIES The village was immediately behind the British front line of 20 November 1917 (see Map 6). Axes such as this road were important arteries for the supplies and stores needed to initiate and sustain great offensives. In order to keep routes open, infantry battalions were rotated on 'pioneer duties' which were basically 'humping and lifting' activities. One such battalion that was working in exactly this area was the 1st/5th Cheshire Regiment. Its history records the following 'At the beginning of November it soon became evident that something was brewing as the Battalion was employed nightly with two Field Companies (Royal Engineers) of the 62nd Division on widening the main Cambrai road by corduroying (re-inforcing the surface with logs) the north side of the road from Beugny (you drove through it just before Louverval) to Bousies. This work which was pushed on with feverish haste, was completed on the 20th.'

Four days later the Cheshires had to move back. 'The action of the enemy became much more lively and aggressive, so much so that the Battalion had to evacuate Boursies which had become a shell trap. The cook-house received a direct hit from a shell which killed a Sergeant cook . . . one field cooker was completely put out of action and a second considerably damaged.'

The village memorial is a Poilu standing on top of a column and unusually the figure is brightly repainted from time to time. One interesting detail is the gas mask, which is rarely seen on memorial figures.

Continue to the next crossroads and turn right on the D19 to Hermies. Take the Havrincourt road out of the village and stop just before the bridge over the Canal du Nord.

CANAL DU NORD At the time of the battle this part of the canal was dry as it was still under construction. The front line ran alongside, parallel to the western edge of the canal just here, so you are standing at the right spot to begin your assault on the Hindenburg Line. Your route from here follows pretty well the exact advance of the 51st (Highland) Division. Ahead of you is the village of Havrincourt and to its right Havrincourt Wood. The front line, as Map 16 shows, bent eastward so that the wood was on our side and the village on the enemy side. The 51st hid some 10,000 men in and around the wood and prepared routes forward, dressing stations and, 'as cavalry were also detailed to take part in the operations, six water points with a capacity for watering 7,000 horses per hour.' (A cavalry division had about 10,000 horses).

Continue to Havrincourt village.

The supporting artillery was moved up on the night of 17 November, the tanks were brought into Havrincourt Wood on the night of 18 November and the infantry moved into line on the night of 19 November. In the early hours of

20 November the tanks moved out in front of the infantry assembly trenches and lined up on a white marker tape. There were 70 of them in the divisional force.

On the small road that leads past the church and turns sharply east is a memorial column to the 62nd Division whose axis came through here. They also captured the village in 1918.

Take the DI5E/D92 Flesquières road out of Havrincourt.

At 0630 the advance began. Fifteen 18-pounder batteries dropped a mixed HE and smoke creeping barrage in front of the division and two 4.5 howitzer batteries put a standing smoke screen on to Flesquières Ridge where you are now driving.

Continue to the British Cemetery on the right. Stop.

FLESQUIÈRES HILL CWGC CEMETERY The only significant delay on the first day was around Flesquières in the 51st Division sector. The divisional history describes the German defences thus, 'The area through which the Division was destined to advance was traversed by three separate trench systems each forming integral parts of the Hindenburg system. Of these the first . . . was composed of a maze of wide, heavily wired trenches . . . in rear of the front system and just south of the village of Flesquières lay the Hindenburg support system, composed of two lines of heavily wired deep trenches connected with each other and with the front system.'

The 51st broke through the first part of the Hindenburg Line on 20 November but didn't penetrate the Support Line here until the following day, a 'failure' that has two simplistic explanations. First, General Harper, commanding the division, did not follow the drill which had been worked out for tank/infantry co-operation. He had his tanks advance in fours, line abreast, instead of in threes in 'V' formation, and his infantry advanced behind the tanks in extended order, not in file as laid down. This may have resulted in heavier casualties, but a more serious mistake was that, having broken the first line, General Harper stopped to reorganize and his tank crews switched off their engines and got out. This had been part of the original plan, but the other divisions had exploited their initial success and continued to advance. After a 20-minute delay the 51st started to advance towards Flesquières Ridge at 0855 hours but by this time the friendly artillery support had moved on and enemy fire was coming down on the attacking force.

Second, German fire from Flesquières Château area was steadily knocking out the division's tanks. In his Dispatches General Haig wrote, 'Many of the hits upon our tanks at Flesquières were obtained by a German artillery officer who remaining alone at his battery, served a field gun single handed until killed.'

Some authorities doubt the existence of the German gunner, who came to be known as 'the Phantom Major'. Others, like airman Arthur Gould Lee, were certain. He wrote in his diary for 28 November 1917, We walked to Flesquières and examined the scene at the corner of the Château wall where the Hun artillery major and a handful of men had held up the advance on the 20th by catching the tanks at point blank range as, one by one, they topped the brow of the slope to his front. It was an amazing sight. In a crescent, a few hundred yards long, facing his grave, lay a whole line of disabled tanks. One German source named the gunner as Unteroffizier Kruger and between them the various authorities say the number of tanks destroyed was between 7 and 16, a feat unequalled until the exploits of Wittman in Normandy in 1944.

The cemetery is triangular in shape. The great cross is roughly central on the road side and standing beside it you have views across the ground over which the 51st and 62nd Divisions advanced. Bourlon Wood is visible on its hill beyond Orival Wood and clearly commands entry into Cambrai, whose spires can be seen to the right on a clear day. At the back of the cemetery at the apex of the triangle is a special memorial to men of the 63rd Royal Naval Division whose graves have been lost. Burials were started here by the 2nd Division in 1918 alongside a German cemetery. The German burials were later moved. An idea of the degree of confusion in the fighting that followed the Cambrai attack may be gathered from the fact that of the 810 graves here 74 per cent contain unidentified bodies.

Continue to the next road junction turning left towards Bourlon Wood which is visible on the horizon. At the British cemetery on the left stop.

ORIVAL WOOD CWGC CEMETERY   The cemetery is beside a small wood that has the same shape today as it had at the time of the battle. It was begun during the fighting for Cambrai and enlarged after the war by burials brought in from around Flesquières. On the left is a special memorial to those who were originally buried in Flesquières Château cemetery and at the back are twenty German graves including men from the German Naval Division. In the far right hand corner is the grave of Chang Te Hsun of the Chinese Labour Corps. The most notable headstone here is that of the poet Lt Ewart Alan Mackintosh MC of the Seaforths, author of the collections *A Highland Regiment* and *War, the Liberator*. Regarded as a typical 'Gael', he was a popular and sensitive officer (see also the Arras section of the Vimy tour), who became engaged to Sylvia Marsh in 1916 while teaching 'bombing' to the Cambridge Corps of Cadets.

'The days are long between, dear lass.
Before we meet again,
Long days of mud and work for me,
For you long care and pain.

But you'll forgive me yet, my dear
Because of what you know,
I can look my dead friends in the face
As I couldn't two months ago.'

These were the words he wrote 'To Sylvia', on returning to the front from a 'cushy' job in Cambridge – only to be killed here on 21 November.

Continue via Anneux to the crossroads with the N30 main Cambrai road. Go straight over, following signs to the Canadian Memorial, Bourlon Wood.

BOURLON WOOD AND ITS MEMORIALS This wooded hill commands the routes to Cambrai and here the Cambrai offensive foundered. Here too a valiant band of little men proved themselves worthy of every adjective for bravery and in so doing were destroyed. They were the Bantams, the 40th Division.

There were originally two Bantam Divisions, the 35th and the 40th. They were made up of small but sturdy men, 5 ft to 5 ft 3 in tall and with a minimum chest measurement of 34 in, but owing to a lack of suitable reinforcements the 35th lost its Bantam status at the end of 1916. When the 40th moved up from pioneering duties (of the work of the Cheshires earlier) four of the battalions were of normal-sized men. On 21 November the church bells rang out in London in celebration of the news of the great victory at Cambrai. It was a mistake. Bourlon had not fallen. On 23 November the 40th (Welsh) Bantam Division was ordered forward to take over the offensive on Bourlon Wood and its Prussian Guard from the 51st Division. In three days of intense hand-to-hand fighting the Welsh took the wood but never managed to take the village. At the end of 72 hours the division had lost 4,000 men. It was destroyed. Although the 40th then lost its Bantam status, in recognition of its magnificent record at Bourlon, the C-in-C allowed the division to retain its cockerel emblem, together with two acorns symbolizing its sacrifice in the wood.

The Canadian memorial up the slope is a Canadian granite block of the pattern seen at Courcelette on the Somme and at Hill 62 in the Ypres Salient. It commemorates the Canadian Corps' crossing of the Canal du Nord on 27 September 1918 during the Hindenburg Line offensive and the subsequent advance to Mons and Germany.

The Bourlon Wood Cemetery is signed along a muddy path past a cruciform memorial to Frenchmen killed in the Second World War. It was begun by the Canadian Corps in October 1918 and has some 245 burials, mostly Canadian. The register reveals that many of the soldiers were of UK origins, being second or even first-generation Canadians, like Corporal William Gibbs of the 78th Battalion (Manitoba) Regiment who had fought in the Boer War with the 2nd Bn Royal Scots Fusilliers.

Continue to Cambrai.

MAP 17

THE KAISER'S OFFENSIVE
21 March – 5 April 1918

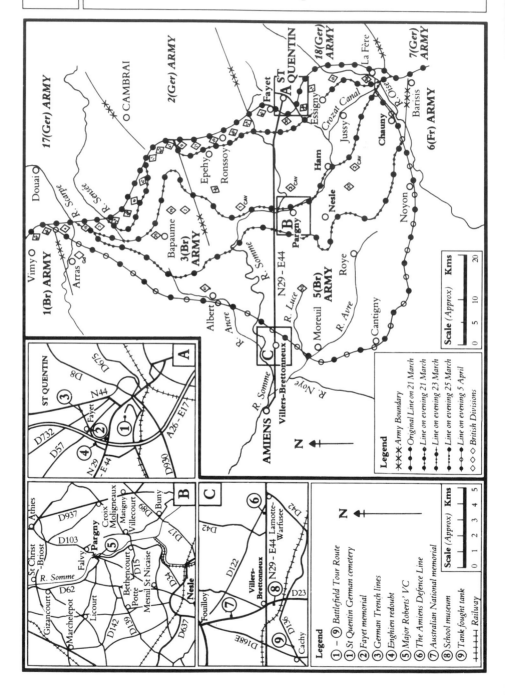

Legend

✳✳✳ *Army Boundary*

○━○━ *Original Line on 21 March*

●━●━ *Line on evening 21 March*

●━●━ *Line on evening 23 March*

━━━ *Line on evening 25 March*

━○━○ *Line on evening 5 April*

◇ ◇ ◇ *British Divisions*

Scale (Approx)   Kms

0   5   10   20

Scale (Approx)   Kms

0   1   2   3   4   5

Legend

① – ⑨ *Battlefield Tour Route*

① *St Quentin German cemetery*

② *Fayet memorial*

③ *German Trench lines*

④ *Enghien redoubt*

⑤ *Major Roberts' VC*

⑥ *The Amiens Defence Line*

⑦ *Australian National memorial*

⑧ *School museum*

⑨ *Tank fought tank*

+++++ *Railway*

THE KAISER'S OFFENSIVE

21 MARCH–25 APRIL 1918

'It will be an immense struggle that will begin at
one point, continue at another and take a long
time. It is difficult, but it will be succesful.'
Ludendorff to the Kaiser.

'We move through St Quentin at a trot and the British
are hardly firing . . .. Everything has gone brilliantly.'
Lt Herbert Sulzbach (German Artillery Officer), Diary entry, 21 March, 1918.

'You must admit, General Gough, that your troops,
sometimes left their positions before they
should have done.'
Lord Milner to General Gough GOC 5th Army.

'With our backs to the wall and believing in the
justice, of our cause each one of us must fight
on to the end.'
From Field Marshal Haig's Order of the Day, 11 April 1918.

SUMMARY OF THE BATTLE

Following a five-hour bombardment by over 6,000 guns, one million German soldiers attacked along a front of nearly 50 miles opposite the British Third and Fifth Armies. Gough's Fifth Army, between Amiens and St Quentin, gave way and when the offensive was finally halted, in fighting that involved the world's first tank versus tank battle, Ludendorff had penetrated 40 miles into the allied lines, taken over 1,000 guns and inflicted more than 200,000 casualties. German casualties, however, were also nearly 200,000. General Gough was made the scapegoat for the near defeat of the Fifth Army.

OPENING MOVES

After the failure at Cambrai the BEF went into a defensive mode and began to construct positions in depth similar to the Germans. A forward lightly held zone was meant to delay the attacker, while behind it was a main battle zone held in strength and depth. In both zones small redoubts (defended positions) and

131

machine-gun posts were to be scattered like cherries in a madeira cake. The battle zone was generally to be separated from the forward zone by a gap of two to three miles and was to be 2,000 to 3,000 yards deep. Four miles further back still was a rear zone, effectively a second position to which the defence could retire if need be. All of these positions had to be prepared and as it attracted the lowest priority the rear zone in many places was hardly more than a belt of wire known as the Green Line.

The British C-in-C, Haig, reasoned that the most critical part of his line was in the north, shielding the Channel ports and he put 46 divisions to cover what amounted to two-thirds of his front. The remaining third, on the right, was covered by Gough's Fifth Army which mustered 14 divisions. Already thinly spread compared to the north, the Fifth Army was given a further 25 miles to cover which were taken over from the French early in 1918. Foch also wanted Haig to contribute nine divisions to a central allied reserve to be controlled by Foch. Haig refused. Instead he made a 'gentleman's agreement' that each would come to the other's aid with six divisions after five days' notice if the need arose.

On 29 November 1917, hostilities ceased on the Russian front. A week later Rumania stopped fighting. The Germans now had spare forces which they could move to the Western front. In the period up to the opening of the Kaiser's Offensive their strength rose by 30 per cent. British strength, compared with the summer of 1917, fell by 25 per cent.

Ludendorff held a conference, ironically in Mons on 11 November 1917, at which the plans for the *Kaiserschlacht* were discussed. He decided to strike first in the area of Arras and St Quentin where the ground would be firmer than in Flanders. He also chose to attack the British whose forces, he believed, had been weakened by Passchendaele and whose generals, he felt, were more inept and less flexible than the French. In addition he introduced a wholly new tactical philosophy. Ludendorff adopted an attack concept originated by Captain Geyer, that of a light tactical assault unit, the infantry group, made up from a few riflemen, mortar teams, engineers and light machine-guns. These groups of storm troopers incorporated in a thin screen would move forward to probe and penetrate enemy defences, by-passing any centres of opposition according to circumstances and not limited by a rigid timetable. The main attack force, following behind and reinforced with its own under-command field artillery, would overcome any resistance remaining. In addition, artillery tactics were also revised. Von Hutier had introduced the idea of silent registration on the Eastern Front and it had been used with great effect at Caporetto. His chief gunner was Oberst Georg Bruchmüller and he now became the great conductor and orchestrated a score for the March artillery programme that was to confirm his nickname, 'Breakthrough Bruchmüller'.

Bruchmüller's plan began with silent registration and consisted of seven phases, six of them between 0400 and 0940 hours, the jump-off time, the seventh being a creeping barrage. He defined the targets to be hit, the intensity to be achieved, the explosive/phosgene gas mixture to be used, and the duration, of each phase. Training for the attack, 'Operation Michael', was intensive and thorough. Steadily Ludendorff built up his strength. By the night of 20 March the German superiority in infantry was four to one and the more than 6,000 guns standing by for Bruchmüller's overture were a larger assembled force of arms than those of the British on the Somme on 1 July 1916, the British at El Alamein in October 1942 and the Allies against Saddam Hussein in February 1991 all added together: *Der Tag* was about to dawn.

WHAT HAPPENED

At 0930 hours on 21 March 1918, after 5 hours of Bruchmüller's itemized bombardment, 3,500 mortars opened rapid fire on the British front line defences. Five minutes later in thick mist the storm troopers advanced. 5th Army communications had been destroyed, battalion positions and redoubts were cut off and by-passed. Not only did the defenders know little about what was happening, they could see little. By nightfall, the Germans had penetrated the forward zone on both Fourth and Fifth Army fronts and were consolidating in the battle zone. Gough withdrew his right wing 7 miles to behind the Crozat Canal (shown on modern maps as the St Quentin Canal between Ham and Chauny see Map 17) and asked the French for permission to blow the railway bridges. They refused.

The following morning the Germans continued their assault, the mist still protecting them. By the end of the day the Fifth Army's centre had been broken and all of its meagre reserves committed. On the night of 22 March Gough decided that he must pull his remaining forces behind the line of the River Somme and make a stand there. The line held for 3 days but the German tide would not be denied. The Fifth's retreat continued. On 23 March German long range railway guns started to shell Paris. The French considered pulling back to defend their capital and Haig looked at the possibility of abandoning the Fifth Army and moving the Third Army north to protect the Channel ports. But the German advance was slowing. Their roads forward were clogged with traffic and constantly harassed by the RFC. Their soldiers, who had been on short rations for many months and whose clothing and equipment was of poor quality, were overwhelmed by the richness of captured British food and supplies and engaged in wholesale looting. Rudolph Binding, the German writer who took part in the advance recorded in his diary on 28 March, 'There were men driving cows . . . others who carried a hen under one arm . . . men carrying a bottle of wine under their arm and another open in their hand . . . men staggering . . . men who could hardly walk . . . the advance was held up and there was no means of getting going again for hours.'

On 26 March, in emergency sessions, Clémenceau, Foch, Milner, Haig and others conferred under the chairmanship of President Poincaré at Doullens. The initial mood of impending defeat was shattered by Foch, who proclaimed, 'I will never surrender.' Haig promised Poincaré that he would hold Amiens and when Foch was appointed Supreme Commander of the allied forces on the Western Front, Haig willingly acquiesced to the position of Number Two. The headlong retreat of the Fifth Army however needed a scapegoat. Ignoring the fact that Gough had warned of his shortage of men both for fighting and for preparing defences, had warned of the too-extended frontage that he had to hold, had warned of the certainty of the location of the coming attack and had asked repeatedly for reinforcements, he was relieved of his command. Two days later Rawlinson took over from him in the field with the HQ staff of the Fourth Army. On that same day the German advance was virtually spent. The Third Army north of the Somme threw back the German efforts against Arras. Ten miles in front of Amiens, just to the east of the village of Villers Bretonneux, the tired Germans were fought to a standstill by the 1st Cavalry Division.

On 3 April Gough met Haig before returning to England. The meeting was brief. Haig said that the orders for Gough's removal had not come from him, that there would be an enquiry into the actions of the Fifth Army and its Commander and that Gough would have 'every chance' to defend himself. Haig concluded by shaking hands. 'I'm sorry to lose you Hubert,' he said. 'Goodbye'.

Already Australian troops, rushed down by Haig from the north, were arriving around Villers Bretonneux. When the Germans attacked again at dawn on 4 April it seemed momentarily as if the village must fall, but an Australian bayonet charge tipped the scales. The 40 miles advance was over.

The Germans paused to gather their strength. At GHQ Haig realized that the situation was critical and asked Foch to take over some part of the front held by the British and Commonwealth forces. Foch agreed to move a large French force towards Amiens and on 11 April Haig, worried about the morale of his tired and overstretched troops, issued a 'Special Order of the Day' which was addressed to 'All Ranks of the British Army in France and Flanders'. It said, 'Three weeks ago today the Enemy began his terrific attacks against us on a 50 mile front . . .. Many amongst us now are tired . . .. There is no other course open to us but to fight it out! Every position must be held to the last man: there must be no retirement. With our backs to the wall, and believing in the justice of our cause, each one of us must fight on to the end . . .'.

In the dawn mist of 24 April the 4th (Ger) Guards Division and the 228th Division supported by 13 tanks came down the hill towards Amiens. Again the Australians took them on, pinching out the village on the morning of Anzac Day, 25 April, just hours after the first ever tank-versus-tank battle. (Three days before the Australians had buried Baron Manfred von Richthofen, the 'Red Baron', at Bertangles, with full military honours. An Australian anti-aircraft battery claimed the victory – so did the Canadian pilot, Captain Roy Brown. Von Richthofen had 80 kills.)

Ludendorff had written off Operation Michael on 4 April and switched his attention to Neuve Chapelle, where the fury of Operation Georgette fell upon the unfortunate Portuguese 2nd Division on 9 April. Amiens was safe.

THE BATTLEFIELD TOUR

The tour begins at the German cemetery at St Quentin and from there moves to the German jump-off trenches at Fayet. It then follows the retreat of a typical British infantry battalion to the Somme at Pargny and there traces the details of an action which led to the winning of a vc. The retreat continues to Villers Bretonneux – the Australian National Memorial and cwgc Cemetery and school – and ends east of the village where tank fought tank for the first time.

Total time   4 hours 30 minutes
Total distance   75 miles
Map   IGN Laon/Arras 1:100,000

At the junction of the St Quentin ring road extension of the N44 with the N29 Amiens roads immediately west of the city, follow signs to 'Deutsche Friedhof'.

ST QUENTIN GERMAN CEMETERY   Over 6,000 named burials marked by small black crosses with up to four soldiers in a grave are gathered here, mostly from the 1918 offensive. Inside the entrance on the left-hand border of the cemetery is a memorial wall carrying the names of almost 2,000 missing with no known grave. A short flight of steps flanked by two larger than life Graeco-Roman soldiers leads to a central panel with laurel wreath and sword, headed by the words 'Resquiescat in pace' – Rest in peace.

Return to the N44 junction. Continue straight across on the N44 and take the first turning left on to the D57. In Fayet village turn right at the obelisk war memorial.

FAYET MEMORIAL   A small plaque on the memorial records the British 6th Divisions' part in recapturing the village in September 1918, as well as the German offensive in March of that year.

Continue north-east through the village to the crossroads with the D732.

You are now 150 yards behind the British front line trench system and facing the Germans.

Continue straight across the crossroads into the cutting. As the cutting flattens out, some 200 to 300 yards later, on the top of the plateau you reach the area of the German front line trench and have crossed No Man's Land. There may be a caravan parking area on your right. Stop.

GERMAN TRENCHES   The trench lines here ran almost due south for about 2,000 yards and at this point were barely 100 yards apart. The British force between here and the northern edge of St Quentin (the cathedral should be visible to your right) was the 2nd/8th Worcesters, part of 182nd Brigade of 61st Division of the Fifth Army. These were forward zone positions. The battalion put two companies forward, A and B, each covering a front of about a mile with their company HQs in Fayet village (B Coy) and 1,500 yards south of it (A Coy). D Company was nominated as a counter-attack force and centred on Fayet village, while C Company and battalion HQ occupied a central redoubt about a mile behind the lines.

The Regimental History described the defences as 'for the most part merely shallow ditches not more than waist deep. Neither labour nor materials had been available to improve the defences. There was but scanty wire protection save around the actual defensive posts.'

What happened here is described now in selected extracts from the *Regimental History*. On the night of 20 March a raiding party went into the German trenches. 'The raiders brought back prisoners from three different German regiments. Those prisoners stated that the German army would attack the next day . . . the Corps Commander decided to put into force the pre-arranged dispositions for meeting an attack. The order to man the battle stations reached HQ 61st Division at 0435 and at that very minute all along the line the German artillery opened fire . . .. For several hours the platoons of the 2nd/8th Worcesters endured the bombardment. The mist torn only by the blaze of the shell bursts and then thickened by their smoke, hid everything from the eyes of the crouching sentries. Gas shells added their fumes to those of the high explosives and the survivors groped in the trenches, half-blinded by their gas masks . . .. On every side parties of the enemy's infantry came looming through the mist . . . instead of advancing in regular waves they worked in infiltration . . . the forward posts were overwhelmed one by one.'

All of the Worcesters' companies were decimated, small bands of survivors struggling back to battalion HQ: 'a ring of small defensive posts connected by a trench . . . from 1020 attack after attack beat against the defences . . . the enemy closed in from every side . . . two-thirds of the defenders had been killed or wounded . . . ammunition ran out . . . the German infantry charged in with the bayonet and the remnants of the defenders were compelled to surrender.' It was 1730. What the gallant Worcesters did not know what that Holnon, the village a mile or more behind them, had been taken and passed by the enemy seven hours earlier. Altogether the battalion lost 19 officers and 560 men on that day, almost exactly the same total as the Tyneside Scottish lost at la Boisselle on the first day of the Somme.

To your left about 100 yards away across the fields, is an arc of wood. In that wood original German jump-off trenches still remain and, crops permitting – be very careful not to damage anything that may be growing – it is possible to walk to them across the field. You can therefore stand exactly where the Kaiser's battle began.

Drive back to Fayet war memorial. Turn right and then left at the bottom of the hill in the direction of Holnon. Immediately after the road crosses the motorway there is what appears to be a rectangular wooded area about 100 yards off the road to your right. Stop.

ENGHIEN REDOUBT The area enclosed by trees is in the precise form and position of a British redoubt called Enghien (presumably based upon an earlier French fortification, since Enghien was the name of the Marshal of France who gave Vauban his opportunity to become France's greatest fortifications exponent). The northern boundary of 2nd/8th Worcesters was the road along which you are driving. This is a typical redoubt formation. One thousand yards due south of here was Ellis Redoubt where the Worcesters had battalion HQ. Redoubts were meant to be mutually supporting and the ground between them covered by machine-gun fire. The mist prevented that. The redoubt was held by the 2nd/4th Oxs and Bucks, who with a few Worcester stragglers, survived until 1630 on 21 March.

Continue to Selency on the N29. Turn right towards Amiens.

As you make your way towards Amiens in the line of the retreat, two literary, personal accounts will considerably add to your understanding of what it was like to have taken part in this momentous and often terrifying event. First there is Colonel Rowland Feilding's moving *Letters to a Wife*. In 1918 this sensitive and popular Regimental officer was commanding the 1st Civil Service Rifles. His account of the battalion's withdrawal from Ronssoy to Bray is dramatic and realistic, describing the high casualties, the pitiful refugees who fled before the armies, and his own wounding and treatment. Second, there is Sir Herbert Read's *In Retreat*, published in 1925. Read was a Captain in the Yorkshire Regiment, and served with distinction, winning the DSO and the MC. *In Retreat* is both coolly factual and vivid. It describes men as 'dazed', 'haggard'; the fighting as 'bloody', 'hellish', 'ghastly'. We share the light relief of his battle-weary group when a forager brings (no questions asked about its provenance), 'French bread, butter, honey and hot, milky coffee in a champagne bottle! We cried out with wonder: we almost wept. We shared the precious stuff out, eating and drinking with inexpressible zest.' Of such contrasts are battles made.

Immediately after crossing the Somme at Brie, turn left on to the D62 and continue to Pargny village. As the road enters the village, it runs abruptly left as the buildings begin. Stop.

PARGNY When the German attack opened, the 1st Battalion of the Worcesters was at Moringhem 6 miles east of St Omer. Next morning they and the whole of 24th Brigade marched to St Omer and entrained at midday, reaching Amiens that night. After a short delay the train continued to Nesle (see Map 17) where the troops got out at 0230 hours on 23 March in darkness. The Worcesters marched north and took up positions on the west bank of the Somme covering Pargny. Their task was to hold the river line and to cover the retreat of the Fifth Army. Very early in the morning the route across the Somme, through the village, became congested with refugees and by 1400 hours battalions of the Fifth Army began to stream back closely followed by the Germans. That evening about 2000 hours Germans began to cross the Somme by the bridge at Pargny, which had been incompletely blown. Major (acting Lt Col.) F. C. Roberts of the battalion, seeing what was happening, gathered about 45 men, where you now are, determined to drive the enemy back across the river.

At 2100 hours Major Roberts' party set off towards the bridge on an action that was to win him the VC. You can walk the route as you read the story in Major Roberts' own words, 'We started off with fixed bayonets and magazines loaded. For the first hundred yards or so we went in two parties in single file on each side of the main road at the walk and as quietly as possible. The first sign I had of the enemy was some shouting from houses we were passing and then both machine gun and rifle fire from windows and doors, with small parties dashing into the streets and clearing off in the direction of the bridge. Once this started we all went hell-for-leather up the street firing at anything we saw and using the bayonet in many cases. Every man screamed and cheered as hard as he could and, by the time we reached the church, the village was in an uproar – Bosches legging it hard for the bridge or else chucking their hands up. In the churchyard itself the hardest fighting took place – tombstones being used as if in a game of hide and seek. After clearing it we had a few moments rest and went smack through to the bridge where a crowd of Bosche were trying to scramble across. Some did and some didn't. That more or less ended it – we actually captured six light machine guns, fifteen to twenty prisoners and killed about eighty. Our own losses were heavy.'

You now need to head for Villers Bretonneux, which you may do either by returning to the N29 Amiens road by retracing your steps to Brie or by continuing south to the D337 and turning right. Either way you will eventually pass through the small village of Warfusée-Abancourt on the N29.

WARFUSÉE-ABANCOURT   The German advance towards Amiens was so rapid that, fearful for the safety of the city, General Gough decided to occupy an old French defensive position, the 'Amiens Defence Line', which had been constructed in 1915 (see Map 17). It was 8 miles long and ran across the St Quentin–Amiens road immediately west of this village. On the night of 25–6 March an ad hoc force about 3,000 strong was gathered to occupy the position under the command of Major General C. G. S. Carey and it became known as 'Carey's Force'. Among the patchwork of small units involved were two companies of American 6th Regiment engineers from the US 3rd Division, totalling some 500 men. The Americans occupied the line from the road to the wood about 1 mile to your right (north) and came into action on the night of 27 March. They were probably the first Americans to fight in the line. The Prime Minister, Lloyd George, referred disparagingly to the rapid withdrawal of Gough's 5th Army and gave undue importance to the action of Carey's Force by saying that 'it closed the gap to Amiens for about 6 days' and that it had been formed on the initiative of General Carey. In fact it and other similar forces had been formed by Gough – Carey's Force had been created while was on leave in England!

Continue to Villers Bretonneux.

Just before you enter the town there is a marker stone on the left, indicating the closest that the Germans got to Amiens and held for 24 hours, though on 25 April the German tank thrust burst through the village and down the hill towards Amiens where it was stopped and sent back (see below).

In the centre of Villers Bretonneux turn right and follow signs to the Australian Memorial. Park.

AUSTRALIAN NATIONAL MEMORIAL AND FOUILLOY CWGC CEMETERY Unveiled by King George VI on 22 July 1938 the memorial consists of a wall carrying the names of almost 11,000 Australians who have no known grave and a 100 ft high central tower which can be climbed. The superintendent who lives alongside the cemetery has a key to the tower. If you intend to climb up it, allow an extra 20 minutes. The memorial was designed by Sir Edwin Lutyens and due to delays occasioned by lack of funds it was the last of the Dominion memorials to be built. The original plan for the memorial had included a 90 ft high archway, but presumably this was omitted for financial reasons. The memorial bears the scars of Second World War bullets and the top of the tower was struck by lightning on 2 June 1978 and renovated extensively. By facing directly away from the Memorial on a clear day, the Cathedral in Amiens can be seen. How near the Germans came!

Return to the crossroads with the N29 and continue straight across. Turn right at the first junction on to Rue Victoria and on the left, after the next junction, is Villers Bretonneux School. Stop.

VILLERS BRETONNEUX SCHOOL The links between Villers Bretonneux and Australia have been strong since the end of the First World War. Until recent years veterans regularly returned on Anzac Day. The town is twinned with Robinvale and reciprocal visits are frequently made. In the Town Hall is a permanent exhibition which includes a kangaroo. In 1993 four new memorials were planned in the town by the Australian Government – at the National Memorial; by the Town Hall; in the main square and at the school. These plaques, including a 'sister' version at the Australian War Memorial in Canberra, were designed to include a relief map of the battle area and to emphasize the youth connections between France and Australia. Funding for the plaques came from sponsors whose names could be placed at the bottom right-hand corner. A similar project placed plaques in Gallipoli over the 75th Anniversary of the ANZAC landings. The school was rebuilt with the funds raised by the schoolchildren of Victoria, Australia, and even today the schoolchildren of Villers Bretonneux learn 'Waltzing Matilda'. Above the school is a museum, recently much improved with funds from the *Département* who encourage the town's ambition to become a major focal point for remembrance of the First World War. Opening times, which are as yet somewhat irregular, are posted on the door. Outside the school is an obelisk recording the story of its building project.

Return to the crossroads of the N29 and D23 and turn left. Continue through the town and downhill to the crossroads with the D168E. Turn left towards Cachy and immediately before the village turn sharp left on the D168 towards Villers Bretonneux. Drive for 500 yards and stop.

TANK VERSUS TANK   In the fields to your left and to your right on the slope up towards Villers Bretonneux the world's first tank versus tank battle took place. At 0345 hours on 24 April 1918 German artillery began an HE and gas shell barrage on British positions in the town and on the feature on which the Australian National Memorial now sits. The attack began at 0600 hours and, led by 13 A7V tanks, the Germans inflicted heavy casualties on the East Lancashires of 8th Division in the area around the railway station. By 0930 four A7Vs were making their way across the fields towards where you now are. Earlier that morning three British Mark IV tanks, lagered in the wood which you drove through from the N29, were ordered to move to this area forward of Cachy. They too were moving this way at about 0930. Commanding one of the British tanks was Lt Frank Mitchell and in his book, *Tank Warfare*, he told what happened:

'Opening a loophole I looked out. There, some three hundred yards away, a round squat-looking monster was advancing, behind it came waves of infantry, and farther away to the left and right crawled two more of these armed tortoises . . .. So we had met our rivals at last. Suddenly a hurricane of hail pattered against our steel wall, filling the interior with myriads of sparks and flying splinters . . . the Jerry tank had treated us to a broadside of armour-piercing bullets . . . then came our first casualty . . . the rear Lewis gunner was wounded in both legs by an armour-piercing bullet which tore through our steel plate . . . the roar of our engine, the nerve-wracking rat-tat-tat of our machine guns blazing at the Bosche infantry and the thunderous boom of the 6 pounders all bottled up in that narrow space filled our ears with tumult while the fumes of petrol and cordite half stifled us.' Mitchell's tank attempted two shots at one of the A7Vs. Both hit, but seemed ineffective. Then the gunner tried again 'with great deliberation and hit for the third time. Through a loophole I saw the tank heel over to one side then a door opened and out ran the crew. We had knocked the monster out.'

Before the day was over seven of the new British Whippet tanks charged into the German infantry and the advance stopped. The Germans however were now poised on the high ground. If Amiens were to be saved they had to be moved. That evening in darkness relieved only by the light from burning buildings in the town the Australian 15th Brigade north of the N29 and the Australian 13th Brigade where you are now attacked either side of Villers Bretonneux. In the morning of 25 April, three years to the day after the Gallipoli landings, the two brigades met in the area of the marker stone. The German effort was over. Frank

Mitchell, who won the MC for his part in the tank action, was particularly proud that this first tank versus tank encounter was won by his tank, No.1 Tank of 1st Section, A Company of the 1st Tank Battalion. When the war was over, Mitchell, tongue in cheek, recalling that the tanks were called 'landships' and that naval crews are entitle to prize money for sinking enemy ships, applied for prize money for himself and his crew for having knocked out an enemy 'landship'. The War Office descended into a puzzled silence and then turned his application down.

General Sir Hubert Gough (whose, father, uncle and younger brother were all awarded the VC) was never given another command. His only military action came with the Home Guard in the Second World War. Controversy about his 1918 performance continued until his death in 1963, aged 92. He never pressed for the enquiry that Haig had promised but remained convinced that in time he would be vindicated and recognized as the saviour of the Fifth Army. Today he is seen as having been in the wrong place at the wrong time.

MAP 18	THE AMERICAN FIRST ARMY OFFENSIVE AT ST. MIHIEL
	12–16 SEPTEMBER 1918

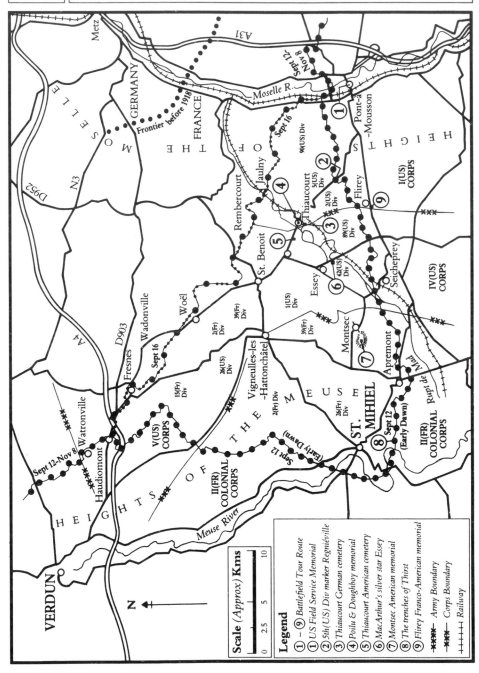

Scale (Approx) Kms

0   2.5   5   10

N

Legend

① – ⑨ *Battlefield Tour Route*
① *US Field Service Memorial*
② *5tht (US) Div marker Regniéville*
③ *Thiaucourt German cemetery*
④ *Poilu & Doughboy memorial*
⑤ *Thiaucourt American cemetery*
⑥ *MacArthur's silver star Essey*
⑦ *Montsec American memorial*
⑧ *The trenches of Thirst*
⑨ *Flirey Franco-American memorial*
✳✳✳ *Army Boundary*
✳✳ *Corps Boundary*
++++ *Railway*

ST MIHIEL

12 SEPTEMBER 1918

'Marshal Pétain . . . sent down to the First Army, two
days after the battle, about 800 French officers and
NCOs to see for themselves how the American troops
had succeeded in crossing this hitherto considered
impassable obstacle (barbed wire) . . .. A French officer
told me afterwards that the evidence on the ground
convinced him that our infantry had walked over the
wire, but he thought perhaps they were assisted in this
remarkable performance by the size of their feet.'
George C. Marshall, Memoirs.

'When the word finally went back to the United States
that I had been wounded it said I had been hit in the
Toul sector. I had to be sure everyone realised this was
a section of France, not my anatomy.'
Mark Clark.

SUMMARY OF THE BATTLE

On 12 September 1918 the American First Army under General 'Black Jack'
Pershing carried out its first offensive. More than half a million Americans
supported by some 110,000 French attacked and within 36 hours reduced the
German St Mihiel Salient. American losses were about 7,000, German 20,000.

OPENING MOVES

America declared war against Germany on 6 April 1917 and on 26 May 1917
Major General John J. Pershing, who got his nickname 'Black Jack' from having
commanded negro troops in the Spanish-American War, became C-in-C of the
American Expeditionary Force (AEF). In response to urgent appeals from the
French and the British, the Americans gathered together Regular units to form
the 1st Division and sent it to France. The main body arrived at St Nazaire on
26 June 1917, two weeks after Pershing and his staff landed at Boulogne.

In October 1917, preliminary training over, one battalion from each regiment
in the 1st Division was sent into the line with the French for ten days' experi-

ence. The sector chosen, Toul, had been a quiet one for three years and on 23 October 1917 a battery of the 6th Field Artillery fired the first American Army round of the war. There were by now four American divisions in France – all opposite the St Mihiel Salient in Lorraine, each about 28,000 strong. There was the 1st Regular, the 2nd (mostly Marine), the 26th, a National Guard force mainly from Massachusetts and the 42nd 'Rainbow', with men from every state in the Union. Its Chief of Staff was Douglas MacArthur.

Pershing made clear to the Allies that he did not want his troops to go into battle until they were fully trained, and that they would remain under American command and fight as such. It was a policy he may have inherited from the King of France when he sent troops to help George Washington to fight the British at Yorktown in 1781. Pershing was a hard taskmaster and he emphasized to staff and soldiers alike that they were training for open warfare and not for life in the trenches. By the end of the year there were about 180,000 American troops in France but they had not yet fought together in large groups. On 20 April 1918 the first 'American' contest took place. It may well have been designed by the Germans to try to undermine the confidence of the untried Americans. Early in the morning behind a divisional barrage some 2,000 Germans emerged from their positions around Montsec (see Map 18) and headed towards the Dough-boys of the 26th (Yankee) Division. The fighting centred around the village of Seicheprey 5 miles east of Montsec. The Germans took it that day. The Yankees took it back the day after. They had proved that they could fight, although they lost many men as prisoners. All the Doughboys (who probably got their name from their days in the Mexican Wars, when their uniforms got covered with white adobe dust) needed was more experience.

A month later on 28 May, the 28th Infantry Regiment of the 1st Division attacked German positions at Cantigny, 20 miles south of Amiens. They took the village in less than an hour and with the help of the 18th Infantry held on to it through 48 hours of German counter-attacks. It was a clear victory for the Americans in France. Those Doughboys who fought at Seicheprey and Cantigny saw themselves as an élite – just as did the 'out since Mons' Tommy.

However, Pershing's 'All American Force' concept was not holding firm and, with the breakthrough of German forces at the Chemin des Dâmes on 27 May in Operation Blücher, part of the Kaiser's Offensive, he was persuaded to allow his five divisions to be used as supports in the Marne area. Co-operation between the Allies was the name of the game and Pershing allowed his troops to cement the tired bricks of French divisions. On 31 May the US 3rd Division stopped the Germans at Château-Thierry. On 4 June the US 2nd Division halted the enemy at Belleau Wood and recaptured it on 25 June. Pershing, though, wanted his men back. He had had in mind, since the entry of America into the war, that the first offensive by the American Army should be against the St Mihiel Salient. By July 1918 there were one million Doughboys in France and their C-in-C wanted to bring them all under his control. At an Allied Commanders' conference on 24 July his proposal to reduce the salient in order to cut the Metz–Maubeuge railway was agreed as a 'local attack'. On 10 August Foch, the Allied Supreme Commander since Doullens on 26 March, finally gave into Pershing's frequent and forceful demands that there should be an American 1st Army. It was a supreme, dreamed-for moment for Pershing. Five days later he upgraded the St Mihiel plan to a 15-division assault designed to 'strike the heaviest blow possible and secure the maximum results'.

On 30 August Foch tried to scale down the American attack and he and Pershing had a head-on disagreement. Foch wanted to split the Americans in two, putting one half with the French in the Argonne and the other in Champagne. Pershing flatly refused. He would agree to fight in the Argonne, he said, but as an American Army under American control. Even so, before that his Army would have its first battle, and that would be a limited offensive at St Mihiel to pinch out the German salient. Foch had no alternative but to agree, and he did so formally on 2 September. The Doughboys had ten days to get ready for their first fight in an all-American operation.

WHAT HAPPENED

The Americans were spread from the Channel to Switzerland. Six divisions were with the French on the Aisne, two with the BEF at Ypres and others just arriving or training behind the lines. Pershing set about assembling them.

The German-occupied salient, triangular in shape, lay about 20 miles southeast of Verdun. Its base was roughly 25 miles between Pont à Mousson and Verdun and it pointed about 15 miles into allied territory to the little town of St Mihiel. Since their arrival in 1914 the Germans had constructed considerable trench, wire and bunker defences. The staff planning for the attack was done by Colonel George C. Marshall and the idea was to hit both flanks of the triangle with overwhelming force. The plan called for the main assault by the American I and IV Corps to be against the southern face and three hours later a second diversionary attack on the western side by the US V Corps together with the French 15th Colonial Division. At 0100 hours on 12 September 3,000 guns opened fire with HE, following up as the light improved, with smoke. At 0500 the main assault went in led by French Renault tanks and low flying aircraft. So intense was the bombardment that the German Crown Prince said that 'it exceeded anything we had known at Verdun and on the Somme'. The American advance through the wire was extraordinarily rapid. Just after dawn the following day elements of 26th Division from the western assault made contact at Vigneulles-les-Hattonchâtel with men of the 1st Division from the southern assault. The salient had been pinched off and the 1st Army had taken some 16,000 prisoners and over 440 guns. Two days later Pétain's officers arrived to try to work out why Americans had done so well.

The Battlefield Tour

The tour begins at Pont à Mousson at the south-eastern corner of the salient and crosses the jump-off lines in the US 1st Corps area to the Thiaucourt German and American cemeteries. It goes on to the American memorial on Montsec then to the remarkable German trench lines in the Aprémont Forest, ending at the Franco-American memorial in Flirey.

Total time   4 hours 30 minutes

Total distance   52 miles

Map   IGN 11 Nancy/Metz/Luxembourg 1:100,000

Pont à Mousson is easily reached from either of two signed exits from the Metz–Nancy autoroute. Cross the river east to west into the central square. Stop.

PONT À MOUSSON   Almost central in the square (which is surrounded by picturesque arcades) is a memorial fountain in Renaissance style. It is a reconstruction of the original fountain, damaged during the war, which was erected by the American Field Service after the war as a memorial to its dead. The Field Service was a group of volunteer ambulance sections that joined the French Forces shortly after the war began (cf. Ernest Hemingway's *Farewell to Arms*) later reinforced by vehicle sections after America entered the war. When the AEF reached Europe the strength of the Field Service was about 2,000. At the end of 1917 most personnel were enlisted or commissioned into the American Army but the Service did not serve with US forces. On the Western Front it remained with the French until the end of the war. There is also a memorial plaque to nurses of the Field Service in St. George's Memorial Church in Ypres in Belgium.

The town was taken by the Germans in 1914 but quickly recaptured by the French and held until the end of the war despite regular shelling by German artillery.

Take the D958 west out of Pont à Mousson passing a French Military Cemetery on the right in Montauville and then fork right on the D3 to Régniéville. Stop at the next crossroads with the D75 where there is a deteriorating marker column on the right.

RÉGNIÉVILLE   The village no longer exists. It was one of a considerable number that were so utterly destroyed during the war that they were never rebuilt. By continuing on foot for 100 yards over the crossroads in the direction of travel, remains of the old village churchyard may be found in the wood to the right. The wooden marker at the cross roads is one of many put up by the American 5th Division shortly after the Armistice. Very few survive, despite an attempt in the late 1980s by the superintendent of the US Meuse-Argonne Cemetery to have them listed and maintained. It is understood that the American Battle Monuments Commission is considering a renovation programme.

The crossroads going left and right run over or beside the line of the American I Corps forward trenches. Your direction of travel is the direction of attack towards the German lines barely 400 yards up the road. The 5th Division led off here and, despite fierce machine-gun fire from the woods, broke through the barbed wire, crossed the enemy trenches and by nightfall had moved three miles up the road towards Thiaucourt.

Continue on the D3 to Thiaucourt village and immediately after passing under the railway bridge turn left and follow the signs to the German cemetery.

THIAUCOURT GERMAN CEMETERY   Facing across the road and away from the cemetery it may be possible to see the hill of Montsec in the distance about nine miles away and the white American memorial surmounting it continues to be a good orientation marker for the rest of the tour.

The cemetery was extensively renovated during the 1980s and most of the grave markers are black crosses. Here and there between the crosses headstones mark the resting place of Jewish soldiers. More than 8,700 named soldiers are buried with a further 2,970 in a mass grave. At the bottom left of the cemetery some isolated old stones mark the grave of soldiers from the 1870 conflict and beyond them is a row of individual 1914–18 headstones and opposite them a plinth upon which a German eagle once stood. The villagers here, having been invaded in 1870, 1914 and 1940 were not prepared to be overlooked by this symbol of German might and destroyed it. Even half a century after the end of the Second World War the gardeners who look after the cemetery are not popular in the village and there have been instances of vandalism of the mass grave.

Return to the village and continue up hill.

THIAUCORT POILU–DOUGHBOY MEMORIAL   This is on the left as the roads begins to rise. The French Poilu and the American Doughboy are shaking hands. It is a most photogenic memorial, its small surrounding garden always immaculately tended, and well worth a stop. The 2nd Division entered the village on the afternoon of the first day of the battle and dug in to the north of it for the night. The village was an important link in the German railway supply system and one of the main objectives of the US I Corps which captured eleven field guns here loaded on to railway flats.

Continue out of the village to the American Military cemetery on the left. Stop.

AMERICAN ST MIHIEL (THIAUCOURT) CEMETERY   Like all American cemeteries in Europe this one has a resident English-speaking superintendent who has an office in the cemetery and keeps regular opening hours. There is a comfortable visitors' room, with leaflets about the cemetery, the cemetery registers, visitors' book and toilets.

Each one of the 4,153 soldiers buried here has a white Italian marble headstone – either a Latin cross or a Jewish star of David. In the centre of the cemetery is a large sundial in the form of an eagle. At the end of the north-west axis from the eagle is a sculpture by Paul Manship showing a typical young American officer in field uniform. The main architectural feature of the cemetery, designed by

Thomas H. Ellet, of New York, is the memorial building marked by two flags at the far end of the main avenue. On the left within the peristyle is a chapel with altar and beautiful mosaic walls featuring the national colours of America and France and the Angel of Victory, with Doves of Peace. To the right, again through bronze doors with striking 'Doughboy's head' handles, is a room with a magnificent coloured marble wall map illustrating the St Mihiel campaign. The scale of the map is 1:100,000. The cemetery is marked upon it and you can readily follow the route you have driven and also the route you have yet to drive. On the end walls, carved in black marble panels are the names of those soldiers missing with no known grave. Beyond the building Montsec is visible on a clear day.

Continue past the cemetery to Béney-en-Woevre and turn left on to the D904 to Essey village. In the centre turn right on to the D28.

ESSEY VILLAGE The main square is named after Colonel Driant, the commander in the Bois des Caures at the opening of the Verdun battle. The village is in the centre of what was the area for the 42nd (Rainbow) Division. One of the division's two brigades, the 84th, was commanded by Brigadier General Douglas MacArthur. He went over the top with his men and in or around this village he met Major George Patton. Both remained upright as if daring the other to acknowledge the danger of German artillery fire and MacArthur later claimed that Patton did flinch briefly and that he said to him, 'Don't worry Major, you never hear the one that gets you.' MacArthur's front line leadership here earned him his fifth silver star for gallantry in action.

Continue to Richécourt and there turn right on to the D119 and follow signs to the American Memorial at Montsec. Park.

MONTSEC AMERICAN MEMORIAL This hill offers visibility over much of the Salient and observers on it directed German artillery fire. The American fire plan included a great deal of smoke around Montsec in order to blind the enemy. The hill itself was honeycombed with tunnels and protected by belts of barbed wire. Traces of the trench systems still remain around the memorial.

The memorial, which commemorates the capture of the St Mihiel Salient and other American operations, is a circular colonnade – a classical design like the Jefferson memorial in Washington and strikingly similar to the First World War memorial in Atlantic City. It was inaugurated in September 1931, when many relatives travelled from the United States. Within the circle, set on a stone plinth, is a bronze relief map laid out to match the ground and three small Sèvres porcelain illustrative plates. It is totally possible, on a clear day, to match the map to the view, and set into the floor below the columns are the points of the compass. Carved in and around the memorial are the names of the French and American units that took part in the operation, the names of villages liberated by the Americans, battle honours and notices in French and English, including one that explains how the memorial was damaged in the Second World War.

In good visibility the American cemetery that you visited earlier may be seen across the water to the north–east, though, because of the trees on the hill, you may need to stand in the car park to see it. In the far distance to the south and swinging westwards are the heights of the Meuse. St. Mihiel is due west of here.

George Patton commanded the American-manned tanks used in the operation and 26 years later (but for 9 days) as Commander of the liberating 3rd Army in 1944, he came back. As always he was chafing at what he saw as delays in advancing.

'Montsec has a huge monument to our dead,' he wrote. 'I could not help but think that our delay in pushing forward would probably result . . . in the erection of many other such monuments'. There was little delay in 1918. The Americans had a precise task at St Mihiel. Their next offensive was almost upon them and they had precious little time to prepare for it.

Drive to the bottom of Montsec and turn sharp right (not back through the village) onto the D12 via Loupmont to Aprémont.

APREMONT   Near the church is a memorial fountain to those Americans who fell here. It was donated by Holyoke, Massachusetts.

Continue past the church north-west on the D907 in the direction of St Mihiel. After passing on the right a memorial to Frenchmen shot by the Germans in the Second World War and the entrance to a military style encampment (there is a German cemetery within it) the road bends sharply right. Signed left up a small road are 'les Tranchées de la Soif'. Follow the signs and park at the first opportunity. Put on wellies if it is wet and be prepared for a slippery but fascinating twenty minutes walk.

APREMONT FOREST MEMORIALS AND TRENCHES   The trench system here is probably the most comprehensive 'real-state' complex to be found anywhere on the Western front. It was constructed by the Germans and the detailed earthworks of front-line support and communication trenches are locked together by concrete shelters and command posts and the whole wooded area is peppered by shell holes. At the beginning of the walk is an obelisk commemorating the achievement of the French VIII Corps in taking this position and at about the halfway point of a circular walk that brings you back to where you started is a memorial commemorating the bravery of a small number of French soldiers who were cut off here and probably gave the area its name, 'Trenches of Thirst'. To the right of the path that continues the walk past the memorial and back to the start point, some 20 ft into the woods is a well-preserved line of deep concrete bunkers.

Return to the main D907.

To the left is St Mihiel which was captured by the Germans on 24 September 1914 but which was not attacked during the offensives in 1918. The Germans abandoned it and it was entered by the French 26th Division on 13 September.

Turn right. Go back through Aprémont on the D907 via Bouconville to the D958. Continue in the direction of Pont à Mousson to the memorial on the right in Flirey village.

149

FLIREY Before entering the village you passed the remnants of railway embankments and it was in those that the American 89th Division had its headquarters. The village was just behind the assault line, the attack going from your right to left. The American 1st Army's achievement was quite remarkable and came from the offensive attitude encouraged by Pershing, the energy and enthusiasm of the soldiers, the thorough and professional staff work and the intricate co-operation of infantry, tanks and aircraft. Some 2,000 allied aircraft under 'Billy' Mitchell, who was to become well known in the Second World War, provided air support. That Ludendorff had ordered the gradual evacuation of the salient on 8 September and that some of the heavier German weapons had been withdrawn is, however, relevant. Doubtless the attitude of the German defender was less stubborn since he knew that withdrawal was imminent but as the memorial, erected by the people of Lorraine shows, the French were in no doubt about the capabilities of their American allies. The Germans also knew that the game was almost over. In their first all-American battle the Doughboys had 'walked over the wire', On the side of the memorial are listed the American divisions that fought in the area. By the end of the following day, 13 September, the Americans had pinched off the salient. Pershing's faith in an all-American army was vindicated. It was his 58th birthday.

THE AMERICAN MEUSE-ARGONNE OFFENSIVE
26 SEPTEMBER–14 OCTOBER 1918

'There is a general opinion that the Americans went
into the Argonne and ended the war. This is simply not
true. From September 26 until November 1 the AEF
had a very rough time,'
Henry Berry, Make the Kaiser Dance

'The only way to begin is to commence.'
George C. Marshall, Memoirs

SUMMARY OF THE BATTLE

On 26 September 1918 under the overall strategic direction of Marshal Foch the Allies began a co-ordinated pincer attack against the Germans on the western front between Ypres and Verdun. The American 1st Army as the southern pincer fought along the heights of the Meuse and into the forest of the Argonne. It was a bloody affair. By the time of the Armistice the Americans had lost some 117,000 men, almost 20 per cent more than the Germans.

OPENING MOVES

On 24 June 1918 Pershing, Pétain and Haig met with Foch and he outlined his ideas for a grand September offensive along the front from Ypres to Verdun. The Americans were to be in the south around Verdun, the French in the middle and the British opposite and south of Ypres. Meanwhile, while the great affair was being organised, a number of smaller offensives were to be launched. One opened on the Somme on 8 August when the British Fourth Army (containing Australians and Canadians) and the French First Army came out of the early morning fog on to von der Marwitz's 2nd Army. By the end of the day advances of up to 8 miles had been made and the Germans had lost some 27,000 men. The official German account described the day as 'the greatest defeat which the German army has suffered since the beginning of the war'. Ludendorff wrote later, 'August 8th was the blackest day of the German Army in the history of this war.'

Another of the 'smaller' offensives was the American action at St. Mihiel. Foch had wanted to dissolve the Americans into his master plan but Pershing

MAP 19	THE AMERICAN MEUSE – ARGONNE OFFENSIVE 26 SEPTEMBER – 1 OCTOBER 1918

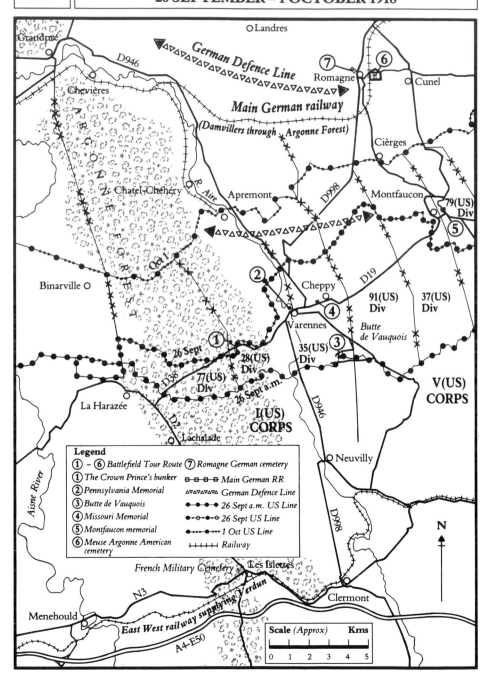

Legend

① – ⑥ *Battlefield Tour Route* ⑦ *Romagne German cemetery*
① *The Crown Prince's bunker* 🔲🔲🔲🔲 *Main German RR*
② *Pennsylvania Memorial* △▽△▽△▽△ *German Defence Line*
③ *Butte de Vauquois* •–•–•–• *26 Sept a.m. US Line*
④ *Missouri Memorial* •–○–•–○ *26 Sept US Line*
⑤ *Montfaucon memorial* •••••• *1 Oct US Line*
⑥ *Meuse Argonne American cemetery* +++++ *Railway*

refused. Foch backed down but Pershing had to compromise too by agreeing that his 1st Army wold not push on past the base of the salient and that his objectives would be limited so that it could then take part in the master plan.

Meanwhile, following the 'black day', Ludendorff offered the Kaiser his resignation. It was refused. However, communist agitation and strikes were causing major difficulties in Germany and by the middle of August the Kaiser and Ludendorff were speaking of the need to sue for peace. Yet Ludendorff managed to withdraw his forces away from the constant allied attacks without letting the Allies break through. It was a trying time. By the first week in September the Germans had lost all the territory that they had won in the March offensive and Ludendorff began to show signs of strain, swinging wildly from optimism to pessimism. His stepson Erich, a flyer, had been killed on 21 March and Ludendorff had had to identify the exhumed body. Personal and national tensions were testing him to breaking point.

Foch's master plan was almost a mirror image of the German March offensive, with massive blows planned to take place at different times and different places along the Western Front. Four were planned altogether to be launched on consecutive days. The first would be a joint Franco-American affair on 26 September 1918 which the Doughboys would call 'The Mews Argonne', but the Americans had to move a long way from St Mihiel. It would be no easy task to move them, let alone launch the offensive. Four days before the battle of St Mihiel began the First Army Operations Officer, Lt. Colonel George C. Marshall, was told to prepare the movement order to have the Army moved away from St Mihiel and in position for an attack on 25 September south of the Argonne forest. He had never prepared such an order before.

WHAT HAPPENED

George Marshall later wrote, 'About 10 minutes consideration made it apparent that to reach the new front in time to deploy for a battle on 25 September would require many of these troops to get under way on the evening of the first day of the St Mihiel battle . . .. This appalling proposition rather disturbed my equilibrium and I went out on the canal to have a walk while thinking it over . . .. After half an hour of meditation [I] returned to the office still without any solution . . . I called a stenographer and started the dictation of the preliminary order . . . I started with the proposition that the only way to begin is to commence . . . In less than an hour I . . . had completed the order.'

Marshall's order worked. By midday on the second day of St Mihiel troop movements to the Meuse-Argonne were under way. There were only three usable roads over which to move half a million men, 2,000 guns and more than 900,000 tons of supplies and ammunition. Yet it was done, and almost entirely by night. Three army corps, each with three divisions in line and one in reserve were in position and ready to go. The fire support was to be provided by 2,700 guns and some 190 small French tanks, 140 manned by Americans, would accompany the infantry.

At 0230 hours on 26 September the opening bombardment began. Three hours later the First Army went over the top in dense fog. This was no repeat of St Mihiel. Three of the divisions had never been in combat before, five had not completed their training. Like Marshall with his movement order, they had not done anything like it before. The ground over which they had to advance was churned as if by a giant's plough from bombardments as far back as Verdun. Thick belts of wire and tangled woods made almost impassable by fallen trees contributed to a growing confusion. The energy and enthusiasm of the troops took them through the first German positions but their lack of experience prevented them from fully exploiting their gains. Over the next two days the Americans continued to move forward but German resistance was stiffening. Casualties were heavy and communications broke down. Ludendorff might have had his doubts about victory, but the German soldier was fighting well. On 29 September the Americans went on the defensive in order to reorganize. The French Fourth Army, which had attacked with the US First Army, did little better.

By 1 October the advance stopped between 7 and 10 miles into the German lines. Altogether the French and the Americans had taken 18,000 prisoners but Foch was disappointed and tried to reinforce the Argonne offensive with another French army. Pershing would not agree. The Americans began attacking again on 4 October and while they made gains Foch commented that they were 'inferior to what it was permissible to expect'. In mid-October Prime Minister Clémenceau wrote to Foch about what he called the Americans 'marking time' and Pershing's 'invincible obstinacy', and canvassed Foch's opinion on whether he should 'tell President Wilson the truth and the whole truth concerning the situation of the American troops.' Foch did not agree with Clémenceau, having, as he said, 'a more comprehensive knowledge of the difficulties encountered by the American Army.' In a written reply Foch kept to the bare essentials and ended his letter, 'There is no denying the magnitude of the effort made by the American Army. After attacking at St. Mihiel on September 12th, it attacked in the Argonne on the 26th. From September 26th to October 20th its losses in battle were 5,158 men – in exchange for small gains on a narrow front, it is true, but over particularly difficult country and in the face of serious resistance by the enemy.'

THE BATTLEFIELD TOUR

The tour begins at les Islettes, 20 miles west of Verdun and passes the French Military cemetery there before entering the Argonne Forest. Subsequently it visits the Pennsylvania memorial at Varennes, the Butte de Vauquois, the

American memorial at Montfaucon, the American Meuse-Argonne cemetery and the German cemetery at Romagne, where it ends.

Total distance   38 miles
Total time   4 hours 30 minutes
Map   IGN 10 Reims/Verdun 1:100,000

Take the Ste. Ménéhould exit from the A4 Autoroute de l'Est and drive east on the N3 to les Islettes and the crossroads with the D2. Turn left here and follow signs to the French cemetery. Stop.

LES ISLETTES   The Germans entered the village on 3 September 1914 but were driven out two weeks later. They made continuous efforts to retake Les Islettes which sits on the important east–west railway from Verdun, but failed. It became a major supply and stores centre and was on the French-American Army boundary at the start of the battle. The cemetery was created as a concentration cemetery in the region of la Biesme. It has 2,206 named burials from the Argonne battlefield and covers an area of 1,100 square metres. There is no mass grave. The cemetery was relandscaped and the graves remarked in 1957.

Continue on the D2 into the Argonne Forest.

The road is heading directly towards the German front line. To a first approximation the French Fourth Army is on the left and the American First Army on and to right of the road for about 19 miles to the east.

After Lachalade turn right on the D38 signed to Varennes.

About half a mile up the road you cross the front line of 26 September (see Map 19).

A further 3 miles on the country becomes particularly steep and wooded and the road bends dramatically right as a track leads backwards to your left. It may be signed 'Abris du Kronprinz'. The location is marked on the IGN map. Follow the signs by car if dry and if the barbed-wire fences have been removed. (They come and go.) If wet you'll need 4-wheel drive. It is a confusing journey but if you persevere you should arrive at the remains of a concrete bunker after about half a mile.

THE ABRIS DU KRONPRINZ   This structure with its styled 'bay window' is said to have been used as an HQ by the Crown Prince. It sits at about the limit of the first day's advance by the Americans and on the boundary of the 28th and 77th Divisions. It was finally taken on 28 September and subsequently used as 77th Division HQ. The area was also known as 'Champ Mahaut.'

Return to the D38 and continue towards Varennes.

As the road leaves the forest there is dramatic and abrupt evidence of the change in terrain. Many Americans believe that the Meuse-Argonne battle took place in the forest. It did not. To attack an entrenched enemy in such countryside would have been folly. The plan was that the French Fourth Army would attack northwards along the western edge of the forest and the First Army northwards along the eastern edge where you now are. The forest is cut by the valley of the River Aire at Grandpré about 8 miles north of here and the idea was that the

French and Americans would meet there and in so doing pinch out the Germans in the forest without having to assault them head on. There was fighting in the Argonne, of course, but the main effort was made some 5 miles further east around Montfaucon. The Americans eventually reached Grandpré on 14 October after many days of fierce and protracted struggle.

The incredible exploits of America's most decorated First World War soldier, Sergeant Alvin C. York (the Audie Murphy of his day) took place nearby. A rip-roaring, hell-raiser from Tennessee, York was converted to become a God-fearing, non-smoking teetotaller – almost a conscientious objector. Yet on 8 October York, serving as an Acting Corporal with the 82nd Division, discovered that as his senior officers and NCOs were progressively killed, he was in charge of his platoon, sent to attack the far flank of the German position.

York decided to use Tennessee turkey shooting procedures and started, one by one, to pick off the German machine-gunners opposing them from the rear, killing about fourteen. He then called on the remainder to surrender, eighty men did, and as York marched them in, by the expedient of holding his Colt to the German Major's head and forcing him to order all enemy they passed to surrender, his bag mounted to an astonishing 132. He was awarded the Medal of Honor and was much used in fund-raising and recruiting drives in the U.S.A. On the centenary of his birth, the State of Tennessee erected a memorial to Sergeant York in front of the Town Hall of Chatel Chehery (see Map 19). Several of his relatives attended the unveiling.

Another American legend of the First World War was the story of 'The Lost Battalion', which in actual fact was neither a battalion, nor lost! According to Major General Robert Alexander, Commander of 77th Division, 'On 3 October a detachment of 550 men (comprising elements of the 306th Machine Gun Bn, 307th and 308th Inf) under the command of Major Charles W. Whittlesey, were cut off from the remainder of 77th Div (New York's Own) and surrounded by a superior number of the enemy near Charlevaux in the Forest d'Argonne, from the morning of October 3, 1918 to the night of October 7, 1918. Without food for more than 100 hours, harassed continuously by machine gun, rifle, trench mortar and grenade fire, Major Whittlesey's command, with undaunted spirit successfully met and repulsed daily violent attacks by the enemy. They held the position which had been reached by supreme efforts under orders received for an advance, until communication was re-established with friendly troops. When relief finally came, approximately 194 officers and men were able to walk out of the position. Officers and men killed numbered 107. Although three Congressional Medals of Honor were awarded for this action – to Major George G. Murtry, Captain Nelson M. Holderman and to Whittlesey himself, Whittlesey was never able to overcome his feelings of guilt for the loss of so many of his men and in 1921 he committed suicide. A memorial to the 'Lost Battalion' was erected at Charlevaux Mill on the D66 (see Map 19).

Continue into Varennes past the local history museum on the left (irregular opening hours) and immediately after there is a large memorial on the left.

PENNSYLVANIA STATE MEMORIAL, VARENNES The area is maintained as a park, at the far end of which is a funeral urn capping a symbolic eternal flame and flanked by two colonnades. Varennes was taken by midday on 26 September by the 35th Division and a number of tanks led by Major George Patton. The town was on the divisional boundary with the 28th Division who fought on the lower ground overlooked by the memorial and indicated by the orientation markers. Many men from Pennsylvania served in the 28th Division. On the 28th Division side of the hill scramblers can find the remains of bunkers and tunnel entrances, but it is safer to take our word for it.

The town is famous as the place where Louis XVI and Marie Antoinette were taken by the French revolutionaries in June 1791. They were spotted in their carriage at Ste Ménehould (where you may have come off the motorway) by M. Drouet the local postmaster who rode through the Argonne Forest to Varennes to rouse the populace. The fugitives were arrested at the Bras d'Or Inn near the bridge. The inn does not exist today but a memorial plaque is on the house on the site.

Continue down the hill and cross the River Aire. Turn right before the church on to the D38 signed to Avocourt. After 1½ miles turn right on to a small road signed to Butte de Vauquois. Stop in the parking area and walk to the top.

BUTTE DE VAUQUOIS At the top is a lantern monument to 'Les Combattants', the soldiers who fought underground here. Relics of barbed wire and metal spikes of *cheval de frise* (named from anti-cavalry spikes used in the 1594 Siege of Groningen in Friesland) can be found. The Germans call them 'Spanish Horseman'. The Tricolore which will probably be flying marks the site of the original village of Vauquois and all around are the craters from the explosions which destroyed it during the years of mine warfare that preceded the attack of 26 September. At that time both American and German front-line trenches crossed the hill and 5 hours before the assault the Americans evacuated theirs and saturated the heights with HE, gas and smoke artillery fire. The 35th Division then pushed forward either side of the hill leaving the defenders and mopped them up later that day.

Return to Varennes and turn right on to the D946. Continue straight on when the D946 turns sharp left and follow signs to Cheppy.

MISSOURI STATE MEMORIAL Before the bridge into Cheppy is the figure of Victory holding a laurel wreath. This represents the State Seal of Missouri and was erected by the State in honour of her sons who died in the Great War. The village became HQ for the 35th, 1st and 42nd Divisions and eventually for V Corps.

Turn right in Cheppy to take D19 (not the D19c) to Montfaucon. Follow signs to the American Monument and park in front of the steps.

MONTFAUCON MEMORIAL   This 180-ft high Doric column of Italian granite with its figure of 'Liberty' on top is the largest American war memorial in Europe. The figure faces the jump-off line of the First American Army on 26 September and from the viewing platform at the top the flag above Fort Douaumont to the south-east at Verdun can be seen. Much of the Meuse–Argonne battlefield is visible, too, of course, including the big American cemetery to the north at Romagne which is the next stop. Around the wall at the top are direction indicators which help orientation, but if you feel able to climb the 234 steps, do not forget to take your binoculars, map and camera. . . . Even in less than perfect visibility the ruins of Montfaucon (Falcon Hill) village can be seen at the base of the column from a bird's eye view. Inside the column at the bottom is a vestibule with American and French flags, a coloured wall map showing the Meuse–Argonne offensive and explanations in French and English. The monument, designed by John Russell Pope, was erected by the US Government and commemorates the 47 days of fighting in the Meuse–Argonne between 26 September and 11 November 1918.

In the woods around the memorials are concrete bunkers and trenches. An expedition on foot is recommended. There are German fortifications which had been prepared over four years from 1914. On 26 September, the first day of the offensive, American troops of the 37th and 79th attacked the hill at about 1800 hours but were unable to take it. The two divisions attacked through a rainstorm at dawn the following day and by midday the Montfaucon was theirs. In the village the State of Ohio built an alms house as a memorial to the 37th Division, many of whose soldiers came from the State.

Opening hours for the memorial are 0900–1200 and 1300–1730 in the summer and 0800–1200 and 1300–1700 in the winter, but it is closed on Mondays, Tuesdays and French holidays.

Drive north on the D104 via Cièrges and follow signs to the American Meuse–Argonne cemetery. Drive to the reception centre and stop.

THE AMERICAN MEUSE–ARGONNE CEMETERY   The centre is manned during normal office hours and contains the Superintendent's office, the cemetery registers, a visitors' book and a comfortable rest room with toilets. Like all such centres, it displays a picture of the President of the United States and an example and brief history of the George Washington medal, now known as the Purple Heart. Please pick up a leaflet showing the plan of the cemetery here, and a copy of Joyce Kilmer's poem 'Trees'. Sgt Kilmer fought with the 165th (Rainbow) Division, was killed in action on July 30 1918 and is buried at Oise-Aisne US Cemetery.

This is the largest American military cemetery in Europe, some 14,200 soldiers being buried here, almost 5,000 more than in the well-known American Second World War Cemetery overlooking OMAHA beach in Normandy. Although most of the burials are of soldiers who fell in the '47 days', in 1922 some were transferred from the Vosges and from occupied Germany. The major works on the cemetery were finished in 1931, the layout being symmetrical about a broad avenue that connects the reception and the chapel that can be seen in the distance at the top of a steep slope. It is possible to drive around the cemetery to the chapel area.

Amongst the white marble crosses and Stars of David there are some Medal of Honour winners, with their names picked out in gold. Another grave of note is that of Frank Luke, the famous 'Balloon Buster', who is buried in Plot A, Row 26, Grave 13.

The chapel has large entrance doors over which bas relief figures represent Grief and Remembrance, and the carved heads of American soldiers are worked into the design of the door's column capitals. Inside is a marble floor at the back of which is an altar within a semi-circle of flags of the allied nations. Subdued and coloured light comes in through the beautiful stained-glass windows which carry the designs of the American divisional and higher formations. On either side of the chapel are loggia carrying the names of nearly 1,000 soldiers missing with no known grave, and in the west loggia is a marble map showing the progress of the Meuse–Argonne campaign and a separate panel carries the names of the missing from the American expedition to Northern Russia. The landscaping of the cemetery, which was approved by General Pershing, began in 1929 and the architectural work was done by York and Sawyer of New York. In the area administered by the Superintendent there some 90 private memorials and details are held in the office.

Leave the cemetery by the opposite gate to the one by which you entered. Continue to the village of Romagne and there follow signs to the 'Deutsche Friedhof'. Stop.

ROMAGNE GERMAN CEMETERY   There is a remarkable visual contrast between this cemetery and the one you have just left – even on a bright day. This one is sad, sombre and dark, with few, if any flowers. The central chapel is heavy and squat, as if trying to hide. The overwhelming impression is one of mourning and regret, while at the American cemetery the message seems to be of pride. It is interesting to reflect upon whether there is a 'right' way to remember and honour the war dead, and whether national characteristics wittingly or unwittingly show through in the chosen designs. French statuary tends to be dramatic, remembering the élan and sacrifice of conflict. British cemeteries strive to remember the individual.

There are 1,412 burials here, one-tenth of the number at the American Meuse–Argonne cemetery that you have just visited.

The village, which was a large German supply depot, was taken by the 32nd Division on the morning of 14 October 1918, and held by them, despite a German counter-attack that night following a heavy gas bombardment. It then became the headquarters of the 90th Division and subsequently III Corps headquarters until the Armistice.

| MAP 20 | **BREAKING THE HINDENBURG LINE** *29 September 1918* |

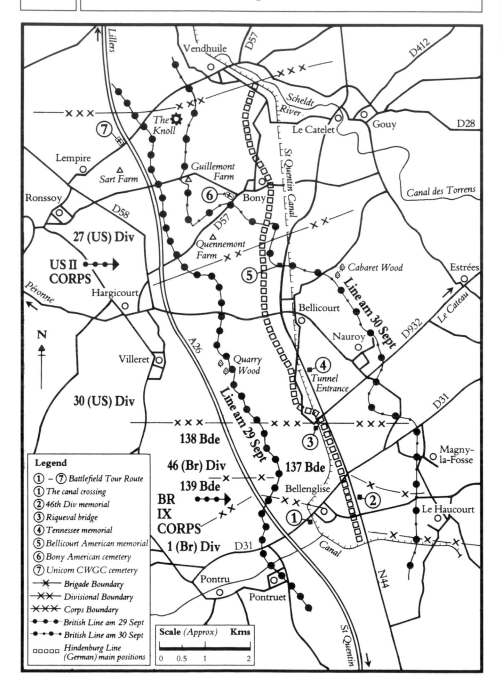

Legend

① – ⑦ *Battlefield Tour Route*
① *The canal crossing*
② *46th Div memorial*
③ *Riqueval bridge*
④ *Tennessee memorial*
⑤ *Bellicourt American memorial*
⑥ *Bony American cemetery*
⑦ *Unicorn CWGC cemetery*

✻✻✻ — *Brigade Boundary*
✻✻✻ — *Divisional Boundary*
✻✻✻ — *Corps Boundary*
•—•—• *British Line am 29 Sept*
•—•—• *British Line am 30 Sept*
ooooo *Hindenburg Line (German) main positions*

Scale *(Approx)* **Kms**

0   0.5   1   2

BREAKING THE HINDENBURG LINE

29 SEPTEMBER 1918

'The British had given us a big half tumbler of rum
before the charge and thank God for that. The
Americans would never have done that . . .. We didn't
actually take the tunnel, the Australians accomplished
that, but we'd softened it up for them.'
Sgt M. D. Cutler, American 27th Division

SUMMARY OF THE BATTLE

At 0555 hours on 29 September the British 46th Division and the American
27th and 30th Divisions set off behind a creeping barrage to attack the
Hindenburg Line defences along the St Quentin Canal tunnel complex. The
46th Division broke the line by nightfall and the Americans, fighting with the
2nd, 3rd and 5th Australian Divisions, did so on the following day.

OPENING MOVES

Since his appointment at Doullens as Supreme Commander, General Foch had
been working towards a co-ordinated joint offensive involving all allied forces.
Neither the Americans nor the Belgians had been present at Doullens (though
the stained-glass memorial window in the Hôtel de Ville where the historic
conference took place suggests an American representative) but they willingly
co-operated with Foch's strategic plan. General Pershing, however, first insisted
upon seeing through his ideas for the St Mihiel Salient attack.

The grand offensive was scheduled to begin over four days and included:

26 Sept.   at 0525 hours the French Fourth and American First Armies would
attack in the Argonne

27 Sept.   at 0520 hours the British First and Third Armies would attack
towards Cambrai

28 Sept.   at 0600 hours King Albert's Army Group would attack in Flanders

29 Sept.   at 0555 hours the British Fourth Army would make a direct assault
on the Hindenburg Line

On 16 March 1917 the Germans began a major withdrawal along a front of 60
miles from Arras to Soissons. As they moved back into the new defensive
positions that they had spent many months preparing, they laid waste to the

countryside much as General Sherman had done in America almost sixty years earlier. The Germans called their new defences the 'Siegfried Line' but probably through an inaccurate debriefing of a German deserter our intelligence sources took the name to be 'Hindenburg Line', and that stuck. Almost exactly halfway along the new line was the major town of St Quentin and worked into the defences to its immediate north were a canal and tunnel complex stretching from Bellenglise to Vendhuille (see Map 20). To break that complex was the task of the British Fourth Army under Rawlinson. It was probably the most formidable part of the whole Hindenburg Line.

WHAT HAPPENED

Starting around the middle of September the 4th Army began a number of local attacks against the Hindenburg Line in order to establish good positions for the major offensive on 29 September. The American 30th Division, which entered the line on 24 September, immediately came under artillery fire and over the next two days was engaged in fighting to complete the elimination of the German outpost line, a process begun by the British.

The American 27th Division came into the line on 25 September to find that the British had been unable to take the ground from which the 27th was supposed to make its assault on 29 September. The strong points in the German position were The Knoll, Guillemont Farm and Quennemont Farm (see Map 20). On 27 September the 27th attempted to take these positions leading off with tanks and artillery at 0530 hours but by the end of the day, with heavy casualties and small bodies of men left isolated across the battlefield, no significant progress had been made. In the confusion of the battle there were many acts of heroism – one in particular merited the Congressional Medal of Honor – America's highest award for gallantry. Lt. William B. Turner took charge of one small group of lost men and single-handed, armed only with a pistol, rushed and destroyed a German machine-gun crew that was firing on them. He then led a charge upon another machine gun and when his pistol ammunition ran out he seized a dead soldier's rifle and using the bayonet led his group across four enemy trenches until he was killed. He is buried at Bony American cemetery, which you will visit.

On the day of the main assault all three forward divisions set off at 0555 hours in fog and under heavy rain clouds. The 30th began at great speed but through lack of experience they did not mop up as they went. Once the Americans had passed over them the Germans came out of deep bunkers and attacked them in the rear. The Australian 5th Division who were supposed to have passed through the Americans now had to retake the ground over which the 30th had already advanced. The situation was extremely complicated because with the Americans somewhere ahead of them and all mixed up with the Germans, the Australians were unable to make full use of their artillery support. The 27th

Division had a particularly hard time to start with because their artillery support, supplied by the British, came down behind, instead of upon, the German strongpoints at The Knoll and Guillemont and Quennemont farms in fear of hitting troops still isolated in the area from the fighting on 27 September. So intense was the German machine-gun fire that the 107th Infantry Regiment had 995 casualties in the day, the heaviest American single day unit loss of the war.

Nevertheless, by noon The Knoll, and the area of the present American cemetery and Quennemont Farm, had fallen to the Americans and the 3rd Australian Division. Early in the afternoon the Australians began to pass through in order to continue the offensive. The combination of vigour and inexperience which dictated the activities of so many of the Doughboys now led them to join up with the Aussies and some men had still not returned to their units two days later. Sir John Monash who was commanding the Australians spoke highly of the Americans and wrote, 'It was found to be a matter of some difficulty to induce these men to withdraw from the fighting and to rejoin their own units so keen were they to continue their advance.' The 27th Division won more Medals of Honor than any other division. The 46th Division forced a crossing of the canal at Bellenglise making use of the early morning fog. The assault brigade, the 137th, was commanded by Brigadier J. V. Campbell, VC who had won his decoration as a Lt Colonel in 1916. The attack, on a three battalion front, was led with great dash, the quality which had earned Campbell his VC and by 0830 hours the division was across the canal and established on the east bank. At the end of the day the Fourth Army had penetrated the strongest part of the Hindenburg Line to a depth of some 6,000 yards and on a frontage of 10,000 yards. It was the beginning of the end for the Hindenburg Line and for Germany. The Armistice was 42 days away.

THE BATTLEFIELD TOUR

The tour begins at Bellenglise with the assault crossing of the St Quentin Canal, moves to the 46th Division Memorial, then to the Riqueval Bridge and the tunnel entrance below the Tennessee Memorial. The next stop is the American National Cemetery at Bony and the tour ends at Unicorn CWGC cemetery.

Total distance   12 miles
Total time   3 hours 20 minutes
Map   IGN 4 Laon/Arras 1:100,000

Take the N44 north out of St. Quentin and after crossing the canal turn left on the D33 to Bellenglise. Follow the signs top Vermand. Immediately after crossing the canal again on leaving Bellenglise turn off the road to the right on to hard standing on the west bank of the canal. Stop.

THE BELLENGLISE CROSSING   You are now standing alongside the boundary between the 1st and 46th Divisions (see Map 20) and on the western bank of the canal, the side from which the attack began. The assault crossing by the 46th

Division was made across the canal along a line from here northwards to the Riqueval Bridge. The German defences were formidable. On this side of the canal was the outpost line of fire positions, trenches and wire which had to be cleared before the canal itself could be tackled. The canal ran in a deep cutting between almost perpendicular banks 30–50 ft high over the divisional front from Riqueval to about 500 yards north of here from where it runs virtually at ground level. Where you are now the canal was practically dry but on average between here and Riqueval it ran to a depth of 5–6 ft. The bridge crossing points had well-sited concrete emplacements and beyond lay the main Hindenburg Line of deep interconnecting trenches, thick belts of barbed wire and fortified villages.

As a preliminary to the main assault the 138th Brigade made an evening attack on the outpost line on 27 September and occupied the German trenches west of the canal. Once the positions had been consolidated the 137th Brigade relieved the 138th. At 0700 on 28 September a heavy German counter-attack forced the brigade out of some of the captured positions and the aggressive attentions of red-painted enemy aeroplanes kept heads down during the day. Nevertheless preparations went on for the 29 September action, but not always helped by our own side. Communications forward were mostly by line and this was frequently broken by enemy shell fire, but one British cavalry unit totally destroyed the communications forward from divisional HQ by cutting out 100 yards of the main cable to use as a picket line for its horses.

The canal was seen as a main obstacle and special mud-mats, collapsible boats, rafts and life-belts from the Boulogne cross-Channel steamers were supplied to the troops and rehearsals in their use took place at Brie Château on the Somme on 28 September. On the night of 28–29 September all of these materials were carried forwards by the divisional engineer field companies to as close to the canal as possible. The assault brigade, the 137th (Stafford), was also moved forward to positions along a taped-out forming-up line 200 yards behind the start line for the creeping barrage. The assault was planned on a three battalion front, starting with the 1st/6th Staffords here, then the 1st/5th South Staffords and on the left (farthest north) the 1st/6th North Staffords. Behind them, splitting the divisional area between each other, came the 138th and 139th Brigades as follow-up forces.

As the barrage opened just before 0600 hours the Staffords leapt out of their trenches and poured down the slopes towards the canal through thick mist. They overwhelmed the German defenders and quickly reached the west bank of the canal. Here the 1st/6th South Staffords attacked in four company waves, one behind the other on a one company front of 400 yards. The canal was almost dry, men and officers wading across shielded from enemy fire by the fog. After a short delay in gaining the far bank they pushed on to their phased objectives – the Blue and Red lines – overcoming enemy resistance in Bellenglise en route. All three battalions advanced to timetable, the centre battalion using all their flotation equipment to cross deep water in the canal and the left battalion taking the bridge at Riqueval. Two and a half hours after they had left their trenches the 137th Brigade had gone through the German outpost line, crossed the St Quentin Canal, broken into the Hindenburg Line and taken over 2,000 prisoners. Its own casualties were 580 officers and men. Quite a day.

AUSTRALIAN 4TH DIVISION MEMORIAL On the hill beyond you to the north-west is a memorial obelisk to the Australian 4th Division which took the high ground in a preparatory assault on 18 September.

Drive back through Bellenglise to the N44 and turn right. Some 200 yards later, as the hill rises to its crest, there is a memorial on the left. Park, but beware: the traffic makes it a very dangerous place to stop.

46TH DIVISION MEMORIAL This is the area that was known as Bellenglise Mill and the original memorial to the division which was erected shortly after the war was a tall wooden cross. The present memorial fell into disrepair and a fund to restore it was raised in the mid–1980s by East Midlands TAVR Association. The 46th was a Midlands territorial division that arrived in France in February 1915 and stood by as a reserve for the battle of Neuve Chapelle. It went on to fight at Hill 60 in the Ypres Salient, at the Quarries during Loos and at Gommecourt in the diversion for the Big Push on the Somme. On 29 September 137th Brigade of the division took this area, 139th Brigade followed up and by 1730 hours advanced troops of the 32nd Division were passing through to continue the pursuit.

Turn around and drive north on the N44 to the junction with the D932 to Estrées. Stop on the N44 to the left. There is a small track through the bushes on the left. Walk through it.

RIQUEVAL BRIDGE The bridge is the boundary between the British IX Corps and the American II Corps. It was in the 46th Division area and was the top end of the 800 yard frontage attacked by the 1st/6th North Staffords. It was known that the bridge was a main supply route for the Germans west of the canal and that on the night of 28 September it was still intact. Therefore, it was decided that one company of Staffords under Captain A. H. Charlton should attempt to seize the bridge. On the morning of the attack the visibility was so bad that Charlton had to lead his group forward by compass but as they scrambled down the slope towards the western end they were fired on by a machine-gun in a trench short of their objective. Charlton took nine men and silenced the machine-gun with bayonets and then raced for the bridge. Four Germans, who formed the firing party for the bridge, came out of cover and headed for the demolition charges. Charlton's men won the race, shooting all four Germans and cutting the leads to the charges. The whole company then stormed over the bridge and cleared out enemy posts and trenches on the far side. If you had looked carefully into the bushes on your way in you would have seen bunker on your right. Have a look as you leave.

One of the most famous photographs of the war was taken here three days later when Brigadier Campbell stood on the bridge and addressed men of his brigade. It is an interesting exercise to try to work out which side of the canal the photographer was standing.

Continue on the N44 to a sign saying 'Souterrain de Riqueval' (not the 'viewpoint') and park on the left near a small memorial column.

TENNESSEE MEMORIAL AND TUNNEL ENTRANCE The small memorial was erected by the State in memory of the 'Tennessee troops of the 59th and 60th Brigades of the 30th Division who broke the Hindenburg Line on September 29th 1918'. The 30th Division was made up from National Guard units from North and South Carolina and Tennessee and it rejoiced in the nickname 'old Hickory' after Andrew Jackson who had been born in Carolina. The tunnel entrance is below you and by carefully descending the path, which is maintained on the edge of disintegration, it is possible to stand beside the canal and look into the tunnel.

The American 30th Division, supported by tanks, advanced quickly on 29 September with three regiments forward on a 3,000-yard front and overwhelmed three lines of trenches and barbed wire as well as sealing off this entrance. However, the Germans had constructed many exits through the roof of the tunnel over its 4-mile length and once the Americans had passed they came up and attacked from the rear.

This is still a working canal and overhead wires provide electricity for the barges and for lighting. The Germans had had heat, ventilation and light in the tunnel, which was dry, and they added chambers in the walls to use as storerooms, offices and medical facilities, etc. It is possible to walk into the tunnel along a small footpath, but discretion is the better part of valour because feelings of disorientation can occur after about 25 yards. As you climb up again you should be able to spot the remains of German bunkers on the west side that protected roof exits.

Continue through Bellicourt village to the large memorial on the left. Stop.

BELLICOURT AMERICAN MEMORIAL This splendid memorial sits directly over the top of the Bellenglise tunnel and when the foundations were being prepared passages leading to the tunnel and several underground rooms at different levels were found. The tunnel was built by Napoleon between 1802 and 1810 and the low ridge upon which the monument stands was formed by spoil from the original excavations. On the front of the memorial are the figures of Victory and Remembrance flanking an American eagle and below them are the names of battles and the inscription 'Erected by the United States Government in Commemoration of those American units which served with the British Armies in France during the world war.'

The 27th and 30th Divisions trained and fought with the British in the Ypres Salient in 1918, and below the Wijtschate Ridge just north of Kemmel Hill they have their own memorial commemorating their actions from 18 August to 4 September 1918. The other side of the memorial here overlooks the 30th Division area and beyond it to the right the 27th Division area. By using the map on the monument, the orientation table beside it and the map in this book, a very good idea can be gained of the progress of the fighting. A little careful searching of the horizon to your right front should reveal an American flag flying just to the right of some trees. This marks the location of the American cemetery which is in the 27th Division area and is your next stop. The two American divisions had more than 7,500 casualties in this area and many lie in the Bony cemetery.

Continue on the N44 and at the next crossroads turn left and follow signs to the American cemetery. Go to the reception centre.

THE AMERICAN CEMETERY, BONY A temporary cemetery was established here in October 1918 for the burial of those killed in the Hindenburg Line fighting. American policy allows repatriation of their war dead's remains and today some 1,850 burials are left, including some men who fought at Cantigny.

The reception centre houses the normal visitors' room (with registers) and toilets. From it a path leads to the tall flag pole in the centre of the cemetery. It is always an inspiring sight to see the Stars and Stripes or the Tricolore flying in their respective military cemeteries and many British visitors express regret that our own flag does not fly in our military cemeteries. It is a matter of practicality. We have so many cemeteries, nearly all of them without immediate local super-vision – that it would be impossible to administer the provision and maintenance of flags. However, it should at least be possible to fly our flag at Tyne Cot, our largest military cemetery. The official reason for not doing so is that the Union flag does not represent all of the nations commemorated. Indeed the Canadians fly their flag at Vimy and the Australians theirs at Villers Bretonneux, rather than the Union flag. After the American Civil War a day in May was set aside as 'Memorial' or 'Decoration' Day to honour those who died. American War dead are remembered and ceremonies are held or flags placed at all memorials and cemeteries in Europe by the American Overseas Memorial Day Association. The Association is based in Paris and was founded in 1930 and is non-profit making. The date of the Memorial Day activities varies slightly, but is as close as possible to the original date of 30 May.

There are a number of Medal of Honor winners buried here, their names picked out in gold, including 2nd Lt William B. Turner, whose bravery you read about earlier. Only 137 of the burials are those of unknown soldiers, although seven of these are in one grave. At the bottom or eastern end of the cemetery is a memorial chapel, inside which the names of 333 soldiers with no known grave are inscribed. Above the bronze doors of the chapel is an American eagle with spread wings and inside are a number of flags beside the altar all illuminated by the light from coloured side panels. The cemetery architect was

George Howe of Philadelphia and the sculptor of the bas relief on the outside of the chapel tower, and the two eagles facing the road, was Frenchman Marcel Loyau.

Continue on the D57, resisting motorway signs. At the junction with the D58 turn right to Lempire and in the village turn right again on to the D28, direction Vendhuile. Continue to the British cemetery on the left just before the motorway.

UNICORN CWGC CEMETERY   The cemetery lies just on the American side of the corps boundary between the British III and the American II Corps. Up ahead, just beyond the motorway and to their right of the road is the area of 'The Knoll', one of the fortified positions that gave the 27th Division such trouble. Burials began after the Hindenburg battle, when men of the 18th Division were buried in what is now the first row of 28 graves on the right. The burials were actually made by the 50th (Northumberland) Division and the cemetery was named from their divisional emblem. After the Armistice the cemetery was extended by bringing in burials from the surrounding area. There are now some 650 graves, 78 from Australia and 409 unknown. There is a vc winner buried here and it is perhaps appropriate to end this last battlefield tour with an extract from his citation as a tribute to all those who fought. Courage defies absolute definition. In the end, in its finest form, it probably derives from a sense of responsibility towards one's fellow humans. Everyone who served in this war, on whatever side, had to struggle with personal and private fears. Some came through that struggle better than others and rose above the ordinary. A small number of those received our nation's highest honour. Corporal Weathers did. This is his entry in the cemetery register:

WEATHERS, Cpl. Lawrence Carthage, 1153, vc. 43rd Bn Australian Inf. Died of wounds 29th Sept. 1918. Son of John Joseph and Ellen Frances Johanna Weathers; husband of Annie E. Weathers, of 'Te Kopuru' Main Avenue, Frewville, South Australia. Native of North Wairo, New Zealand. An extract from the London Gazette, no. 31082, dated 24th Dec. 1918, records the following:- 'For most conspicuous bravery and devotion to duty on the 2nd September, 1918, north of Peronne, when with an advanced bombing party. The attack having been held up by a strongly held enemy trench, Cpl. Weathers went forward alone under heavy fire and attacked the enemy with bombs. Then, returning to our lines for a further supply of bombs, he again went forward with three comrades and attacked under very heavy fire. Regardless of personal danger, he mounted the enemy parapet and bombed the trench and, with the support of his comrades, captured 180 prisoners and three machine guns. His valour and determination resulted in the successful capture of the final objective, and saved the lives of many of his comrades.'

Please sign the visitors' book.

TOURIST
INFORMATION

It is the ironic fate of a guide book that some information given in it will inevitably become out of date as soon as it is published. For instance, it may surprise the reader that new memorials are constantly being erected on the battlefields. Established ones are often dramatically altered by new landscaping by the Commonwealth War Graves Commission or to make way for motorways or high-speed trains.

Print a direction using road numbers and the French may decide to alter the system of numbering and send the pilgrim on interminable diversions (*déviations*), which often abandon the driver part way along. Recommend a restaurant and the brilliant chef may have departed in a huff. Advise on a hotel and the *patron* may have done a moonlight flit. Give opening hours for tourist offices and they may well have invented new, rare 'off season' times.

The information and advice we will, therefore, give here will be of a general, rather than a particular, nature – with the exception of a few favourite haunts we cannot resist mentioning. But please do not blame us if you should be faced with the dreaded 'Under New Management' sign.

The very best advice if you are well organized is to go carefully through the itineraries that you intend to follow in this book, then *contact the appropriate national tourist offices in London or New York well before you leave*. Give them, if possible, at least *one month*, list all the major towns you intend to visit, and request the following information, with relevant brochures (tourist literature is now of a generally high and helpful standard):

1   Addresses and phone numbers of local tourist offices with likely opening times. These can be erratic, and we have found that whatever the information you may be given about them, the optimum time for getting in is 1000–1200 and 1400–1600 during the summer time. The most reliable and helpful offices in the battlefields areas are listed below.

2   Listings of local hotels, bed-and-breakfast homes, self-catering lets, restaurants, museums, camping sites, etc, also maps and town plans. Staff are often discouraged from giving personal recommendations, but you can smile and try.

3   Specific information about battlefield routes: in both France and Belgium there are well-marked *circuits*, signed *Route '14–18, or Circuit de Souvenir*, etc., often with useful accompanying literature.

4   General tourist information/local attractions/cultural events/festivals, etc. The serious student of the battles may well wish to avoid the latter – the area will be congested, local hostelries full.

You will often have more success if you *write in* for this information, rather than phone or call in person for it. In mid-season there are often queues and staff can be harassed and occasionally somewhat off-hand.

FRANCE

Note: When phoning France add the following prefixes: ex-UK 01033; ex-USA 01133

FRENCH GOVERNMENT TOURIST OFFICES

UK   178 Piccadilly, London W1V 0AL Tel: 071 491 7622 (but it's difficult to get through) Fax: 071 493 6594
USA   610 Fifth Avenue, New York, NY 10020 Tel: 010 1 212 757 1125

The French produce a *marvellous* booklet, *The Traveller in France: Reference Guide*. This is updated every year. It contains just about all the basic information you need to know before going to France: on currency, passports/visas, medical advice, electricity, metric measurements and sizes, banking and shopping hours, phoning, motorways, driving, caravanning, camping, hotels, self-catering, *Gîtes de France*, local tourist offices (*syndicats d'initiative*) signed 'i' for information, maps, food and drink, etc., how to get there by car, ferry, rail and air, car hire, with relevent phone numbers. It is absolutely essential. Please send a large SAE and £1 in stamps.

ACCOMMODATION IN FRANCE

New hotels are springing up in France like mushrooms – especially in the 2- and even 1-star category: chains like Ibis, Urbis, Campanile, Fimotel, Balladins, Liberté, Vidéotel, Open Hotel, Formula 1. Often conveniently sited on access roads to main towns, they are functional, with private bathrooms – the lower the star rating, the tinier the space – and the basic essentials; usually very clean, and good value for money but with little atmosphere or personality. The 2-star hotels usually have restaurants serving restricted menus.

In the 3/4-star category the groups Altea, Holiday Inn, Mercure, Novotel, Pullman-Sofitel are reliable, if somewhat predictable, with spacious, well-equipped bedrooms (usually standard and identical throughout the hotel) and bathrooms, restaurants, parking (some with swimming pool). They are sited on motorway access roads, with a few in city centres.

For something more individual, with character and personality, often privately owned, the hotels grouped under the banners *Château Acceuil*, *Logis de France*, *Relais du Silence* and those marketed under the Best Western banner are worth investigating. Not all have restaurants, but when they do they are normally very good. Not all rooms have en suite bathrooms and may vary in size and furnishing – check carefully when you book. Because of this non-standardization they vary from 2 to 4 stars. For absolute luxury, try Laura Ashley's old French home, the Château de Remaisnil, Doullens Tel: 22 770747.

The words *auberge* or *hostellerie* often indicate a patron-run establishment with superb restaurant but more basic accommodation.

UK and French central reservation telephone numbers for the above groups are listed in the *Traveller in France Reference Guide*.

LOCAL INFORMATION/TOURIST OFFICES

Somme

The Somme is glorious: great rolling agricultural plains give way to the picturesque valleys of the Somme and the Ancre – a paradise for the huntin', shootin', fishin' fraternity. Their summer cabins nestle beside the wooded banks and pools. Local specialities are eels (*anguilles*), duck (*canard*) pâté, guinea fowl (*pintade*) and fresh vegetables from the *hortillonages* (small allotments on the rich mud islands of the Somme at Amiens) are marvellous – when you can track them down – so is the *Ficelle Picarde* (a savoury pancake with ham, mushroom and cream).

Somme Departmental Tourist Office, 21 rue Ernest Cauvin, 80000 Amiens   Tel: 22 922639   Fax: 22 927747   Efficiently run by Director Ann-Marie Goales. Tourist information and advice for the whole of the Somme area. Excellent literature. Open normal office hours only.

Albert   This is absolutely central for the battlefields. Try the Hotel de la Paix if food is more important to you than mod cons in the bedroom. Patron is the delightful Monsieur Duthoit, 45 rue Victor Hugo, 80300 Albert   Tel: 22 750164.

Amiens   Makes a good base and has a variety of hotels, from many 2-star individual hotels, and much-of-a-muchness chains – Balladins, Fimotel, Ibis, Liberté, Open Hotel, Vidéotel; to the 3-star Grand Hôtel de L'Univers (no restaurant); the newly and expensively refurbished Carlton (which was the lovely old Carlton Belfort where Siegfried Sassoon and other notables stayed) in the Station Square; and the Novotel with outdoor pool in the suburb of Boves (with a 2-star Campanile and 1-star Formula 1 nearby). Recommendations for atmosphere are the Hotel Postillon (but no restaurant), 17 Place au Feurre (near the Cathedral – which you should visit as it has many First World War memorial plaques as well as being a superb gothic structure). Tel: 22 914617 or the Logis de France Le Prieure (with an excellent restaurant), 17 rue Porion Tel: 22 922767.

A trip by boat along the Somme from Amiens will help you imagine what it might have been like to have been aboard a hospital barge. Bâteau Le Picardie Tel: 22 921640.

Assevillers Useful motorway stop on Autoroute du Nord, Calais–Paris. Shop, tourist information, caféteria, fast foods, pleasant restaurant. Next door is the 3-star Mercure Hotel with outdoor pool and extra large bedrooms (it was a 4-star hotel originally). It is ideal for the Somme, for Kaiser's Battle, even Hindenburg Line tours. Tel: 22 841276.

Peronne Now that Peronne has opened the only official Museum of the Great War on the Somme, known as *l'Historial de la Grande Guerre*, a visit to this historic and interesting town becomes a *must* and is well worth the deviation. Housed in an imaginative, custom built structure which buts on to the ancient castle, the Museum which opens 1000–1900 hours every day from 1 May – 30 September, otherwise closed on Mondays, is divided into four halls: 1. Before the War. 2. From the entry into War–1916. 3. From the Battle of the Somme to the Armistice. 4. After the War. There is also an Audiovisual Hall which tells the story of the July 1916 battle through the eyes of British veteran (and poet) Harry Fellowes. The Historial offers interesting worksheets for children. It plans to become a centre for research on the 1914–18 War. There is a bookshop and caféteria. An entrance fee is payable. Tel: 2283 1418   Fax: 2283 5418. Just around the corner, at 42 Place Louis-Daudre, is the 2-star Saint-Claude Hotel. Most well-equipped rooms have en suite bathrooms Tel: 22 844600   Fax: 22 844757. It has an excellent restaurant.

Pas de Calais

Arras This makes the best base for Vimy, and for Neuve Chapelle, le Cateau and Cambrai too, if you prefer not to move and don't mind a bit of daily motoring. You could even do the Somme from Arras. It is also an ideal place to eat. All around the station square is a variety of restaurants and cafés – from 'quick snack' (and what better for lunch than a *Croque Monsieur* or half a *baguette* with *jambon de Paris* or *Camembert*) to the gourmet restaurant at the Station (which also had a modest buffet). The 'Astoria' is a good compromise. A new Conference Centre has been built in the square, with a 3-star Mercure Hotel (Tel: 21 238888   Fax: 21 233707). The Hotel Moderne, Bvd Faidherbe   Tel: 21 233957   Fax: 21 715542 is fine too. The *places* (squares) with their picturesque Flemish baroque arcades, also offer a variety of eating possibilities. Beneath the Grand' Place is a huge car park. Beneath the Gothic Town Hall and Belfry Tower are the *boves* – underground tunnels and chambers much-utilized in the First World War. Inside is a Tourist Office, Tel: 21 512695.

Cambrai This is another good lunch stop, with a traditional Grand' Place, Town Hall and Belfry Tower and loads of restaurants. There are 2-star Campanile (Tel: 27 816200) and Ibis (Tel: 27 835454   Fax: 27 818166) hotels on the Route de Bapaume and the more glamorous 3-star Chateau de la Motte Fenelon,. Allée St Roch (Tel: 27 836138   Fax: 27 837161). Local speciality is the sweet known as *'Bétise de Cambrai'*. Tourist office, Tel: 27 782690.

There are 3-star Novotel Hotels at Henin-Douai-Lens (Tel: 21 751601   Fax: 21 758859 on the Paris-Lille Autoroute) and at Valenciennes (Tel: 27 442080 Fax: 27 31143 on the Paris-Brussels Autoroute) and a 2-star Campanile (Tel: 21 288282   Fax: 21 424133, on the Route de la Bassée) which could be useful for Loos, Cambrai, Neuve-Chapelle.

Verdun-Reims

Reims   This is a lovely place to stay for the Verdun/Meuse-Argonne/St Mihiel battlefields – a good excuse to see the marvellous cathedral and indulge in champagne. Hotels in the 3/4-star international standard are plentiful, e.g. Novotel Reims Tinqueux (Tel: 26 081161   Fax: 26 087205   swimming pool), Mercure Reims Est (Tel: 26 050008   Fax: 26 856472). For more atmospheric hotels, contact the Tourist Office, Tel: 26 472469.

Metz   This is a good alternative – another glorious cathedral and the usual range of good hotels, e.g. Novotel Centre (Tel: 87 373839   Fax: 87 361000 swimming pool), Novotel Hauconcourt (Tel: 87 804111   Fax: 87 803600 Swimming pool), Mercure Metz Nord (Tel: 87 325279). Tourist Office, Tel: 87 756521.

Verdun   The tourist office here has excelllent literature/maps/suggested routes for the battlefields, hotel and restaurant lists. Place de la Nation, 55100O Verdun. Tel: 29 861418. The best hotel in the town is the 3-star Coq Hardi, with *superb* cuisine (Tel: 29 863636   Fax: 29 860921   8 Avenue de la Victoire). The 3-star Bellevue (Tel: 29 863636   Fax: 29 860921   1 Rond-Point du Maréchal de Lattre de Tassigny) is more modest.

Lille area

Lille and its surroundings make a handy base for touring the Ypres Salient and even Mons. It is an interesting city, too, with some superb restaurants. Full details and listings from the Comité Departmental de Tourisme du Nord, 15–17 rue du Nouveau Siècle, 59800 Lille. Tel: 20 570061   Fax: 20 575270. There are Novotels at Lille Aéroport (Tel: 20 979225   Fax: 20 973612   swimming pool), Lille Centre (Tel: 20 306526   Fax: 20 300404), Lille Lomme (Tel: 20 070999 Fax: 20 447458   swimming pool), Lille Tourcoing (Tel: 20 940770   Fax: 20 940880   swimming pool) and Mercures at Lille Centre (Tel: 20 510511   Fax: 20 740165) and Lille Lomme (Tel: 20 923015   indoor pool).

Maubeuge

The Mercure Maubeuge is ideal for the Mons tour (Tel: 27 649373   swimming pool).

BELGIUM

Note: When phoning Belgium add the following prefixes: ex-UK 010 32; ex-USA 011 32.

BELGIAN GOVERNMENT TOURIST OFFICES

UK   Premier House, 2 Gayton Road, Harrow, Middx. HA1 2XU   Tel: 081 499 5379

USA   745 5th Avenue, New York, NY 10151   Tel: 010 1 758 81 30

The Belgian Tourist Board produces some attractive and helpful booklets – but not one composite one like the French. You will need a selection of the following: Flanders; Belgium: Historic Cities (which includes Mons and Ieper (Ypres) – this has details of how to get to Belgium, on local museums and attractions – and hotels (a new list every year). *Beware* – the French and Belgian versions of place-names are very different. You can be driving through France heading for Lille and when you cross the border into Belgium it disappears from the signposts to be replaced with Rijsell. Other traps are: Ypres-Ieper; Anvers-Antwerpen; Courtai-Kortrijk; Roulers-Roeselare . . .. Flemish is generally spoken in the Ieper area today, but English is widely understood and spoken. You must not leave Belgium without sampling some of their legendary *'frites'* – quite irresistible with mayonnaise. Mussels are very popular – especially for family treats at lunchtime on Sunday. Pepper steak is also a favourite and the pancakes are yummy, as are leek flans and chicken stew. In fact Belgian cuisine is very good indeed. Beer drinkers, of course, have a choice of literally hundreds of beers, from light (blonde) beers to thick almost treacley black concoctions like that brewed by the Trappist monks. And then there are Belgian chocolates . . ..

LOCAL TOURIST/INFORMATION OFFICES

Ypres   The Tourist Office is handily situated in the Cloth Hall in the Stadhuis, Grand' Place, B-8900 Ieper   Tel: 57 200724. The staff are very helpful; and they produce their own booklet of tourist information in English, which is very comprehensive. They also sell guidebooks and maps. There is a separate leaflet for hotels and restaurants. It's difficult to have a bad meal in the cafés and restaurants around the Grand' Place, but if you choose an environment with starched tablecloths, gleaming cutlery and glass, it can take a long time. You may prefer to settle for lunch of chips and mayonnaise, or sausages. Hotels are the Regina (Tel: 57 219006   in the main square, gourmet restaurant); the Hostel St Nicholas (Tel: 57 200622 along Boterstraat, few bedrooms, superb restaurant); the Ariane (Tel: 57 218218   a short stroll from the Grand' Place, very smart decor); and the Rabbit (Tel: 57 217000   on the industrial estate; pleasant modern decor). (See also *Lille.*)

There's nearly always something going on in Ieper – a fair, walking and motor races, festivals (notably that of the Cats – second Sunday in May, fun for children but impossible if you want to do a quiet battlefield tour at this time). The surrounding villages, too, have their annual knees-up for witches, cheese, beer . . .. The Belgians can be very jolly.

Mons   Again, an easily accessible Tourist Office in the Grand' Place, No. 20, 7000 Mons   Tel: 65 335580. Their literature, usually available in English, is most helpful. The War Museum has its own leaflets and there is a leaflet called 'Mons–Belgium Centre of Military Interest'. It lists monuments, cemeteries and points of interest on the First World War battlefields and another called 'Notes on the Mons Battlefield'.

For a town of its size, Mons is woefully short of good hotels. You'd do better in Lille or Maubeuge, where there are Mercure, Novotel type hotels (see above), as well as more 'local' hotels. Eating is another matter. Typically the Grand' Place has a huge variety of restaurants and cafés serving good, hearty Belgian cooking. Mons is very fond of folkloric pageants, parades and festivals (e.g. the Lumecon – the Combat between St George and the Dragon on Trinity Sunday; St Waudra, Mons' patron Saint who has his own procession). The proximity to SHAPE, with it mixture of nationalities, gives Mons a cosmopolitan flavour.

WAR GRAVES ORGANIZATIONS

Principal memorials and war graves cemeteries to be found on the battlefield tours are described within the tour itinerary of each chapter.

COMMONWEALTH WAR GRAVES COMMISSION

The British and Commonwealth memorials and war cemeteries were erected and are maintained by the Commonwealth War Graves Commission (CWGC), established by Royal Charter (as the Imperial War Graves Commission) on 21 May 1917. Its duties are to mark and maintain graves of the members of the forces of the Commonwealth who died in the Great War, and the memorials of those with no known graves. It was the inspiration of a volunteer Red Cross Major, Fabian Ware, who became the Commission's first Director-General. The Commission's Chairman was Lord Derby and Rudyard Kipling sat on the Board. It is sad and ironic that his close and energetic ties with the Commission failed to help him to identify his son's body after he had been declared 'Missing' at Loos (see *Loos*).

The Commission chose a uniform headstone (2 ft 6 ins high, 1 ft 3 ins broad) bearing, when known, the regimental badge, name, rank, number, date of birth and death, religious emblem (e.g. Latin Cross, Star of David) and a personal inscription which the family could choose. At first the Commission actually charged the bereaved family 3½d per letter for this inscription. When it become apparent that even this modest fee was beyond the means of some families, the charge became 'voluntary'.

The stones were laid out, for the most part, in straight lines, 'giving the appearance of a battalion on parade'. Gardeners trained at Kew planted beautiful flower beds in front of each line. The most prestigious architects of the day – Sir Herbert Baker, Sir Reginald Blomfield, Sir Edwin Lutyens (described respectively as 'gentle', 'temperamental' and 'brilliant') were commissioned to design the cemeteries and memorials. Blomfield designed the great white 'Cross of Sacrifice' surmounted by a bronze (nowadays it is plastic, so many bronze swords were being stolen) Crusader's sword, which stands out so proudly from nearly every cemetery. Lutyens designed the 'great fair stone of fine proportions' known as 'the Stone of Remembrance' which is present in most large cemeteries. Kipling chose its inscription from Ecclesiasticus, 'Their name liveth for ever-more', and the inscription on the headstone of every unidentified burial, 'A soldier (sailor/airman, etc.) of the Great War, Known Unto God'. Each sizeable cemetery has a Visitors' Book which the reader may care to sign. The future maintenance of the cemeteries (to be preserved, according to the Commission's Charter 'in perpetuity') will depend upon the support of future Governments of the participating nations – the United Kingdom about 80 per cent, the rest being distributed proportionally, according to the number of their burials, between Australia, Canada, India, New Zealand and South Africa. Pakistan has already opted out.

The number of signatures in the Visitors' Book (happily growing in number with each successive year over the past ten years or so) indicates the high level of interest today. The gardeners, too, appreciate your personal comments, so please sign if you can. The Registers are a mine of information. They summarize the burials by nationality and then list them in alphabetical order, reproduce the citation from the *London Gazette* for Victoria Cross winners, contain a map and, usually, a history of the battles in the area and of the cemetery. Copies may be bought from the Commission's headquarters at 1 Marlow Road, Maidenhead, Berks   Tel: 0628 34221. Their French area HQ is at Rue Angele, 62217 Beaurains, near Arras   Tel: 21 710324. They also keep cemetery registers and stock the over-printed Michelin maps which show the location of First World War cemeteries: the sad mosaic of death which clearly defines the old front line, each cemetery indicated by a numbered purple dot. At Beaurains the Commission's stonemasons, blacksmiths, carpenters, gardeners, mechanics and other craftsmen who maintain the cemeteries and memorials so lovingly, have their base. They, the area superintendents (whose names and addresses will be found in the cemetery's Visitors' Book) and the gardeners are dedicated people, often second and now even third-generation descendants of the men who came out after the war to do the fearful work of creating the peaceful 'Silent Cities' you see today.

AMERICAN BATTLE MONUMENTS COMMISSION

The Commission was created by an Act of Congress in March 1923 to erect and maintain memorials and graves to American War Dead in the United States and overseas. Later the responsibility was limited to foreign sites only. After the First World War, eight military cemeteries were established and a memorial chapel was erected in each, as well as eleven monuments and two bronze tablets to record the achievements of America's armed forces. Its first Chairman was General Pershing and General Mark Clark also held the position.

The cemeteries are: Belgium – Flanders Fields, Waregem; France – Aisne-Marne, Belleau; Meuse-Argonne, Romagne; Oise-Aisne, Fère-en-Tardenois; St Mihiel, Thiaucourt; Somme, Bony and Surêsnes; UK – Brookwood. A total of 29,265 known burials, 1,655 unknown and 4,452 missing men are commemorated. The remainder of the American dead were repatriated, at Government expense, at the request of the family. (After the Second World War the percentage of War Dead repatriated from both Wars was 61 per cent). The graves are marked by white marble crosses or Stars of David, laid out in perfect symmetry on emerald green grass. Much controversy ranged about the Imperial War Graves Commission's decision to mark graves with a headstone (rows of which some irate mothers likened to so many milestones) rather than a cross. The stone's greatest virtue is its flexibility from the point of view of a religious emblem. It can bear a Latin Cross, a Star of David, Hindu, Chinese or Muslim characters or, if the man is an atheist or an agnostic, nothing. The Americans impose a religious symbol on everyone, and make no concessions to Buddhists, Hindus or any other religion or non-religion. One sometimes even sees a Star of David on an unknown soldier's grave. When asked how this could happen one superintendent told the authors, 'We knew the percentage of Jewish soldiers in the Great War, so when a group of unidentified soldiers was brought in for burial, every, say, eleventh, would be deemed to be Jewish.'

On each marker is the serviceman or woman's name, rank, unit, date of death and home State. There are no details about his or her age, and there is no room for any further information, such as the British personal message (another plus for the headstone – there is so much more room for information than on a cross).

The magnificent cemeteries, which proudly proclaim 'Honour to our glorious dead', are immaculately maintained. The Stars and Stripes fly over each one. Every cemetery has a splendid visitors' room, furnished with armchairs and carpets and there are always toilets. The Registers and Visitors' Books are kept there, with details of the cemetery and the burials there. A resident American Superintendent is on hand to help relatives and other visitors. The cemeteries are open every day. On Memorial Day each grave in each cemetery is decorated with the Stars and Stripes and the national flag of the host country.

The Commission's offices are at:

United States	**France**
Room 2067, Tempo A	68 rue 19 Janvier
2nd and T Streets, SW	92 Garches
Washington, DC 20315	France
USA	
Tel: 010 1 202 693 6067	Tel: 010 33 1 970 0173

Volksbund Deutsche Kriegsgräberfürsorge
(The German War Graves Welfare Association)

Their address is Werner-Hilpert Strasse 2, 3500 Kassel, W. Germany. The organization is similar in function to the Commonwealth War Graves Commission and the American Battle Monuments Commission in that it maintains the war cemeteries and memorials to the German War Dead from the First World War onwards and assists relatives in locating and, in many cases, visiting the graves. For more information on German cemeteries in the Salient and in France, see the *Battlefield Tour* sections above.

The visitor will soon discover that there is not the uniform design which one finds in the British cemeteries. The markers vary from flat tablets, as in Langemarck, to upstanding squat stone crosses, to black metallic crosses. Jewish soldiers are marked with a headstone which bears the Star of David. The markers have scant information, sometimes only a name, with occasionally a rank, regiment and date of death. Most cemeteries have a mass grave, the names of the unidentified, missing soldiers probably buried therein being listed on bronze panels or wooden walls. Under the majority of the markers more than one, sometimes eight or ten, soldiers will be buried. There are two reasons for this. It signifies 'comradeship in death' and also, on a practical note, the Germans were not allocated as much territory in which to bury their dead as were the Allies. In most German cemeteries there is a small memorial chapel, and often there will be some statuary – normally of bereaved parents or comrades. Some have reception rooms, sometimes with toilets, and postcards and literature about the cemetery in German and in the language of the host country. There will be a register in alphabetical order and usually a visitors' book to sign. Oak trees, symbolizing strength, are a usual feature. There is a marked lack of flowers and colour in most German burial grounds. They are sad, mournful places – but then the death of a soldier *is* sad and mournful.

SECRETARIAT D'ETAT CHARGE DES ANCIENS COMBATTANTS ET DES VICTIMES DE GUERRE

(French Ministry for War Veterans and Victims)

This is the organization which administers and maintains French War cemeteries, known as *Necropoles Nationales*. Address: 37 rue de Bellechasse, 75700 Paris Tel: 1 45 568131

After the First World War the War Ministry reorganized the *Office National des Sepultures*, which looked after French War graves from Napoleonic times. This was, and the present organization is, financed by a budget allocated by the Government for veterans and war victims.

There are 108 cemeteries in France and 884 cemeteries, plots or individuals buried abroad in 69 countries (12 sites in the UK). The French graves are marked by stone crosses with metal plaques which bear the inscription *'Mort pour la France'* (Died for France) and the soldier's rank, name, regiment and date of death. Very often there are rose bushes in front of each line of crosses and the Tricolore normally flies over the cemetery. French Colonial troops are marked by a shaped headstone. A mass grave, or ossuary, is a feature in many cemeteries. Some have memorial chapels in which commemorative plaques are paid for by the families. At Rancourt on the Somme there are some marvellous plaques to commemorate French heroes (winners of the Croix de Guerre, the Legion d'Honneur, etc.) and, in a side chapel the wonderfully personal original grave markers, some with portraits, porcelain flowers and so forth, kept when the cemetery was standardized. Often French cemeteries contain burials from both World Wars. Many nationalities are represented, sometimes members of the French Foreign Legion. Some First World War cemeteries were started during the war. Others were made in the early 1920s and even as late as the 1980s solitary burials were being exhumed and concentrated into the larger cemeteries. The harrowing work of identifying the bodies, often undertaken by the family from pathetic personal possessions, is realistically portrayed in Bertrand Tavernier's film *La Vie et Rien d'Autre* ('Life and Nothing But').

BIBLIOGRAPHY

Aitken, Max. *'Canada in Flanders'*, Hodder and Stoughton, 1916.

Albert, King. *'War Diaries'*, William Kimber, 1954.

Allinson, S. *'The Bantams'*, Howard Baker, 1981.

American Battle Monuments Commission, *'American Armies and Battlefields in Europe'*, US Government, 1938.

Ascoli, D. *'The Mons Star'*, Harrap, 1981.

Babington, A. *'For the Sake of Example'*, Leo Cooper, 1983.

Bailey, O. F. and Hollier, H. M. *'The Kensingtons'*, Old Comrades, 1935.

Banks, A. *'A Military Atlas of the First World War'*, PBS, 1975.

Barnes, R. M. *'The British Army of 1914'*, Seeley Service, 1968.

Baynes, J. *'Morale: A Study of Men and Courage'*, Leo Cooper, 1987.

Bean, C. E. W. *'Anzac to Amiens'*, Australian War Memorial, 1946.

Bergonzi, B. *'Heroes Twilight'*, Constable, 1965.

Berry, H. *'Make the Kaiser Dance'*, Doubleday, 1978.

Boraston, J. H. *'Sir Douglas Haig's Despatches'*, J. M. Dent and Sons, 1919.

Carew, T. *'The Vanished Army'*, William Kimber, 1964.

Coombs, R. *'Before Endeavours Fade'*, After the Battle, 1981.

Cooper, D. *'Haig'*, Faber & Faber, 1935.

Corbett-Smith, A. *'The Retreat from Mons'*, Cassell, 1917.

Farrar-Hockley, A. *'Goughie'*, Hart-Davis, MacGibbon, 1975.

Farrar-Hockley, A. *'Death of an Army'*, Arthur Barker Ltd, 1967.

Foch, F. *'Memoirs'*, Heinemann, 1931.

Gibbs, P. *'The Pageant of the Years'*, Heinemann, 1946.

Gliddon, G. *'When the Barrage Lifts'*, Leo Cooper, 1987.

Goodspeed, D. J. *'Ludendorff'*, Hart-Davis, 1966.

Gough, H. *'The March Retreat'*, Cassell, 1934.

Gough, H. *'The Fifth Army'*, Hodder and Stoughton, 1931.

Grieve, W. G. and Newman, B. *'Tunnellers'*, Herbert Jenkins, 1936.

Griffith, W. *'Up to Mametz'*, Gliddon Books, 1988.

Holmes, R. *'The Little Field Marshal'*, Jonathon Cape, 1981.

Horne, A. *'The Price of Glory'*, Penguin, 1964.

Hughes, C. *'Mametz'*, Orion Press, 1982.

Joffre, J. *'Memoirs'*, Geoffrey Bles, 1932.

Jones, D. *'In Parenthesis'*, Faber & Faber, 1969.

Lehmann, J. *'The English Poets of the First World War'*, Thames & Hudson, 1984.

Liddell Hart, B. H. *'History of the First World War'*, BCA, 1973.

McKee, A. *'Vimy Ridge'*, Souvenir Press, 1966.

Marshall, G. *'Memoirs of My Service in the Great War 1917–1918'*, Houghton Mufflin, 1976.

Marshall, S. L. A. *'The American Heritage History of World War 1'*, Bonanza, 1982.

Mereweather, J. W. B. and Smith, F. *'The Indian Corps in France'*, John Murray, 1919.

Middlebrook, M. *'The First Day on the Somme'*, Penguin, 1971.

Moran, C. M. W. *'The Anatomy of Courage'*, Constable, 1945.

Moore, W. *'Gas Attack'*, Leo Cooper, 1987.

Pershing, J. J. *'My Experiences in the World War'*, Hodder & Stoughton, 1931.

Stacke, H. F. *'The Worcestershire Regiment in the Great War'*, The Regiment, 1928.

Sulzbach, H. *'With the German Guns'*, Frederick Warne, 1981.

Taylor, A. J. P. *'The First World War'*, Hamish Hamilton, 1963.

Taylor, H. A. *'Goodbye to the Battlefields'*, Stanley Paul, 1928.

Terraine, J. *'The Great War'*, Hutchinson, 1965.

Toland, J. *'No Man's Land'*, BCA, 1980.

Travers, T. *'The Killing Ground'*, Allen & Unwin, 1987.

Tuchman, B. *'August 1914'*, Constable, 1962.

Warner, P. *'Passchendaele'*, Sidgwick & Jackson, 1987.

Watt, R. M. *'Dare Call it Treason'*, Chatto & Windus, 1963.

Williamson, H. *'The Wet Flanders Plain'*, Gliddon Books, 1987.

Wyrall, E. *'The Somerset Light Infantry 1914–1919'*, Methuen, 1927.

INDEX